PROFESSIONS AND PATRIARCHY

How have middle-class men tried to restrict women's access to the professions? *Professions and Patriarchy* brings together sociological and feminist concepts to explore the social sources of professional power and to investigate how gender segregation in employment is generated and sustained.

Focusing on the historical roots of the current gender hierarchy in the health care professions, Anne Witz shows that the gender-blindness of prevailing neo-Weberian and neo-Marxist approaches to the study of professions has not been helpful in analysing the relation between gender and professional projects. She argues that the gender of occupational groups embroiled in professional projects and inter-professional rivalries is not fortuitous, but a necessary factor in explaining both the form and the outcome of professionalisation strategies. By examining the strategies of medical men, midwives, nurses and radiographers in the emerging medical division of labour in the latter half of the nineteenth and early twentieth centuries, Dr Witz shows how class and gender have interacted in complex ways to produce hierarchies of power and prestige in professional work.

Challenging and original, *Professions and Patriarchy* develops a new and incisive critical sociology of professions. It will be of great interest to students of the sociology of work, the sociology of health and medicine, and women's studies.

Anne Witz is lecturer in sociology at the University of Birmingham.

INTERNATIONAL LIBRARY OF SOCIOLOGY
Founded by Karl Manheim

Editor: John Urry
University of Lancaster

PROFESSIONS AND PATRIARCHY

Anne Witz

London and New York

First published in 1992
by Routledge
11 New Fetter Lane, London EC4P 4EE

Simultaneously published in the USA and Canada
by Routledge
a division of Routledge, Chapman and Hall Inc.
29 West 35th Street, New York, NY 10001

Typeset by LaserScript, Mitcham, Surrey
Printed and bound in Great Britain by
Mackays of Chatham PLC, Chatham, Kent

British Library Cataloguing in Publication Data
Witz, Anne, 1952–
Professions and patriarchy. – (International library of sociology)
1. Employment. Equal opportunities
I. Title II. Series
331.712

Library of Congress Cataloging in Publication Data
Witz, Anne, 1952–
Professions and patriarchy/Anne Witz.
p. cm. – (The International library of sociology)
Includes bibliography references and index.
1. Professions – Sociological aspects. 2. Professions –
Great Britain. 3. Sexual division of labor – Great Britain.
4. Women in medicine – Great Britain – Social conditions.
5. Medical personnel – Great Britain – Social conditions.
I. Title. II. Series.
HT687.W57 1991
305.5′53′0941 – dc20   91-13905
CIP

ISBN 0–415–05008–1
0–415–07044–9 (pbk)

To my late father
Charles Louis
Witz

CONTENTS

ACKNOWLEDGEMENTS

Thanks are due to the staff of various organisations and libraries: at the universities of Lancaster and Exeter, and particularly the interlibrary loan staff; the Royal College of Midwives, the Royal College of Nursing, the General Medical Council and the Society of Radiographers for kindly allowing me access to their libraries, and the Society of Radiographers for allowing me access to archival material.

Many people have been involved in this work over the years. I am particularly grateful for the stimulating and supportive environment provided by the Department of Sociology at the University of Lancaster during the early stages of this project. In particular, Sylvia Walby provided constant support and encouragement, and I have valued our many conversations over the years. I also benefited enormously from a community of scholars in constant dialogue in settings as diverse as the Departmental Seminar and the Moorlands pub. Special mention must also go to Mike Savage, Jane Mark-Lawson, John Urry, Brian Longhurst, Alan Warde, Sue Penna and Martin O'Brien, all of whom at some point in time have provided invaluable support ranging from comments on drafts, proof reading to somewhere to live, and to Celia Davies for insightful comments on an earlier version of this work. I was also fortunate enough to be part of a dynamic network of women researchers who were active in the Women's Research Centre, including Penny Summerfield, Penny Tinkler, Janet Finch and many more splendid women. Thanks are also due to all the members of the Lancaster Regionalism Group.

My colleagues in the Department of Sociology at the University of Exeter were also generous in their support, as were the staff of the Social Science Data Processing Unit and the various women involved in the Women's Staff Group and Feminist Reading Group. Special thanks must go to Jo Shaw, Helen Kay and Helen Hintjens and to all the women with whom I shared many a Friday night drink.

Finally, there are some very special and more personal debts of gratitude. First and foremost to my late father, Charles Witz, and my mother, Marie Witz, for their unwavering support through the precarious life course that marks an academic career, as well as to my sister, Teresa, who has provided me with bed and board on many a research trip to London libraries. And to a medical man, Dr Andrew Broad, for whose healing skills and dedication to his profession I am eternally indebted. It is Mike Savage who has acted as 'man-midwife' to this work, and has provided invaluable and insightful comments on my work at all its myriad stages. I have gained a great deal from our intellectual collaboration and long friendship.

INTRODUCTION

'Professions' and 'patriarchy', despite having a splendidly alliterative ring, are two words that are rarely put together. In the burgeoning literature on women's employment over the past decade there has been a relative neglect of the history and nature of women's participation in the professions. This book aims to shed some light on this issue by analysing male and female professional projects in the emerging medical division of labour. At a substantive level, it examines the relationship between gender and professionalisation in medicine, midwifery, nursing and radiography. At a conceptual level, it twins two concepts, the rather jaded concept of profession and the newer, fresher concept of patriarchy. This is, then, a work of sociology and of feminist studies.

The 'sociology of professions' has a somewhat dated and staid aura about it, perhaps most associated with fairly turgid and 'Whiggish' accounts of professional men (cf Carr-Saunders and Wilson 1933, Reader 1966). The traditional sociology of the professions was thoroughly criticised by Johnson (1972) as long ago as the early 1970s for uncritically reproducing at the level of sociological knowledge professionals' own definitions of themselves as possessing distinctive characteristics that marked them off from the ordinary run of managers, administrators, clerical workers, and the so-called 'semi-professionals' such as radiographers, nurses and physiotherapists. More recently, much attention has been paid to the relationship between professions and the class structure, and this focus has led to a radical recasting of sociological approaches to the study of professions. But within this new critical theory of the professions, little attention has been paid to the relation between gender and professionalisation.

It has long been recognised that there is an important relation between gender and professionalisation, and indeed this was a focus of analysis in the now displaced functionalist paradigm of profession (cf Etzioni 1969). However, mainstream sociological renderings of this relationship have rarely gone beyond a simple equation between gender and the status, rewards or degree of autonomy enjoyed by practitioners. The overall trend, even in the newer more critical approaches such as those of Freidson (1970a,b, 1986) and Rueschemeyer (1986), has been to rely on explanations which refer to gendered attributes (such as women's association with 'caring' work) in order to read off the subordinate relation of, say, nursing to medicine. There are two problems with these existing approaches. One is that they are static analyses which take the gender of the practitioner as 'already given' and resort to untheorised notions of supposed gender-specific attributes, attitudes and 'problems' which women 'bring to' professional employment. The other problem is that they operate with fairly unreconstructed notions of 'women's role' and have no theory of gender relations beyond a basic, taken-for-granted 'sex role theory'.

When the focus is on women's increasing participation in male-dominated professions, there is a tendency to focus on the problems women have in adjusting to typically male career patterns, problems which are assumed to be largely generated by the difficulties of reconciling a career with a family (Fogarty, Allen and Walters 1981). In short, the 'dual role' problematic, which focuses on conflicts between family and work roles experienced by women and which was the dominant focus in studies of women's employment in the 1960s, lingers on in studies of women in 'top jobs'. And yet this approach has long been subject to considerable critique (cf Beechey 1978) for its voluntarism and neglect of structural factors located within the labour market itself which constrain and limit women's employment. Even Crompton and Sanderson's recent (1989) study of women in pharmacy and accountancy sneaks a voluntaristic, dual role explanation by the back door, although their main focus is on patterns of vertical segregation by sex in occupational labour markets. In short, sociological studies of women's professional work are still prey to what Garnsey (1978) has called 'the fallacy of the wrong level', i.e. reading off women's position in the hierarchy of professional work from their position in the family. More seriously, I think it can be

2

argued that both traditional and critical approaches to the professions continue to reproduce at the level of sociological knowledge professional men's own construction of their gendered self-image.

A sociological analysis of gender and professions which incorporates a more sophisticated conceptualisation of the ways in which gender is itself both socially constructed and a structuring principle is long overdue. The concept of patriarchy is introduced in this analysis of gender and professionalisation in order to structurally ground the category 'gender' by locating it firmly within power relations of male dominance and female subordination. Of course, 'patriarchy' has been a much debated concept, even within feminist studies, since its reemergence as a key concept of second-wave feminism. It has proved at one and the same time a powerful critical tool and a problematic one, tending as it sometimes does to slide into universalism, ahistoricism and ethnocentrism. The formerly more restricted use of the term to refer to the power of the male head of household (the 'power of the father') describes a particular, historically specific form of male dominance. But the concept of patriarchy is now used by contemporary feminist scholars more broadly to refer to gender relations in which men are dominant and women subordinate. It therefore describes a societal-wide system of social relations of male dominance (cf Millett 1972, Hartmann 1979, 1981), not simply those in the family/household. Indeed, an extremely important element of the development of this broader, gender concept of patriarchy has been to establish that patterns of male dominance in modern society do not rest solely on the unequal distribution of power in the family (cf Walby 1986, 1989, 1990a, and 1990b, Hartmann 1979, 1981). It is this broader, gender concept of patriarchy which I use in this analysis of professions and patriarchy, because I believe that, despite the protestations of its critics (Bradley 1989, Crompton and Sanderson 1989, Barret 1987, Acker 1989, Rowbotham 1981), it is able to capture the highly complex and shifting nature of gender relations, teasing out the synchronic links betwen gender relations in various sites of social relations (such as the family, labour market and state), as well as the diachronic shifts in the structure of patriarchy, where the common motif is 'from private to public patriarchy' (Hernes 1987, Borchorst and Siim 1987, Walby 1990a, 1990b).

In Part I the concepts of 'patriarchy' and 'professions' are addressed. Chapter 1 discusses 'dual systems' theorists and explores their contributions to an analysis of women's position in the labour market. These writers all offer superior accounts to those offered by human capital theorists (Mincer 1980), dual and segmented labour market theorists (Doeringer and Piore 1971, Barron and Norris 1976, Gordon, Edwards and Reich 1982), and Marxist approaches, both those that rely on the concept of an ideology of masculinism (Barrett 1987) and those that work within the 'labour process' framework (Braverman 1974, Beechey 1978, 1986, Bradley 1989, Glucksman 1990, Liff 1986, Milkman 1984). The origins and persistence of job segregation by sex in the labour market or labour process are, I believe, best explained within a dual systems framework which explores the intersection between two structuring principles, those of patriarchy and those of capitalism, as the work by Hartmann (1979), Cockburn (1983, 1985, 1986a, 1988), Savage (1985, 1987, 1988a,b), Walby (1986, 1988b, 1990), Mark-Lawson and Witz (1988, 1990), Lown (1990) and Summerfield (1984) demonstrates. I shall, however insist that it is essential to work with a historically sensitive concept of patriarchy.

But the dual systems thesis has been substantiated largely with reference to manual occupations, such as coal miners, engineers, printers, cotton textile workers, and fairly routine forms of non-manual work such as clerical work. It has also been substantiated in cases where male workers are organised into trade unions, rather than in industries and occupations where there is weak union organisation, although this does not provide sufficient grounds to undermine the explanatory potential of dual systems theory, as Glucksman (1990) has recently claimed it does. By comparison, there has been a relative neglect by dual systems theorists of those occupations currently seen as comprising the 'service class' (Goldthorpe 1982, 1987, Abercrombie and Urry 1983). Yet the work of Crompton (1986) and Crompton and Sanderson (1989) clearly establishes the importance of forms of vertical occupational segregation by sex in the service class. We need to consider whether the concepts of 'exclusion', and its corollary 'segregation', which are used in analyses of how organised, working-class men have delimited and constrained working-class women's partipication in paid work, are adequate to the task of analysing processes generating job segregation by sex in professional work. Do we need to complement these with other concepts if we are to understand the specific form assumed by patriarchal practices in professionalising occupations? What are the

4

similarities and differences between the stances and strategies adopted by men in professional organisations and in trade unions? These are some of the issues that are raised in this book.

However, the generic concept of profession is also an implicitly gendered one and we need, first of all, to move onto a less andro-centric terrain within which to locate discussions of professions and patriarchy. This issue is explored in Chapter 2. I shall argue that the first step is to abandon any generic concept of profession and redefine the sociology of the professions as the sociological history of occupations as individual, empirical and above all historical cases rather than as specimens of a more fixed, general concept (cf Freidson 1983). The term 'professional project' is introduced to establish the concrete and historically bounded character of profession. The second step is to conceptualise these projects as strategies of occupational closure, which aim for an occupational monopoly over the provision of certain skills and competencies in a market for services. It is neo-Weberian writers who have used the concept of closure to analyse professional-isation (cf Parkin 1979, Parry and Parry 1976) and chart the links between these and processes of class formation in modern capitalism. What remains to be done, however, is to develop the conceptual framework for an analysis of gender and the closure strategies adopted by professionalising occupations. So, in Chapter 2, I critically develop and refine the conceptual tools of neo-Weberian closure theory in order to unpick the specifically gendered dimensions of closure practices in professionalising occupations. These are exclusionary, inclusionary, demarcationary and dual closure strategies.

It is important to gender the agents of closure strategies and distinguish between male and female professional projects. Indeed, the very fact that women *have* engaged in professional projects has been generally neglected in the sociological literature. Gender clearly makes a difference to both the form and the outcome of professional projects. Finally, these gendered projects need to be grounded within the structural and historical matrix of patriarchy as well as capitalism.

The remaining chapters that make up Part II explore and develop the concepts of closure and arguments about professions and patriarchy developed in these first two chapters. It is the relation *between* gender and closure which concerns me and it is causal processes linking these which I seek to identify. I look at the relation between gender and medical professionalisation through an analysis of women's struggle to enter the modern medical profession in the 1860s and 1870s. Medical men used gendered exclusionary strategies to maintain a male monopoly of registered medical practice in the years immediately following the passage of the 1858 Medical (Registration) Act. Aspiring women doctors, in their turn, replied with an inclusionary strategy. In Chapter 4 I examine inter-occupational relations between medical men and female midwives during the latter half of the nineteenth century, using the concept of demarcation to unpick medical men's stances in relation to midwives, and dual closure to describe midwives' own strategic responses to their tenuous and unregulated position in the emerging medical divisioon of labour. In this and the following chapter on nurses' campaign for a system of state-sponsored registration, I elaborate on the concept of 'dual closure' and argue that female professional projects typically assumed this form. Finally, in Chapter 6, I examine the mixed-gender occupation of radiography during the 1920s and 1930s, a period when it underwent an inexorable process of feminisation. I look at how male radiographers failed to exclude women from formalised routes of access to radiography and, conversely, how women gained and maintained access to radiography training and practice. The concept of gendered internal demarcation is introduced to highlight how processes of vertical segregation within an occupational labour market emerge. In addition, this chapter on radiography and the chapter on the occupational politics of nurse registration both examine the complex interrelation between gender, professionalisation and employer strategies.

Inevitably, because I have chosen to focus specifically on the relation between gender and the occupational politics of closure that have characterised professional projects, there are various facets of professionalisation which remain unexamined, but not because they are unimportant. For example, there are those which would be of interest to Foucauldian scholars exploring the relation between power, knowledge and gender. Indeed, I think there are some interesting ways in which a focus on 'discursive strategies' can be used to illuminate the gendering process at work, such as in the recent work of Pringle (1989) who explores the shifting discursive construction of the secretary over the course of the twentieth century, and the sexualisation of power relations within bureaucratic hierarchies. The concept of discourse seems to me to provide a bridge between hitherto different, and conflicting, explanations of gender divisions in the workplace, between those which used the concept of 'ideology' and others which have adopted a more materialist focus on patriarchal practices. At points in my analysis, I do refer to 'discursive strategies', and now think these are more important than I used to.

Part I

GENDER, CLOSURE AND PROFESSIONAL PROJECTS

1

PATRIARCHY, CAPITALISM AND GENDER RELATIONS AT WORK

There has been considerable debate and disagreement about the concept of patriarchy, both over the precise referent of the concept and whether or not it has any utility in explanations of women's oppression in modern society. Some participants in the debate have exhibited extreme caution regarding the use of the term patriarchy and, at most, seemed prepared to countenance only a historically specific, *generational* use of the term to refer to the power of the father over women and younger men (cf Barrett 1987). Others advocate the use of a broader *gender* concept of patriarchy to refer to a social system of gender relations of male dominance and female subordination (cf Hartmann 1979, 1981, Walby 1986, 1989, 1990b, Cockburn 1983, 1985, 1986a, 1988), and one which persists in modern 'patriarchal capitalism' (Hartmann 1979, 1981) or 'capitalist-patriarchy' (Eisenstein 1979).

In this chapter I shall argue that we need to work with a gender concept of patriarchy which refers to a societal-wide system of gender relations of male dominance and female subordination in order to explain gender divisions in paid work. I acknowledge that this concept may appear as problematic as it is useful, but shall argue that it has enormous explanatory potential if used in an historically sensitive way. The gender relations of patriarchy assume historically, culturally and spacially variable forms, which must be studied in their specificity.

To speak of the patriarchal structuring of gender relations is to describe the ways in which male power is institutionalised within different sites of social relations in society. It is incumbent upon those who argue for the explanatory potential of the concept of patriarchy to specify more precisely: how male power is institutionalised in different sites of social relations – that is, the ways and means, or the 'material', of male power (Cockburn 1983, 1986a); the diachronic interrelationship between the gender relations of patriarchy in each of these different sites at any one point in time – or what Walby (1989, 1990a: 20) refers to as the different 'social structures and practices in which men dominate' and their interrelations; and the diachronic shifts in the social patterning of male dominance over time – or those 'changes in both the degree and form of patriarchy' (Walby 1990a: 23), such as the shift from 'private' to 'public' forms in modern, patriarchal capitalist societies (Walby 1990a, 1990b, Holter 1984, Hernes 1987).

The stance of extreme caution with regard to the use of the concept of patriarchy may be associated with the Marxist-feminist current (cf Barrett 1980, 1987; Rowbotham 1981; Beechey 1977, 1978, 1986; Vogel 1983, Humphries 1977, 1981, 1983, Phillips 1987, Glucksman 1990). Barrett (1987) argues that although categories of Marxism cannot allow an exhaustive account of women's oppression under capitalism, at the same time the concept of patriarchy remains a trans-historical and solely descriptive term when it refers to all expressions of male domination within a society. The concept of patriarchy to which Barrett takes exception is that in current usage among some feminist sociologists and social historians: broadly a *gender* based concept of male dominance. Rowbotham (1981) is similarly troubled by the use of the term patriarchy to distinguish women's subordination as a sex from class oppression, objecting to its use on the grounds of its alleged universality and biologism. Curiously, though, Rowbotham takes the referent of the term patriarchy to which she objects to be the 'power of the father' and yet this is precisely what Barrett regarded as an acceptable, restricted use of the term. Generally though, what we may broadly define as a Marxist-feminist current has been reluctant to reclaim the concept of patriarchy, whilst acknowledging that the family continues to be a site of male power which is inadequately treated within Marxist theory (cf Vogel 1983). Thus Beechey (1977, 1978, 1986) argued that Marxism must acknowledge the centrality of the family-production relation in explaining women's oppression and Barrett (1980) stressed the importance of familial ideology in shaping women's oppression today.

On the other hand, there were those who, albeit in a variety of ways, sought to salvage the concept of patriarchy from theoretical neglect and re-cast it in such a way as to further our understanding of the ubiquity of male dominance and the complexity of gender relations and inequality in the family, the labour market and the state (cf Millett 1972, Delphy 1984, Hartmann 1979, 1981, Eisenstein 1979, 1981, 1984, Summerfield 1984, Braybon 1981, Walby 1985a,b, 1986, 1989, 1990a, 1990b, Westwood 1984, Alexander and Taylor 1981, Lown 1983, 1990, Cockburn 1983, 1985, 1986a, 1986b). In their defence of patriarchy, Alexander and Taylor (1981) argue, correctly, that sexual divisions and antagonisms need to be analysed with concepts forged for that purpose. The gender based concept of patriarchy currently in vogue describes the power relations between men and women, in which men are dominant and women are subordinate, i.e. it speaks of a societalwide system of male dominance, and provides some of these concepts. Inevitably, there have been a variety of divergent formulations of the lynch-pin of such a system and a variety of 'bases' of patriarchy have been identified in the literature. Firestone (1974) specifies biological reproduction, Delphy (1984) husbands' control over their wives' labour within the marriage relation, Rich (1980) compulsory heterosexuality, Chodorow (1978a, 1978b) mothering, and Hartmann (1979, 1981) men's control over women's labour both within and without the household as the underpinnings of male dominance. However, not all writers who argue that women continue to be oppressed within a system of male dominance necessarily utilise a concept of patriarchy. Some writers have used the notion of a 'sex-gender system' and still reserve the term patriarchy for an historically specific form of male dominance where male power is synonymous with fatherhood (cf Rubin 1975), whilst Chodorow (1978a) has distinguished between a sex-gender system and the mode of production, but remains ambiguous as to whether the contemporary Western sex-gender system constitutes a patriarchal system.

For those who have argued that we need a concept of patriarchy as well as capitalism to probe the issue of the specifity of women's oppression, whether in the labour market or elsewhere, the question of their interrelationship becomes central. Eisenstein (1979, 1981) employs a notion of one system of capitalist-patriarchy, arguing that:

> capitalism and patriarchy are neither autonomous systems nor identical: they are, in their present form, mutually dependent. . . . This statement of the mutual dependence of

patriarchy and capitalism not only assumes the malleability of patriarchy to the needs of capital but assumes the malleability of capital to the needs of patriarchy.

(Eisenstein 1979: 22, 27)

It becomes difficult to disentangle the workings of one from the other system, and Eisensteins's formulation of 'capitalist-patriarchy' relies upon a somewhat biologisitic and essentialist notion of 'sex-class' as the unit of patriarchy.

Hartmann (1979, 1981), Cockburn (1983) and Walby (1986, 1989, 1990a), on the other hand, work with a far more robust social constructionist concept of patriarchy.

THE DUAL SYSTEMS FRAMEWORK

Hartmann (1979, 1981) elaborated a dual systems model of separate sets of capitalist and patriarchal relations that interrelate to form a 'partnership' of patriarchal capitalism:

Capitalism grew on top of patriarchy; patriarchal capitalism is stratified society par excellence. . . . Patriarchy, far from being vanquished by capitalism, is still very virile; it shapes the form modern capitalism takes, just as the development of capitalism has transformed patriarchal institutions. The resulting mutual accommodation between patriarchy and capitalism has created a vicious circle for women.

(Hartmann 1979: 230, 298)

This has been a highly influential formulation, broadly adopted by other writers, although with minor differences in emphasis. Walby (1986), for example, argues that Hartmann overemphasises the mutual accommodation of capitalist and patriarchal interests, and understates the conflict between the two. Hartmann defines patriarchy as:

A set of social relations which has a material base and in which there are hierarchical relations between men and solidarity among them which enable them in turn to dominate women. The material base of patriarchy is men's control over women's labor power. That control is maintained by denying women access to necessary economically productive resources and by restricting women's sexuality . . . . the material base of patriarchy, then, does not rest solely on

14

childrearing in the family, but on all the social structures that enable men to control women's labour.

(Hartmann 1981: 14, 12)

Hartmann substantiates her claim that capitalism has been built on top of patriarchy through an analysis of the status of women in the labour market, paying particular attention to job segregation by sex (cf 1979), and through an analysis of the family wage, to which she accords a pivotal role in securing the material basis of male dominance in both the labour market and the family in industrial patriarchal capitalism (cf 1981).

When women participated in the wage-labor market, they did so in a position as clearly limited by patriarchy as it was by capitalism. Men's control over women's labor was altered by the wage-labor system, but it was not eliminated. In the labor market the dominant position of men is maintained by sex-ordered job segregation . . . . Women's subordinate position in the labor market reinforced their subordinate position in the family, and that in turn reinforced their labor-market position.

(Hartmann 1979: 217)

Hartmann (1979) argues that historically it has been male workers who have been instrumental in restricting women's activity in the labour market. Capitalists have played only an indirect role in this process, inheriting job segregation by sex and using it to their advantage through, for example, the substitution of cheaper female labour for male labour and by buying off male workers' allegiance to capitalism with patriarchal benefits. Hartmann argues:

Job segregation by sex . . . is the primary mechanism in capitalist society that maintains the superiority of men over women, because it enforces lower wages for women in the labor market. Low wages keep women dependent on men because they encourage women to marry. Married women must perform domestic chores for their husbands. Men benefit, then, from both higher wages and the domestic division of labour. This domestic division of labour, in turn, acts to weaken women's position in the labor market. Thus, the hierarchical domestic division of labor is perpetuated by the labor market, and vice versa. This process is the present

15

outcome of the continuing interaction of two interlocking systems, capitalism and patriarchy.

(Hartmann 1979: 208)

Hartmann's thesis that patriarchal relations persist within capitalism is further substantiated through an analysis of the family wage (cf Hartmann 1979). This is a wage high enough to support non-working dependents, and the demand for a family wage became a central plank of male trade unionists' wage bargaining strategies from the mid-nineteenth century onwards (cf Barrett and McIntosh 1980). The argument for a family wage may be seen as a necessary corollary of exclusionary practices as men sought simultaneously to exclude women from paid employment and retain their unpaid domestic services in the home.

The overall purpose of Hartmann's analysis is to demonstrate how patriarchal relations have been constituted and sustained within capitalism, both in the sphere of paid employment and in the sphere of the family. One of its major strengths is that women's subordination within these two spheres is seen as dynamically interrelated and reinforcing. Hartmann does not 'read off' women's subordinate status in the labour market from their subordinate status within the family-household. But the real strength of Hartmann's analysis derives from her *materialist* formulation of a theory of patriarchy. Patriarchy is 'a social system with a material base' (1979: 208). Patriarchal relations are *systemic*. Hartmann has drawn upon the Marxist *method* of historical materialism in order to refine a theory of patriarchy, adopting a critical stance towards theories of patriarchy which treat it either as an ideological system autonomous from the economic mode of capitalism (cf Mitchell 1975) or reduce it to biology and reproduction (cf Firestone 1974). The influence of Marxism upon Hartmann comes through in her focus on women's work or labour and her argument that it is men's control over women's work activities which provides the material basis for patriarchy. Hartmann is shifting the emphasis away from what she sees as an overemphasis in radical feminism on biology and reproduction, and towards an emphasis on men's control over what we could term 'material-productive' rather than 'sexual-reproductive' activities. Thus, she insists that 'It is necessary to place all of women's work in its social and historical context, not to focus only on reproduction (Hartmann 1981: 9).

16

Walby (1986) contributes to a further refinement of a theory of patriarchy in two ways. First she proposes a more exhaustive model of patriarchy than Hartmann's, where patriarchy is seen as a societal-wide system of interrelated structures of relatively autonomous patriarchal relations through which men exploit women. Walby (1983, 1986) also substantiates her thesis that gender inequality is a consequence of the interaction of the autonomous sytems of patriarchy and capitalism by exploring how these systems interact in the sphere of paid work, focusing on three contrasting areas of employment: cotton textiles, engineering and clerical work. Developing a new theory of patriarchy, Walby combines the insights of the materialist feminist analyses of Delphy (1984) with that of Hartmann. Like Delphy, Walby (1986) regards the domestic division of labour as a patriarchal mode of production, in which the producing class is composed of women-wives and the non-producing, exploiting class is composed of men-husbands. But Walby moves beyond Delphy (1984), who focuses exclusively on the patriarchal mode of production regarding it almost as a completely self-sustaining mode existing in parallel to and unaffected by the capitalist mode. Walby insists that the patriarchal mode only exists in articulation with another mode of production. Moreover, Walby claims that: 'When the patriarchal mode articulates with the capitalist mode, the primary mechanism which ensures that women will serve their husbands is their exclusion from paid work on the same terms as men' (Walby 1986: 54).

In her most recent publication, however, Walby (1990a) prefers not to use the term 'mode of production' to describe patriarchal relations in the household.

Importantly, Walby (1986, 1989, 1990a), like Hartmann attributes considerable causal powers to patriarchal relations in paid work in sustaining women's subordination throughout society as a whole. Walby's model of patriarchy (1986) prioritises sets of patriarchal relations in domestic and paid work, but identifies other sets of patriarchal relations that are of key significance in defining patriarchy as a system of interrelated social structures. These are patriarchal relations in the state, male violence and sexuality, whilst patriarchal relations in cultural institutions are added in a later (1990a) formulation of the model. The substantive case study material relating to women's employment provides invaluable insights into different types of patriarchal strategies, important variations in the nature of patriarchal relations in the workplace and

17

how these interact, often in conflict with, capitalist relations. Walby identifies two main patriarchal strategies: exclusion and segregation. She provides detailed historical documentation of the patriarchal strategies of organised male workers: in cotton textiles where they were not strong enough to sustain exclusionary strategies and where women maintained access to paid work; in engineering where strongly organised male workers excluded women from skilled work; and in clerical work, where men lost their battle to exclude women but maintained sex segregation. Overall, Walby relies too heavily on the concept of 'exclusion' to capture the form assumed by patriarchal practices in the labour market. As a result, in her eagerness to shift the weight of explanation of women's position in paid employment from the family to the labour market, she underestimates the significance of other forms of patriarchal control in paid employment, particularly those which derive from familial authority relations and yet which do structure women's and men's position in the labour market. I shall return to this point later.

Extending her analysis of the shifting nature of patriarchal relations into the twentieth century, Walby (1990a) goes further than Hartmann, who insisted on the dynamic interrelations between women's oppression in the family and the labour market, to insist that the causal link between family and labour market goes in the reverse direction from that commonly assumed; it goes from the labour market to the family, rather than vice versa. Walby also argues that we have witnessed a shift from 'private' to 'public' patriarchy, where private patriarchy was based on the household as the primary site of women's oppression, and public patriarchy is based principally on public sites such as the labour market and the state. But throughout her work runs a constant emphasis on the significance of patriarchal relations in paid employment, particularly job segregation by sex, in sustaining the web of patriarchal relations in modern society.

Cockburn, in her studies of technological change, gender and class relations in printing (1983), in clothing manufacture, mail order warehouses and medical X-ray work (1985) also provides further grist to the mill for Hartmann's thesis. Whereas Walby (1986) sees exclusion and segregation as distinct outcomes of different patriarchal practices, Cockburn (1985) talks of these in a way which treats the exclusion of women from skilled jobs and their segregation into unskilled and low-paid occupations as

18

related patriarchal practices, as two sides of the same coin. So, for Cockburn, the patriarchal practice of excluding women from compositing was accompanied by their confinement and segregation into book-binding and other print-finishing operations, as men could not prevent employers from engaging women in printing industries, only in particular grades of job.

Cockburn has tended to display an ambivalence about the concept 'patriarchy' which is never entirely resolved, except to concede in one of her latest publications that the concept has been used by feminists not because it is ideal but for lack of another. Utilising Hartmann's 'dual systems' framework Cockburn nonetheless locates her analysis of male dominance and technological change in printing within 'the class relations of capitalism and the gender relations of patriarchy and their bearing upon each other' (1983: 8). Although hesitant about the lack of historical sensitivity of the concept 'patriarchy', when loosely used to mean 'male supremacy', Cockburn thinks it needs more closely defining rather than rejecting outright. Cockburn is also reluctant to prioritise any one set of social relations as the site of patriarchy:

> To say that patriarchal power is exercised only in the family or in directly sexual relations is as blinkered as to suppose that capitalist power is exercised only in the factory. The sex/gender system is to be found in all the same practices and processes in which the mode of production and its class relations are to be found. We don't live two lives, one as a member of a class, the other as a man or a woman. Everything we do takes its meaning from our membership of both systems.
>
> (Cockburn 1983: 195)

Cockburn's study of the struggles around the introduction of new technology into the printing labour process from the late nineteenth century to the present day demonstrates how the strategies of craft organisation and craft control of printing were directed against employers, unskilled workers *and* women. Had nothing but class interest been at stake, the men would have found women acceptable as apprentices, would have fought wholeheartedly for equal pay for women and for the right of women to keep their jobs at equal pay. As it was, the men and their unions sought to have the women removed from the trade. The arguments used by men against women differed from those used against male rivals. They

19

expressed the interests of men in the social and sexual exploitation of women (Cockburn 1983: 151).

Cockburn's analysis demonstrates the virility of patriarchal forms of craft organisation and craft control in printing. She demonstrates how these organisations were utilised in the pursuit of patriarchal strategies of exclusion, and also reveals how masculinist constructions of skill, aided by men's privileged access to technological competence, have further reinforced the exclusion of women from craft privileges. Cockburn's study of male printers' defence of their skills in the wake of technological change such as the more recent transition from hot metal to cold composition technologies provides support for the argument of Phillips and Taylor (1984), who emphasise processes whereby skill labels become gendered, and argue that worker resistance to de-skilling has centred on the preservation of *masculine* skills as the issue providing much of the force to worker's resistance. 'Skill has increasingly been defined against women . . . . It is the sex of those who do the work, rather than its content, which leads to its identification as skilled or unskilled ' (Phillips and Taylor 1984: 63). In her later work, Cockburn (1985) turns to a more detailed examination of the role of male usurpation of technological competence in generating sexually segregated job hierarchies, arguing that:

Technological competence is a factor in sex-segregation, women clustering in jobs that require little or none, men spreading across a wider range of occupations which include those that call for technical training. There is nothing 'natural' about this affinity of men to technology. It has, like gender difference itself, been developed over a long historical period in conjunction with the growth of hierarchical systems of power.

(Cockburn 1985: 9)

But perhaps the most interesting aspect of Cockburn's work is her conceptual distinction between three material instances of male power that are demonstrated by her study of gender relations, skill and technology in the printing trades. The economic is the first instance, as men have benefited more from capitalist development of the printing industry than women and, in addition, their higher earnings and better job prospects are predicated upon women's domestic labour. The physical is another instance of male power, and here Cockburn argues that the attribute of 'strength' is deployed competitively by men and is enhanced by their mono-poly over technical competence. The socio-political is another, in my view critical, instance of male power. Cockburn discusses how patriarchal relations, like class relations, are organised and institu-tional, but asks 'where are the societies, the institutions, the armies that organise men's power?' (Cockburn 1983: 203). Cockburn herself demonstrates how one of the ways in which male power becomes institutionalised within capitalist relations is by means of patriarchal craft unions, which provide the socio-political muscle for the wresting of competitive advantage vis-à-vis women and less organised men.

This emphasis on the socio-political instance of male power picks up on and develops what to my mind is a crucial element in Hartmann's argument concerning the resilience of patriarchal relations within capitalism. Hartmann (1979) argues that it was the ability of men to *organise*, particularly during the formative period of industrial capitalism, which played a crucial role in limiting women's participation in the labour market. Men's organisational knowledge was predicated upon their position in the patriarchal family in feudalism.

> I want to argue that, before capitalism, a patriarchal system was established in which men controlled the labour of women and children in the family, and that in so doing men learned the techniques of hierarchical organization and con-trol. With the advent of public-private separations, such as those created by the emergence of state apparatus and eco-nomic systems based on wider exchange and larger pro-duction units, the problem for men became one of main-taining their control over the labor power of women. *In other words, a direct personal system of control was translated into an indirect, impersonal system of control, mediated by society-wide instit-utions* (my emphasis).
>
> (Hartmann 1979: 207)

Lown (1983, 1990) has also utilised a gender concept of patriarchy and explores the links between capitalist and patriarchal relations in shaping the changes in women's employment patterns in the nineteenth century. Through a detailed historical study of the nineteenth-century Courtaulds silk mill in Halstead, Essex, Lown demonstrates how patriarchal relationships had been a central organising principle in the silk trade thoughout its history from the fourteenth century, when silk production was mainly in the hands of women, who were debarred from the same craft status as men, through to the organisation of production in the mechanised silk mill owned by the Courtaulds family. At Courtaulds paternalistic management enabled employers seeking to utilise female labour to resolve tensions between class and patriarchal interests. Paternalism, argues Lown, was one way in which traditional patriarchal authority relations were carried over into the market relationships of industrial capitalism.

Lown's emphasis, then, is on how employer strategies could contain a complex combination of patriarchal and capitalist interests, as employers sought to utilise female wage labour without undermining the patriarchal privileges of male workers in both the workplace and the family. Lown's work is important because it begins to correct the tendency in both Hartmann's and Walby's work to ascribe patriarchal interests to 'men' and capitalist interests to 'employers', and then seeing these discrete sets of interests as either in partnership, as Hartmann (1979) tends to, or assuming more conflictual forms, as Walby (1986) does. Lown shows how the patriarchal structure of the workforce was ensured through vertical gender segregation, as Courtauld's paternalistic practices served to reward male labour more highly than female labour and enable the development of a male labour élite at the expense of female workers. Lown demonstrates all too clearly how in this instance, the case of Courtaulds mill in the nineteenth century, the interests of male workers and their middle-class employer in the simultaneous restructuring and maintenance of patriarchal privileges in both the workplace and the home coincided. Lown insists too that the combination of patriarchal and capitalist interests contained in 'paternalist strategies' should not obscure the fact that in other sectors of the economy, in different geographic locations and over different periods of time, constellations of patriarchal and capitalist interests varied. Like Walby, Lown argues that, despite sectoral and local variations, strategies generally shifted away from exclusion and towards more and more segregation by the end of the nineteenth century.

BEYOND 'PATRIARCHY OR CAPITALISM'?

Although Lown uses the concepts of patriarchy and capitalism to good effect in her study, another recent contribution by Bradley

(1989) suggests that it is time to move beyond the 'capitalism and patriarchy' debate. Bradley's own case studies of the historical development of the sex typing of jobs in primary production (agriculture, fishing, mining), the secondary sector (pottery, hosiery, shoemaking) and in services and professional work show how processes of sexual segmentation and resegmentation have been integral features in shaping the division of labour in each of these sectors. Bradley concludes, however, that capitalism impacted on these sexual divisions of labour, increasing segregation and destroying or marginalising women's traditional skills. The 1880s and the 1890s are identified by Bradley as the key periods in laying down the patterns of segregation and sex-typing on which current patterns of sex segregation in employment are founded.

However, although Bradley's case studies show equally as conclusively as Lown's how familial and workplace gender relations were simultaneously being restructured, her explanatory framework is weaker because she insists on deploying the concept of patriarchy in a far more restrictive sense. She will, for example, only describe workplace relations as patriarchal through 'analogy of the household and authoritarian father to the enterprise or organisation' (1989: 232).

Bradley (1989) seems to want to have her cake but not eat it. Patriarchy seems to her a flawed concept, and one that tends to slide into description. Nonetheless, she concedes that we have to go on talking about patriarchy because there is nothing better. However, we need to abandon the notion of a system of patriarchy or at least operate with a highly modified version of it, and Bradley is critical of Walby's systematising tendencies. Yet at the same time Bradley urges that we keep on trying to develop some form of structural theory and advocates that the way ahead 'is to conceive social structure in terms of many sets of interconnected relationships (class, gender, ethnicity, politics, culture etc.) and to analyse these within the context of their historical development' (1989: 63). But Bradley is reluctant, in the end, to use the term 'patriarchy' to describe a gender system of domination; in fact, as I have already noted, she consistently uses it in the more restricted sense of generational domination. Drawing conclusions from her historical case studies, the pre-industrial family is described as patriarchal, as are control relations in the family division of labour, but when she makes the more general claim that current work arrangements can be described as patriarchal it is with the proviso 'at least if we apply the analogy of the household and authoritarian father to the enterprise or organisation'.

I don't think it is sufficient to use the term patriarchy by *analogy*, because we are clearly using the analogy to point to a gendered division of labour in sites other than the family in which men systematically have more power and advantage than women. In other words, the analogy between, say, gender relations in employment and those in a patriarchal family is drawn precisely *because* we observe relations of male dominance in both. The gender relations of patriarchy describe sets of social relations which are gendered and within which men have more power and advantage than women. They are systemic in the sense of constituting a web of privileges and advantages, which are mutually reinforcing, and which pervade the many sites of social relations and social interaction. Male dominance is, in other words, institutionalised and systemic.

Whilst I applaud Bradley's historical sociological approach to the study of gender relations in employment, her caution about using the concept of patriarchy to analyse the shifting modes of male control in the workplaces she studies seems overly cautious. Bradley is correct to caution against the desire to produce grand, all-encompassing theories of patriarchy, particularly in a climate where the ways we do sociology and think sociologically are undergoing a revolution, as rationalist and ethnocentric tendencies of grand theory building are coming under increasing attack under the impact of the post-modernist critique. This critique is also having an impact on feminist theory more generally, and suggests, as Bradley correctly points out, that the search for overarching 'systems' or 'logics' of patriarchy is misplaced. However, at the same time, this critique does vindicate those critics of either reductionist or universalist accounts of patriarchy, who have insisted that the concept of patriarchy is a conceptual tool which must be historically anchored if it is to aid our understanding of gender relations in industrial, pre-capitalist and capitalist societies. It serves to capture power relations between men and women, but must simultaneously be able to capture shifts in those relations. Indeed, Fraser and Nicholson (1988) suggest that one of the steps to be taken if we are to 'combine a post-modernist incredulity towards metanarratives' with the social-critical power of feminism is to operate with a feminist theory which is 'explicitly historical', and 'attuned to the cultural specificity of different societies and periods' (1988: 100–101). It is not necessary, then, to abandon the power of feminism with its concept of patriarchy to the seamless web of pure description.

There have been other rich and detailed studies of the complex mixture of gender and class conflicts out of which have been forged patterns of sex segregation in the workplace (cf John 1986). Whilst not all these studies explicitly deploy the concept of patriarchy as an explanatory tool, nonetheless they all point to the centrality of gender conflicts in shaping the workplace as we have come to know it. All of these studies document the various exclusionary strategies of organised male workers, although the 'motives' were not always unambiguously or solely 'patriarchal', but sometimes far more complex. The works of Braybon (1981) and Summerfield (1984), for example, have provided empirical documentation of women workers in the first and second world wars, and revealed important conflicts between patriarchal and capitalist interests over the utilisation of female labour during war-time. Braybon locates her analysis solidly within a dual systems framework when she declares that 'the patriarchal system coexists with the capitalist system; the working class have been exploited by the latter, but women have also been oppressed by men of their own or other classes in a multitude of ways' (1981: 12). Both studies challenge the conventional image of women workers entering paid work en masse during the war-time periods, and voluntarily exiting from the paid workforce once hostilities had ceased. Rather, both Braybon and Summerfield explore the complex interrelationship between patriarchy and capitalism and demonstrate how both employers and working men espoused an ideology of female domesticity and, in different and contradictory ways, turned this to their own material advantages; employers to justify paying women less than men, thus facilitating the use of women as cheap labour, and union leaders to resist the employment of women, particularly married women, thus maintaining their patriarchal privileges in both the workplace and the home.

INCLUSION, EXCLUSION AND SEGREGATION

Initially broad and schematic accounts of the historical intersection between patriarchy and capitalism in the structuring of gender relations and sex segregation in employment have given way to considerable and ongoing refinement and modification.

Hartmann's substantive thesis about the vital role of organised working class men in limiting and constraining women's position in the labour market is not without its problems, and has been subject to considerable modification and refinement, as well as vindication.

Walby (1986, 1989, 1990b) and Lown (1990) have both argued that Hartmann's notion of a partnership between patriarchy and capitalism has led her to assume a harmonious articulation between the two and consequently to understate the potential for conflict between the interests of employers and male workers over the employment of women. Lown (1990) has also questioned the tendency to conceptualise 'men' and 'capitalists' as separate categories belonging to distinct systems of social relations, when in fact gender and class intersect in the construction of identity. Cockburn (1983) makes a similar point. Lown and Bradley (1989) both suggest how, in fact, patriarchy and capitalism have not operated as two distinct systems with different agencies, where employers pursue 'capitalist' interests and male workers 'patriarchal' interests. Indeed, both Lown and Bradley show how some employers devised strategies of utilising female labour which combined capitalist and patriarchal interests, describing these as 'paternalist' strategies. For example, in the Bournville chocolate factory in Birmingham the rigid segregation of young female workers supervised by a forewoman was part of a paternalist strategy that extended well beyond the factory gates, as in the case of the Courtauld mill in Halstead.

Debates about protective legislation in the nineteenth and early twentieth centuries have also tended to polarise in evoking either 'class' or 'patriarchal' interests in highly general terms, paying insufficient attention to the historical specificity of the Acts. One school of thought attributes protective legislation to the patriarchal zeal of reformers and the common class interests of both working-class men and women (Hutchins and Harrison 1911, Humphries 1977); others argue (as did some feminists of the period) that the motives of male workers were patriarchal (Walby 1986, Hartmann 1979). However, a careful analysis of the 1842 Mines (Regulation) Act signals caution with regard to general imputations of patriarchal or class interests. The 1842 Mines (Regulation) Act is an example of protective legislation on the part of the state to exclude or restrict women from certain types of work, in this case excluding them from underground mining. It has been cited as an incontrovertibly patriarchal instance of male workers' successful exclusionary strategy (Walby 1986) and it has been cited by Humphries (1977) as evidence to question the assertion that working men's support for protective legislation was patriarchal in both form and effect. In this case, however, the issue was far more complex than either of the above suggest (Mark-Lawson and Witz 1988, 1990). Many coal owners agitating for legislation were much more interested in the economic benefits or competitive advantages they would reap as less modernised competitors would be forced out of business if they could no longer rely on female and child labour; and male colliers in the pits where women worked underground were opposed to the legislation. The structure of local gender relations gave rise to important variations in the stances adopted by both coal owners and male colliers in relation to female labour, and is therefore a highly significant variable, as Savage (1987) in his study of gender and employment relations in Preston at the turn of the century demonstrates convincingly.

A more specific problem with Hartmann's account, and with the 'dual systems' position generally, has to do with the fact that the rate of male trade unionism in the nineteenth century was so low that, if the maintenance of patriarchal relations depended so crucially on the organised pursuit of exclusionary strategies, then 'patriarchal capitalism' could hardly be said to exist before 1900 (Brenner and Ramas 1984, Sen 1980, Mark-Lawson and Witz 1988). This is a particularly important point which suggests that *exclusion* clearly does not exhaust the repertoire of patriarchal practices on the part of male workers. Indeed, most writers agree in identifying a further strategy, generally referred to in the literature as *segregation.* This is best seen as a form of inclusionary strategy, as women workers may not just be excluded from certain jobs or grades of job, but also included in other adjacent or related jobs, usually graded lower or less skilled jobs. In a sense, it is a corollary of exclusion. But there is also another form of inclusionary strategy, which exists prior to both exclusion and segregation, and this is where male control over female labour is exercised within the family system of labour within sites of capitalist production (see Mark-Lawson and Witz 1988, 1990, and Bradley 1989 for more detailed discussion of this mode of patriarchal control).

It is clear that male control over female labour did not operate solely by means of exclusionary and segregationist strategies throughout much of the nineteenth century. The picture was rather more complex than this. The family system of labour was an equally important way in which patriarchal control relations were constituted within the capitalist labour process. The use of family labour, which was very extensive in the seventeenth and eighteenth centuries and associated by Medick (1976) with 'proto-industrialisation', survived as an historically specific mode of patriarchal control in pockets of nineteenth-century industrial capitalism. As a form of internal contract, it enabled the principal male worker to oversee the labour of family members, as well as exercise control over the distribution of material benefits and the allocation of work tasks. Mark-Lawson and Witz (1988, 1990) have examined its importance in nineteenth-century coal mining, and argued that male colliers in localities where the family system of labour existed did not support moves by individual employers at the local level or by the state at the national level to remove female labour from underground working. Exclusionary strategies on the part of working class men were pursued only when women came to be constituted as wage labourers rather than as subsidiary workers in the family system of labour; only when, that is, women are 'proletarianised'. Seccombe also argues that when women worked outside their homes, competed with men on an open labour market, and took home their own wages, then:

> *These* practices were beyond the bounds of patriarchal stricture. They conferred on women . . . a public presence and economic independence which flouted all the traditional norms of women's place in the family households of their fathers and husbands. When *these* employment opportunities began to predominate, and the more traditional types declined, strong sentiment arose against wage labour for women in general.
>
> (Seccombe 1986: 66)

Thus it is possible to identify shifting modes of patriarchal control within capitalist work relations. The family system of labour is a mode of control which operates by way of the inclusion of women within patriarchal authority relations under the direct, individualised control of the husband (or father). It is only when this form of control begins to break down as men and women enter the labour market as individual wage labourers that exclusionary strategies take precedence, but these are premised on the ability of working men to organise collectively and institutionalise male power in sites other than family relations – in the labour market, civil society and the state. So for example, in the case of coal mining, the first national union, the Miners Association of Great Britain and Ireland, was formed in 1842 three days before the date on which the 1842 Act was to be implemented (John 1981) and henceforth men used their collective organisation to bargain around the size of the wage – the only element of control left to them. As Seccombe argues (1986) the development of an ideology of the male breadwinner norm around 1850 served to 'stabilize' patriarchal relations which were threatened by the challenge of wage-earning women. Savage (1987) has also emphasised how patriarchal control in the Preston cotton industry in the 1880s was not necessarily exercised by the exclusion of women workers from weaving, and demonstrates how instead male overlookers drew on their own family members to work as weavers. In late nineteenth-century Preston the labour market was organised by men and structured in their interests, as patriarchal forms of labour control were exercised.

The segregation strategy is generally acknowledged, but not given much attention. As Walby (1986) demonstrates, it was clearly the response of male clerical workers to the increasing recruitment of female labour into clerical work. Cockburn (1983) and Hunt (1985) see the segregation of women into ancillary and less skilled tasks as the corollary of their exclusion from skilled jobs in the printing trades. Mechanisation and technological change were clearly crucial factors in the de-skilling, feminisation and segregation of jobs, in both manual and routine non-manual employment. Nonetheless, the relation between de-skilling, feminisation and gender segregation is a highly complex one, and we cannot assume a simple correspondence between the three processes.

It is possible to identify three major modes of patriarchal control over female labour. First, an *inclusionary* mode, sustained by means of the family system of labour as a form of 'internal contract' within sites of capitalist production, where the labour of women and children is under the control of the male head of household. Second, the *exclusionary* mode, where organised male workers collectively engage in attempts to preserve certain spheres of work together with privileged wage rates, justified by appeal to the ideology of the 'family wage', for themselves and to prevent women from entering these male spheres of employment. Third, a *segregationary* mode where male and female occupations or jobs are demarcated by gender, thus creating a *hierarchical* gendered occupational order. Which mode of control prevails depends upon a number of factors, such as the structure of local gender relations (Mark-Lawson, Savage and Warde 1985, Mark-Lawson and Witz 1988, 1990), rates of technological change (Bradley 1989, Liff 1986), and the nature of industrial and occupational expansion (Glucksman 1985). The inclusionary mode precedes the exclusionary mode in any particular case, because the latter is pursued when women enter the labour market as individual wage labourers rather than as part of a familial group.

The observed shift from exclusionary to segregationary modes is partly the result of shifts in the occupational structure, and partly the result of shifts in strategy. Exclusionary modes predominated in manual forms of employment (once inclusionary modes, if they existed, had broken down), and segregationary strategies may have accompanied exclusion. However, in these instances, gender segregation was not necessarily the outcome of worker strategies, but can equally be seen as 'unintended outcomes' of these – Kreckel (1980) suggests, for example, that unprotected workers, such as in this case excluded women, are prey to employer exploitation as peripheral and unprotected workers. However, segregationary strategies were the predominant response in routine white-collar occupations, where male collective organisation was weak. As yet, however, gender divisions in higher level white-collar work such as professional and managerial positions have not been discussed. This is largely because, I suggest, we may need to develop new concepts to grasp the processes at work here. The concept of exclusion needs to be twinned with a new concept, demarcation, in order to unpick the historical relation between gender and professionalisation, and I shall suggest how we might do this in the following chapter. For the moment, it is sufficient to note the relative neglect of women in non-routine white-collar work.

CLASS AND GENDER IN MIDDLE-CLASS OCCUPATIONS

The studies reviewed above foreground the material underpinnings of working-class women's social position in the formative period of patriarchal capitalism. By comparison, historical sociological research exploring the dynamic intersection between patriarchy and class in shaping middle-class women's lives has tended to focus more exclusively on the ideological underpinnings at work in the confinement of middle-class women to the domestic sphere as, in Neff's (1929) words, 'idle women'. The focus has been more on Victorian middle-class culture and ideology (cf Davidoff and Hall 1987). Of course it can legitimately be argued that, to a certain extent, this difference in emphasis reflects the very different social positions of working- and middle-class women in patriarchal capitalism for 'In an age when women of the lower ranks were notoriously overworked, not only the aristocracy but both the upper and lower middle classes protected the females of their households from any kind of useful employment' (Neff 1966: 186). Neff somewhat overstates her case, and we should not assume that the reality of middle-class women's lives necessarily was one of idleness (Branca 1976); we should not forget, for example, that middle- and upper-class women engaged in activities that were neither home centred nor employment centred, but philanthropic. Nonetheless, I think it may certainly be argued that patriarchal and class interests coincided in the case of middle-class women who were more thoroughly excluded from gainful employment outside the home and confined within the domestic sphere; whereas the relation between patriarchal and class interests for working-class women was far more contradictory and variable. Indeed, those very same bourgeois men whose wives' and daughters' idleness was an indicator of their own success were also recruiting women workers into their mills and factories, as Lown's study of Courtaulds mill graphically demonstrates. Ironically, too, working women were finding themselves increasingly subject to exclusionary forces, in the form of state protective legislation and the hostile campaigns of unionised male workers, whilst middle-class women were beginning to agitate for the right to gainful employment through, for example, the Society for Promoting the Employment of Women which was formed by the 'Langham Place ladies' in 1859 (Holcombe 1973, Strachey 1935).

In fact it is quite clear that, when we look at the comparatively neglected area of middle-class women's work as 'white-blouse' (Anderson 1988, Crompton and Jones 1984, Davies 1979, Walby 1986, Lowe 1987) and professional (Bradley 1989, Holcombe 1973, Corr 1990, Widdowson 1983) workers, then the concepts of exclusionary and segregationary strategies also have a crucial role to play in explanations of middle-class women's work. But women's entry into the more routine areas of non-manual employment, such as clerical work, was somewhat later than men's, beginning in the 1880s (Anderson 1988), whereas in manual work men and women were both sources of labour from the outset, although whether men or women were employed, and in what particular jobs, varied by locality and by industry, as well as being subject to redefinition (cf Pinchbeck 1981).

Overriding importance is given to the 'supply' and 'demand' factors in explaining women's entry into clerical employment (cf McNally 1979, Anderson 1988), whilst new technology and the mechanisation of the office are usually identified as key factors in facilitating the simultaneous de-skilling and sex-typing of jobs as female rather than male (cf Davies 1979). But the battles are seen to be fought primarily at the ideological level (cf Lowe 1987), particularly around the feminisation of new technology such as the typewriter. Walby (1986) and Zimmeck (1986) alone provide a more materialist analysis of gender and clerical work, which focusses on gender struggles over who had access to what jobs. Walby argues that male clerks attempted to exclude women from clerical work, but that they did not have the socio-political muscle to do so. So they turned to segregationist strategies, which were essentially grading strategies, as work done by women was to be of a lower grade than work done by men. In fact, it is on the strength of her analysis of male clerical workers' strategies in the face of the encroachment of female workers that Walby identifies the strategy of segregation. Her other case studies were of manual workers so, although she suggests that we might periodise patriarchal practices as shifting from exclusion to segregation, in fact the later appearance of segregation strategies is very much linked to the later entry of middle-class women into employment.

There are some important gaps in the literature on how men have managed to secure privileged positions in the labour market. The focus has been mainly on working-class men and, for the reasons suggested above, the responses and strategies of working-class men in the face of women workers may not be the same as those of middle-class men. To assume that we can extrapolate from one to the other suggests an underappreciation of the different patterns of middle-class formation and forms of organisation which characterise the growth of middle-class occupations and occupational hierarchies. In fact, existing analyses of gender and middle-class formation have adopted culturalist rather than materialist frameworks (although I don't want to imply these are incompatible). We need to enquire whether and by what means gendered privileges in employment were secured by middle-class men. If we neglect the actions of middle-class men and women in the sphere of the workplace, and see issues of gender segregation as explained solely by 'forces' of supply and demand or by ideological parameters, then we risk slipping back into the 'fallacy of the wrong level' (Garnsey 1978) by over-emphasising the salience of ideological forces shaping women's role in the middle-class family for explaining the nature of their labour market participation. I am not suggesting for one moment that Victorian ideology of 'separate spheres' did not impact differently on working-class and middle-class women, and neither am I denying its salience in explanations of women's lives both in the family and in the workplace. However, I am suggesting that what is lacking is a more *materialist* analysis of gender divisions and anta- gonisms in non-manual work, like the ones we now have of gender segregation in manual work. We need to look at whether gendered patterns of exclusion and segregation operated in the context of middle-class occupational formation.

Accounts of middle-class women's working lives do exist, but they are few and far between. Vicinus (1985) has provided an excellent study of single middle-class women in nursing, school-teaching and colleges, and organised philanthropy. Her focus is on gender-based solidarity between single middle-class women and their separatist strategies for setting up alternative female communities. Holcombe's is the main study to date of Victorian ladies at work, and provides detailed accounts of women's entry into and role in transforming the professions of nursing and teaching, and of their recruitment into the distributive trades, clerical occupations and the civil service. Vicinus emphasises the role of gender-based solidarity between women, particularly in overcoming the stigma surrounding middle-class women working and single women providing for themselves independently of the family, but Holcombe insists that the Victorian women's movement had little impact on women's work.

Rather, the growth in the numbers of middle-class working women was a natural result of the general development of the country's economy, was the answer to the changing needs of an increasingly industrialized and urbanized society. In short, the Victorian women's movement witnessed but did not cause the widening of the avenues of employment for middle-class women.

(Holcombe 1973:198)

Holcombe's 'explanation', if indeed we can call it that, entails reducing women to passive onlookers of the march of economic progress, as they are pulled into the workplace by the mysterious forces of economic change and by the exigencies of industrial capitalist development. The resistance of men to this process only surfaces once women are firmly ensconced in the workplace as teachers, secretaries, clerical workers etc. and centres around issues of equal pay and opportunities. In short, Holcombe's largely narrative account of middle-class women's employment in the late nineteenth and early twentieth centuries lacks any clear conceptual framework which could begin to explain the complex ways in which patriarchy as well as capitalism shaped middle-class women's working lives.

By contrast, the work of Zimmeck (1986, 1988) charts the gender antagonisms that accompanied the recruitment of women into the civil service in clerical grades, and establishes that patriarchal exclusionary strategies operated to ensure that women did not enter the administrative grades of the civil service. These were reinforced by dowry payments to women on marriage in lieu of pensions, as well as by marriage bars (Sanderson 1990). Male careers in the civil service hierarchies were forged on the backs of women, as the employment of women in lower grade mechanical work released men into career paths towards intellectual and administrative work, and indeed enabled the very construction of these career paths.

We need to develop a more conceptually rigorous framework for unpicking the complex trajectory of women's employment in white-collar occupations, particularly the professions which are a relatively neglected area of gendered work. We need to enquire whether and in what ways processes of middle-class occupational formation incorporated gendered strategies. Although bourgeois and patriarchal constructions of women as wives and daughters consigned to the 'private sphere' were extremely powerful forces shaping middle-class women's lives in Victorian Britain, this fact alone does not explain their position in paid employment. In a fascinating study of a much neglected sphere, women's entrance into the professions in America between 1890 and 1940, Glazer and Slater (1987) argue that, whilst the movement towards occupational professionalisation occurred independently of women's interests, nonetheless at the same time women of the new middle class saw the emergence of professions as a historical moment of incomparable opportunity for them. What Glazer and Slater's work shows, as does my work, is that it is vital to locate an analysis of gender relations in professional work within the larger process of professionalisation that was occurring – for the purposes of their study in the later nineteenth century in America, but also slightly earlier in the case of Britain.

I think it is quite possible to show that, just as male power was institutionalised within trade union organisations as the collective work-based organisations of the working class, it was also institutionalised within middle-class occupational organisations. Indeed, the relative ease with which middle-class men had no need to fear female competition for many jobs was precisely because bourgeois men already had exclusive access to many institutional forms in modern society, like the university, professional associations, and of course the state. The battle to secure women's access to education, particularly college education (cf Dyhouse 1981, Strachey 1936), was a necessary corollary of women's entry into middle-class occupations. But, just as middle-class men had many distinctive means of patriarchal domination at their disposal, so too middle-class women when they did seek to gain a foothold or secure a stronger basis in forms of professional work, also had more available means than working-class women. Indeed, one has to seriously question Holcombe's charge that the Victorian women's movement was ineffective in opening up avenues of employment for women. As Vicinus (1985) has demonstrated, at the very least it provided a network of interlinking individuals and support groups which provided campaigning bases. There is clear evidence, presented in my chapter on women's struggle to enter the medical profession, that women's entry into medicine was the outcome of a collective campaign orchestrated by aspiring women doctors, and supported by networks of women sympathisers – Emily Davies and Millicent Garret Fawcett are two names which immediately spring to mind. Vicinus is correct to point to the importance of gender-based solidarities in opening up avenues of gainful employment for women.

CONCLUSION

To summarise my argument so far. It is necessary to broaden our perspective on middle-class women's lives in the formative period of patriarchal capitalism by looking at how gender divisions in middle-class employment were forged. In order to do this, we need to look at the mechanisms of middle-class occupational formation and unpick the gender dimensions of these processes. This will complement the tendency in analyses of the social position of middle-class women to rely wholly on a culturalist framework and the role of patriarchy at the ideological level only. The burgeoning literature on the social position of working-class women has demonstrated how the restructuring of women's roles in the labour market and in the family-household were interrelated processes, and how patriarchal practices operated in both these sites of social relations. We also need to enquire as to whether similar or different processes were operating to demarcate and define gender divisions in middle-class occupations. If so, what were these processes? And how did they effect the terms on which middle-class women entered into and participated in paid work.

My ensuing analysis of patriarchal practices shaping the emerging medical division of labour in the late nineteenth and early twentieth centuries aims to refine and extend our grasp of how, historically, men have organised and acted to limit and control the terms on which women participate in paid work. The focus is on the socio-political and institutional locations of male power in the public sphere, and the extent to which the institutionalisation of male power in this sphere provided a crucial resource in the key historical period of occupational professionalisation.

The substantive focus, then, is on the occupational politics of professionalisation. I draw upon the 'burnished' tools of neo-Weberian closure theory in order to conceptualise the occupational politics of professionalisation as closure strategies, but analyse these along their specifically gendered dimensions by drawing upon the 'freshly fashioned' tool of the gender concept of patriarchy. I shall suggest how it is necessary to distinguish between two key strategies of professional closure, one is *exclusionary* and the other is *demarcationary*. The term 'demarcation' is used in preference to 'segregation' (the term used by Walby, Cockburn and Lown), which I prefer to reserve to describe the structured outcome of closure processes, i.e. job segregation by sex. It is also used because I do not think that when I refer to 'demarcation' I am talking about an equivalent strategy to 'segregation'. For one thing, demarcation strategies were vital corollaries of exclusionary strategies in the emerging medical division of labour; they were not simply residual side-effects of, or last resorts in the face of the failure of, exclusionary strategies, which is how they sometimes appear in discussions of trade unionists' responses to women workers.

There is another important and fruitful difference between my work and existing 'dual systems' analyses of gender divisions between working-class men and women in employment. This has to do with the fact that working men were directly embroiled in the struggle between capital and labour, a struggle that was stacked against them, yet professionalisation strategies are the organisational responses to labour market conditions on the part of class-privileged male actors. This means that men engaged in occupational professionalism will have access to the resources of class as well as gender privilege. In addition, I shall also argue that the institutions of civil society and the state proved critical to the pursuit of professional projects (as Larson 1977, 1979, and Johnson 1982 also argue). So I am able to extend Hartmann's focus on the interrelations between the family and the labour market by looking at other sites where male power was institutionalised, namely civil society and the state. Indeed, I shall suggest how male dominance in the professional division of labour around the provision of medicine was crucially dependent upon the patriarchal structuring of those institutions and organisations that inhabit the sphere of civil society and of the institutional ensemble of the modern state.

In the next chapter I propose that we conceptualise professional projects as historically specific closure projects and argue that we need a theory of professionalisation that can cope with the fact that women as well as men have engaged in professional projects. In other words, it needs to be able to deal with the specifically gendered dimensions of occupational professionalism. This will then give us a better handle on the historical construction of gender segregation, both vertical and horizontal, in professional divisions of labour or middle-class occupations. So another important way in which I hope to complement and extend existing work on gender relations in employment is by showing how gender has provided a resource for solidarity and collective

37

action not just in the case of men, but also for women. I shall propose a framework for analysing closure strategies of professionalisation which not only distinguishes between typical male strategies, but also between typical female strategies.

2

PATRIARCHY AND PROFESSIONS

In this chapter I shall argue that the relationship between gender and professionalisation is a neglected one, and that female professional projects have been ignored in the sociology of professions. One of the reasons for this neglect has to do with the fact that the generic notion of profession is also a gendered notion. This is because it takes what are in fact the successful professional projects of class-privileged male actors at a particular point in history and in particular societies to be the paradigmatic case of profession. I shall argue that it is necessary to speak of 'professional projects', to gender the agents of these projects, and to locate these within the structural and historical parameters of patriarchal capitalism. Professional projects are projects of occupational closure, and I propose a model of occupational closure strategies which captures the historical configuration of the gendered politics of occupational closure.

In this chapter I briefly review the general state of the art of the sociology of the professions before critically elaborating neo-Weberian and neo-Marxist approaches to the study of professions, and the small body of literature that probes the issue of the relation between gender and professions. The neo-Weberian closure model is elaborated critically in order to suggest a model of occupational closure strategies that identifies their gendered dimensions. The neo-Marxist model, with its focus on the structural and historical parameters of professionalisation, provides the springboard for further locating gendered professional projects within the structural and historical parameters of patriarchy as well as capitalism.

PROFESSIONS AND POWER

Johnson's (1972) radical reconceptualisation of a profession as not an occupation per se but a mode of controlling an occupation has provided the new orthodoxy in the sociology of professions. The main trajectory of the sociology of professions in the 1970s and 1980s has been the emergence of a new critical theory of the professions, which has been centrally concerned with the concept of power. The conceptual indissolubility of the concepts of 'power' and 'profession' has provided the central axis of the new critical sociology of the professions.

The precise course of the conceptual revolution in the sociology of professions from the dominance of the 'trait' and 'functionalist' paradigms through to the jostling for position between neo-Weberian and neo-Marxist paradigms is now a familiar tale (cf Crompton 1990). Functionalist renderings of the professions (Parsons 1954) emphasised the distinctiveness of modern professions, locating their development within the rationalising tendencies of the wider society. 'Trait' approaches attempted to identify precisely what constituted this distinctiveness, looking for essential attributes or traits (cf Greenwood 1957). A less static, although related, approach was the 'process' one, which sought to understand what an occupation had to do to turn itself into a profession (Wilensky 1964). This end state was defined in terms of those essential attributes that warrented the assumption of the mantle of 'profession' (Vollmer and Mills 1966). Trait and process approaches ultimately foundered on the sheer diversity of elements that various authors identified as providing the essence of profession, as well as the failure to come up with the same elements. The most frequently mentioned were skill based on theoretical knowledge, provision of training and education, testing the competence of members, organisation, adherence to a professional code of conduct and altruistic service.

Crompton has recently suggested that we may fruitfully retain some of the insights of apparently displaced paradigms, particularly the notion of 'institutional altruism' (Crompton 1990). Indeed, Larson (1979) makes heavy use of the strongly Parsonian link between the rise of professionalism and rationalisation, although she talks of capitalist rationalism, thus displacing its Parsonian (although not its Weberian) overtones. However, Johnson's devastating critique of the loaded ideological, cultural and historical bias of these approaches marked a radical and irrevocable break with them. The kernel of Johnson's critique was that:

> Not only do 'trait' approaches tend to incorporate the professionals' own definitions of themselves in seemingly neutral categories, but the categories tend to be derived from the analysis of a very few professional bodies and include features of professional organisation and practice which found full expression only in Anglo-American culture at a particular time in the historical development of these professions.
>
> (Johnson 1972:26)

Johnson's own proposed framework is now as well known as his critique. It centered around treating profession not as an occupation per se, but as an institutionalised means of controlling occupational activities. Although he initially emphasised different institutional solutions to the uncertainty in any consumer–producer relationship as the basis of a typology of institutional modes of control, distinguishing between collegiate control, patronage and state mediation, Johnson later came to see the relation between professions and the class structure (1977) or the state (1982) as more fruitful points of departure for a sociology of professions. In effect, the emphasis shifted from the ways in which actions become institutionalised to the ways in which they are structurally and historically constrained.

Despite Johnson's own shift towards a more structurally grounded notion of profession, the original focus on the institutionalisation of power relations has persisted and developed under the ambit of neo-Weberian perspectives on professionalisation. A profoundly influential conception of professionalisation has become that it is a strategy of occupational control, and a battery of neo-Weberian concepts have been deployed in the analysis of professionalisation. Freidson (1970a, 1970b) has argued that a profession is an occupation which has successfully struggled for the right to control its own work, and so has been granted legitimate organised autonomy, usually by a dominant élite or by the state. Parkin (1979) has defined professionalism as a strategy of exclusionary closure designed to limit and control the supply of entrants to an occupation in order to enhance its market value. Parry and Parry (1976) have similarly defined professionalisation as a strategy of social closure and a means of collective social mobility, whilst Berlant (1975) has taken the Weberian notion of monopolisation and explored tactics for domination that characterised medical professionalisation. Turner (1987) has defined professionalisation as a strategy of occupational control involving occupational relations of dominance and subordination, and Larkin (1983) has introduced the notion of 'occupational imperialism' to capture processes of dominance and subordination in the medical division of labour.

So far, though, the use of neo-Weberian closure concepts to inform sociological analyses of professionalisation and power has failed to consider the relation between gender, power and professionalisation. The notable exception is Parry and Parry's (1976) analysis of medical professionalisation as a strategy of social closure and collective mobility. They acknowledge both the class and gender dimensions of professional closure in medicine, which became a closed and homogeneous world in both class and sex terms – it was male and upper-middle class. Nonetheless, the gender dimensions of professionalisation are undertheorised compared to its class dimensions. This raises an interesting issue in relation to the deployment of neo-Weberian concepts of social closure and collective mobility which is how implicitly gendered these concepts are. The intellectual sexism of neo-Weberian stratification theory has meant that women do not have a social class (cf Parkin 1971, Giddens 1980), except that derived from their association with a man, as either a father or a husband (cf Acker 1973). But this presents a thorny problem when it comes to the possibility of considering the professionalisation strategies of female occupational groups. After all, if the social class position of women is wholly derived, then how can the professionalisation strategies of female occupational groups be conceptualised as collective mobility projects? How can women move from nowhere to somewhere else in a positional and class structure in which they have no position? It is precisely because of the embedded intellectual sexism and androcentric assumptions of neo-Weberian sociology that Parry and Parry are unable to satisfactorily integrate their analysis of nurse professionalisation into their general thesis about the link between professionalisation, social closure and collective mobility.

It is necessary, then, to build upon the enormous theoretical leaps in our explanation of professionalisation facilitated by the development of neo-Weberian closure concepts through gendering these concepts, and to locate professional projects within patriarchal as well as the capitalist structures emphasised by more neo-Marxist writers such as Johnson. First, we need a more finely tuned model of the variety of closure strategies which may be employed by occupational groups engaged in professionalisation strategies and one which captures their specifically gendered dimensions. This will open the way towards conceptualising 'female professional projects'. It will also correct the androcentric bias in neo-Weberian discussions of professionalisation as a closure strategy.

OCCUPATIONAL CLOSURE AND GENDER

It is, as I have already indicated, the neo-Weberian tradition which has elaborated the concept of closure (cf Parkin 1974, 1979, Murphy 1983, 1985, 1986, 1988) and which has used closure concepts in the analysis of professionalisation (cf Parkin 1979, Berlant 1975, Parry and Parry 1976, Freidson 1970a, 1970b, 1977, 1983, 1986, Waddington 1984, Larkin 1983, MacDonald 1985). But little attention has been paid to the gendered politics of occupational closure, with the notable exception of Crompton (1987).

Crompton (1987) also argues that, when it comes to looking at the position of women in the professions, then it may be more fruitful to develop neo-Weberian closure concepts than Marxist ones. A particularly important point made by Crompton is that apparently individualist exclusion practices clearly incorporate a substantial collective element. In particular, she suggests that the credentialling process is overlaid by gender exclusion, though not just at an individual but also at a collective level. However, Crompton seeks to develop the concept of 'status' in order to provide a better handle on the interplay between gender and professionalism, whereas I prefer to refine the concept of closure itself in order to explore the gendered nature of professional closure strategies. Further, whereas Crompton only seeks to locate the developments of professions within processes of class formation, I further locate these within gender formation in modern society. There is some overlap though. Crompton, for example, observes that the status of a quality, including gender, has to be *actively* maintained and reproduced and I demonstrate some of the mechanisms for doing so within professional work. Also, Crompton suggests that sex-typing occurs in the case of the pro-

43

fessions as the occupation 'crystallises' or emerges as a recognisable, functionally differentiated entity (Murgatroyd 1985). This is precisely what I show, but using 'gendered' closure concepts. I will return to Crompton and Sanderson's (1989) work in the concluding chapter because it examines women in the professions today, so provides clues as to what contemporary forces are shaping women's participation in professional work, and how these may be both similar to and different from those at work in the late nineteenth and early twentieth centuries.

Frank Parkin, one of the major protagonists of neo-Weberian closure theory, offers a baseline definition of modes of closure as different means of mobilising power in order to stake claims to resources and opportunities. A conceptual model of the specifically gendered dimensions of occupational closure will therefore be concerned with how occupational closure strategies provide the means of mobilising male power in order to stake claims to resources and opportunities distributed via the mechanism of the labour market. The bare conceptual bones of such a model of the various occupational closure strategies that may be utilised within the context of professional projects is set out in Figure 2.1. This model turns upon a four-fold distinction between strategies of exclusionary, inclusionary, demarcationary and dual closure. Exclusionary and demarcationary strategies are engaged in by a dominant social or occupational group in the hierarchy of closure, whilst inclusionary and dual closure strategies describe the responses of subordinate social or occupational groups.

Gendered strategies of exclusionary and demarcationary closure

The distinction between exclusionary and demarcationary strategies of closure is suggested by Freidson's (1977) discussion of the Janus-headed nature of the professional power of doctors, who enjoy not only an occupational monopoly but also a position of dominance vis-à-vis related and adjacent occupations in the medical division of labour. This is a distinction between, on the one hand, exclusionary strategies which aim for intra-occupational control over the internal affairs of and access to the ranks of a particular occupational group and, on the other hand, demarcationary strategies which aim for inter-occupational control over the affairs of related or adjacent occupations in a division of labour.

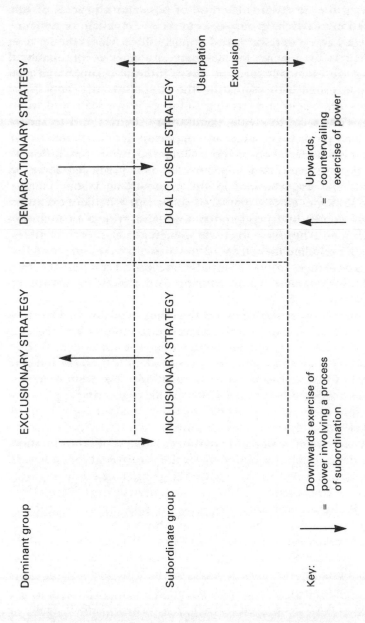

Figure 2.1 Strategies of occupational closure: a conceptual model

Parkin (1979) defines exclusionary strategies of closure as involving the downwards exercise of power in a process of subordination as a social group seeks to secure, maintain or enhance privileged access to rewards and opportunities. This is the sense in which it is used here. Exclusionary strategies of occupational closure are essentially mechanisms of internal occupational control, concerned with regulating the supply of an occupational group's own labour and creating a monopoly over skills and knowledge. They serve to create exclusionary shelters and to secure privileged access to resources and opportunities distributed by the mechanism of the labour market. Gendered forms of exclusionary strategy have been used to secure for men privileged access to rewards and opportunities in the occupational labour market. These strategies employ gendered collectivist criteria of exclusion vis-à-vis women and gendered individualist criteria of inclusion vis-à-vis men. They serve to create women as a class of 'ineligibles' through excluding them from routes of access to resources such as skills, knowledge, entry credentials, or technical competence, thus precluding women from entering and practising within an occupation.

Demarcationary strategies, on the other hand, are mechanisms of inter-occupational control, concerned to monitor and regulate the labour of other, related occupations in a division of labour. Demarcationary strategies are concerned with the creation and control of boundaries between occupations. The term demarcation is introduced by Kreckel (1980) in his pioneering application of closure concepts to processes of labour market segmentation. Kreckel distinguishes 'exclusion', involving the 'vertical' or downwards exercise of power and entailing a process of subordination, from 'demarcation', which involves the 'horizontal' or 'sideways' negotiations between occupational groups whereby separate spheres of competence and control are mutually negotiated (1980: 540). Without necessarily accepting the full import of Kreckel's definition – which is that there is an absence of dominative processes in demarcationary strategies – Kreckel's introduction of the term demarcation does suggest the importance of processes of occupational closure which have to do with the creation and control of boundaries between occupations.

The concept of a demarcationary strategy of closure captures those processes which Larkin (1983) calls 'occupational imperialism' in the medical division of labour. Larkin correctly notes the

46

relative paucity of supplementary concepts referring to inter- occupational domination rather than to intra-occupational domination in the Weberian (and indeed the Marxist) model of professionalisation. The term demarcation used here is similar in its import to Larkin's term 'occupational imperialism':

> Occupational imperialism refers to attempts by a number of occupations to mould the division of labour to their own advantage . . . it involves tactics of 'poaching' skills from others or delegating them to secure income, status, and control.
>
> (Larkin 1983: 15)

> The term 'occupational imperialism' is not intended to connote an ossified skill distribution, but an arena of tension and conflict between groups which is largely shaped in outcome by the differential access of each to exterior power sources.
>
> (Larkin 1983: 17)

Like Larkin uses the term 'occupational imperialism', I shall use the term 'demarcation' to refer to strategies engaged in by dominant social or occupational groups, who have greater access to power resources than those groups hit by demarcationary strategies. Larkin, however, does not systematically analyse the gendered dimensions of occupational imperialism and how the resources of male power may be utilised in the pursuit of demarcationary strategies.

Strategies of demarcationary closure are absolutely vital in the understanding of how unequal gender relations are created and sustained within an occupational hierarchy in the labour market. Gendered strategies of demarcationary closure describe processes of inter-occupational control concerned with the creation and control of boundaries between gendered occupations in a division of labour. They turn not upon the exclusion, but upon the encirclement of women within a related but distinct sphere of competence in an occupational division of labour and, in addition, their possible (indeed probable) subordination to male-dominated occupations. The concept of a gendered strategy of demarcationary closure directs attention to the possibility that the creation and control of occupational boundaries and inter-occupational relations may be crucially mediated by patriarchal power relations. It also establishes that the gender of occupational groups embroiled in inter-occupational, demarcationary struggles, both as architects and as targets of demarcationary practices, is not fortuitous or contingent, but a necessary factor in explaining both the form and the outcome of such strategies. This latter point is sadly neglected by Larkin (1983) in his otherwise excellent study of the medical profession's strategies of occupational imperialism in relation to the adjacent and related paramedical groups of radiographers, chiropodists and physiotherapists in the medical division of labour. The centrality of the relation between gender and inter-occupational relations of domination and subordination is suggested by Donnison (1977), Ehrenreich and English (1973b, 1979), Verluysen (1980), and Hearn (1982, 1987) in relation to midwives and medical men, and by Gamarnikow (1978) and Bellaby and Oribabor (1980) in relation to nurses and medical men.

Gendered strategies of inclusionary and dual closure

Inclusionary and dual closure strategies describe the different countervailing responses of groups who are subject to either exclusion or demarcation. Inclusion describes the upwards, countervailing exercise of power by a social group which is hit by exclusionary strategies, but which, in its turn, seeks inclusion within the structure of positions from which its members are collectively debarred. Dual closure strategies describe the responses of occupational groups hit by demarcationary strategies, but the strategic aim is not to be included in the ranks of the occupational group engaged in demarcationary closure. Dual closure strategies are conceptually and empirically far more complex than this. They entail the upwards countervailing exercise of power in the form of resistance on the part of subordinate occupational groups to the demarcationary strategies of dominant groups, but they also seek to consolidate their own position within a division of labour by employing exclusionary strategies themselves.

This distinction between inclusionary and dual closure strategies owes much to Parkin's and Murphy's refinements to the concept of closure. One of the major ways in which Parkin (1979) expands upon Weber's original concept of closure is by introducing closure strategies other than those of a purely exclusionary kind into the closure framework. The term 'usurpation' is introduced to capture those dimensions of collective action on the part of a subordinate group which assume an oppositional form and involve the countervailing use of power in an upwards direction:

> Usurpation is that type of social closure mounted by a group in response to its outsider status and the collective experience of exclusion. . . . What is entailed in all such cases is the mobilization of power by one group or collectivity against another that stands in a relationship of dominance to it.
>
> (Parkin 1979: 74)

Murphy, another neo-Weberian closure theorist, further distinguishes between different forms of usurpation. Inclusionary usurpation is defined as:

> the struggle by the excluded group to become included as incumbents represented in the present structure of positions in proportion to their numbers in the population. This inclusionary form of usurpation involves the struggle for equality of opportunity and for the shift from collectivist to individualist criteria of exclusion.
>
> (Murphy 1984: 560)

Revolutionary usurpation, on the other hand, aims to change the structure of positions itself, rather than simply to seek inclusion in that structure.

Although there is considerable disagreement between Murphy and Parkin about the precise import of the concept of usurpation, I am nevertheless going to use this term only in a minimal sense of denoting the countervailing, upwards exercise of power on the part of a subordinate group. This is the sense in which Parkin uses the concept of usurpation. An inclusionary strategy is usurpationary in this sense and is so called because the strategic aim of the actors is to be included in a structure of positions from which they are excluded. This is the sense in which Murphy uses the concept of inclusionary usurpation.

The term 'dual closure' is also introduced by Parkin to cover the possibility that 'exclusionary strategies aimed at what Weber calls the "monopolization of opportunities" are frequently employed by one segment of the subordinate class against another, most usually on the basis of race, sex, ethnicity, or some other collectivist attribute' (Parkin 1979: 89). Dual closure strategies entail the use of both exclusionary as well as usurpationary activities. A dual closure strategy is so called because it involves the simultaneous exercise of power in an upwards direction, that is its usurpationary dimension, and in a downwards direction, which is its exclusionary dimension. This is also the sense in which Parkin uses the concept of dual closure.

How then do these concepts help to construct a model of occupational closure strategies that captures the gendered dimensions of professionalisation? A gendered strategy of inclusionary usurpation describes the ways whereby women, who are hit by gendered strategies of exclusion, do not simply acquiesce in the face of patriarchal closure practices, but challenge a male monopoly over competence. They seek to be included in a structure of positions from which they are excluded on account of their gender. It is usurpationary because it is a countervailing strategy, in tension with an exclusionary strategy. It is an inclusionary strategy of usurpation because it seeks to replace gendered collectivist criteria of exclusion with non-gendered individualist criteria of inclusion.

Gendered strategies of dual closure, on the other hand, describe the manner in which women may contest demarcation. They involve a two-way exercise of power, in an upwards direction as a form of usurpation and in a downwards direction as a form of exclusion. Most importantly, they capture the form assumed by what I shall refer to as 'female professional projects' in the medical division of labour – such as, for example, campaigns for state-sponsored systems of registration by midwives and nurses (cf Donnison 1976, Baly 1980, Abel-Smith 1960, Dingwall, Rafferty and Webster 1988).

Dual closure strategies are complex and varied. Along their usurpationary dimensions, they do not have the same inclusionary aims as usurpationary responses to exclusion. So, for example, unlike aspiring women doctors, whose struggle was an inclusionary one, midwives and nurses did not aspire to become fully qualified medical practitioners. So their struggles were usurpationary in the minimal sense, of resisting the demarcationary strategies of medical men. But it is precisely because these campaigns also contained what can only be described as exclusionary elements, that we may speak of 'female professional projects'. They are not simply strategies of resistance to the demarcationary strategies of dominant occupational groups, but they also seek in turn to consolidate their own position in the hierarchy of closure through employing exclusionary devices.

Gender and strategy

The bare bones of a conceptual model of occupational closure strategies have now been set out. The main purpose of this model is to capture the gendered dimensions of these strategies. It will be substantiated on the terrain of the emerging medical division of labour in Part II, when I look at gender and professionalisation in medicine, nursing, midwifery and radiography. But before moving on to consider further aspects of the relation between gender and professionalisation, it is necessary to clarify a few points about the relation between gender, closure and professional projects.

In what sense are strategies gendered? First, the strategic actors are gendered and, second, gendered criteria of exclusion or inclusion may be inbuilt features of closure strategies. The agents of closure practices are gendered so gender may form the basis of solidarity between men or women. Professional projects are, I have argued, strategies of occupational closure and so any assessment of both the form and the eventual outcome of these strategies should consider whether the agents of these were men or women. However – and here closure concepts help us very little – an analysis of the gendered dynamics of professional projects as strategies of occupational closure must also locate these within those patriarchal structures which, historically, have constituted the facilitating or constraining parameters of such strategies. This raises the issue of the relation between strategic action and structural constraints, an issue which is highlighted as a particularly problematic aspect of the use of the concept of strategy in sociology generally by Crow (1989). The term strategy heavily connotes *process* and, whilst this is one of its strengths, it is also one of its potential weaknesses in so far as structures threaten to dissolve into infinitely malleable processes. It is therefore essential to keep in view the interplay between strategy and structure, between actions and resources for action.

As regards the interplay between strategic actions and resources for action, this is the weakest part of neo-Weberian closure theory, which has a tendency to dissolve the possession into the exercise of power. Power is a built-in attribute of closure, so there is a one-sided emphasis on the exercise of power and a neglect of the mere possession of power. This is particularly acute in Parkin's work, although Murphy (1984, 1988) attempts to rectify this overly 'actionist' conception by specifying the structural relations between different rules of closure, which he refers to as the 'deep structure of domination'. Nonetheless, closure theory forecloses a discussion of the social sources of power and this is why closure concepts are only utilised here within a theory of the middle range, i.e. to conceptualise gendered forms of distributive struggle specifically in the arena of the labour market. Weberian concepts are useful, but they do not provide an exhaustive purchase on social reality. As Crompton (1987) points out, one does not have to argue that the positional structure is wholly determined by closure in order to acknowledge that closure strategies have a significant impact. And as Crompton and Gubbay (1977) concluded in their assessment of the relative merits of Weberian and Marxist class theories, the Weberian focus on the distributive mechanism of the market is a useful one, but fails to provide a comprehensive alternative to Marxist class theory, which delves behind relations of exchange to uncover underlying relations of production. Indeed, the growing tendency is for sociologists to combine the insights of Weber and Marx in the class analysis of contemporary society (cf Abercrombie and Urry 1983, Marshall et al. 1988). It has also been argued that a more eclectic framework is appropriate for an understanding of professionalisation and that 'a satisfactory explanation of professionalization as an occupational strategy will come eventually to depend upon both Weberian and Marxist perspectives' (Turner 1987: 139–40). But the gender-blindness of both neo-Weberian and Marxist currents means that gender relations are treated in neo-Weberian closure theory as either derivative or contingent upon the principal form of exclusion in capitalist society, which is private property (Murphy 1984: 557, 1988), and as class derivative in Marxist theory. This gender-blindness frustrates the development of an analysis of the relation between gender and professionalisation.

By referring to gendered strategies and patriarchal structures, I am establishing that gendered actors who are engaged in professional projects as strategic courses of action will have differential access to the tactical means of achieving their aims in a patriarchal society within which male power is institutionalised and organised. There have been resources of power to which women are denied access, and are unable to mobilise. I shall endeavour to keep in view the interplay between strategy and structure by distinguishing between strategic courses of action, which are gendered, and facilitating or constraining structures, which are patriarchal. Gendered strategies and patriarchal structures are mediated through the institutionalisation and organisation of male power within different sites of social, economic and political relations.

But closure strategies are gendered in another sense too. The criteria of exclusion from or inclusion within an occupation may be gendered. Murphy (1984, 1988) refers to 'rules of sexual exclusion' which may, of course, be enshrined in the legal system. I shall refer to these as gendered collectivist criteria of exclusion and shall demonstrate how these do not operate 'informally' as some writers (cf Freidson 1986) suggest, but historically have formed a key plank of closure practices.

PROFESSIONS, CAPITALISM AND PATRIARCHY

So far I have suggested that professional projects are best conceptualised as processes of occupational closure, and have sketched the bare bones of a model of occupational closure strategies that is geared towards capturing their gendered dimensions. In particular, I also stressed the necessity for gendering the agents of professional projects, who are positioned not only within class relations but also within gender relations of dominance and subordination. However, it is also necessary to ground these projects historically within the structural parameters of patriarchal capitalism in order to develop further insights into professionalisation as an occupational strategy and establish the significance of gender for understanding not only the form but also the outcome of these strategies.

Professions and capitalism

The critical neo-Marxist theory of the professions which emerged during the 1970s established the necessity for grounding the rise of professionalism within the historical and structural parameters of competitive, monopoly and welfare capitalism – in short, for analysing the relation between professions and the class structure (cf Johnson 1977, Larson 1977, 1979, Navarro 1978, Ehrenreich and Ehrenreich 1977). But it remains to locate professional projects within the structural and historical parameters of patriarchy as well as of capitalism.

Sociologists generating middle range theories of professionalisation as a process of monopolisation or closure have been criticised (cf Johnson 1977) for considering the social division of labour in abstraction from the specific and determining processes of capitalist social relations. There has been considerable discussion of the relation between professionals and the class structure of contemporary capitalism generally (cf Abercrombie and Urry 1983, Ehrenreich and Ehrenreich 1977, Rueschemeyer 1986, Johnson 1977, Crompton 1990). Professionals have been located in the new middle class (Johnson 1977, Carchedi 1977), in the 'service class' (Abercrombie and Urry 1983) or in the 'professional–managerial class' (Ehrenreich and Ehrenreich 1977). But most attempts to relate professions to the class structure are highly functionalist. Johnson (1977) follows Carchedi in viewing professionals as 'agents of both the collective labourer and global capital'. Professionalism, which Johnson defines as colleague control over work activities, can only arise when these core work activities fulfil the global functions of capital, which are functions of control, surveillance and reproduction of labour power. Ehrenreich and Ehrenreich (1977) also define the professional–managerial class in terms of its major function in the social division of labour, which is 'the reproduction of capitalist culture and capitalist class relations'. But the relation between professions and the class structure is surely far more mediated than this (Gramsci 1971: 12).

Abercrombie and Urry (1983) urge that we reject such a functionalist reading of the relationship between professionals and capitalist relations of production. They point out that intellectuals or professionals are located in part at least in civil society, a sphere where relatively free association may take place, and that, as a result, professionals can to some degree generate and regulate their own forms of knowledge, albeit mediated by the state. They oppose a unicausal, functionalist reading and insist instead that professionalisation has had crucial consequences upon existing forms of structured social inequality, particularly upon the relations between labour and capital. They conclude:

> On the one hand, Marxists have been right to emphasise the increase in the degree to which professionals function for capital, as constitutive elements of the service class; yet on the other hand, Weberians have been correct to emphasise the distinctive market position of professionals which stems in

part from their ability to regulate their particular knowledge-base.

(Abercrombie and Urry 1983: 147)

But we are no nearer to understanding the relationship between professions and patriarchal structures. As Stacey (1981) observes, the narrow focus on production relations of capitalism elides the gender order and the part played by professionalising occupations in sustaining that order. Nor does it offer any way of conceptualising the relation between gender, professionalisation and patriarchal structures.

It is by using Larson's work (1977, 1979) as a springboard that we can begin to locate gendered professionalisation strategies within their structural parameters, although it must be emphasised that Larson herself only investigates the relation between professional projects and capitalist institutions. Larson is unconcerned with gender, let alone patriarchy.

Larson locates the rise of professionalisation within the historical matrix of competitive capitalism, and explores the relationship between professional projects and capitalist institutions such as the state, the free market for services, the labour market, the bureaucratic organisation and the modern university system of higher education. Larson's core argument is that the rise of professionalism has been a phase of capitalist rationalisation. It was in the structural context of competitive capitalism during the latter half of the eighteenth and the first half of the nineteenth centuries that the model of profession was first projected. This first phase of modern professionalisation was therefore an historically specific phase which coincided with the consolidation of the capitalist mode of production: with industrialisation and laissez-faire capitalism. This was followed by a second phase of professionalisation, where the model of profession is superseded by the ideology of professionalism. This ideology functions as part of the dominant ideology of advanced capitalist societies which justifies inequality of status and closure of access in the occupational order. It is an ideology utilised by newly differentiated technical specialities, such as auxiliary specialisms within medicine, and by new occupations located within bureaucratic organisations. The historical transition from a model of profession to an ideology of professionalism describes the strategic shifts of occupational groups as they find themselves in a shifting structural context:

55

the model of profession, divorced from the structural matrix within which it was formed, is adopted as a strategy of occupations which are in radically different situations with regard to the market and to capitalist relations of production than were the classic protagonists of the first professionalisation movement.

(Larson 1979:612)

Larson identifies the core of the professional project as the attempt to secure a structural linkage between *education* and *occupation*; between *knowledge* in the form of the negotiation of cognitive exclusiveness, and *power* in the form of a market monopoly. This, together with her insistence that professionalism was an historically specific organisational movement, is an important contribution to sociological analyses of professionalisation, because profession is treated as a concrete, historically specific *project* with discontinuities in both its substance and its structure.

Larson isolates two key dimensions of the professional project. The first is the creation and control of a professional market which is not structurally subordinated to the capitalist market of employers. The second is the negotiation of cognitive exclusiveness to a body of relatively abstract knowledge susceptible to practical application. Like Freidson (1986) her focus is on both power and knowledge. Professionalisation is essentially about market power and the construction of a formal knowledge base. The structure of the professionalisation process consists in the unification of these two elements, secured within the historical matrix of competitive capitalism and by means of capitalist institutions. Larson emphasises the role of training institutions, particularly the modern university, as the empirical arena within which the link between knowledge and the market is secured.

Professional movements were essentially organisational projects, aimed at a specific form of monopoly based on a complex model of market organisation and control: 'In this model, two sets of elements – specific bodies of technical–theoretical knowledge, and actual or potential markets for skilled services or labour – which therefore admitted relatively independent trajectories are structurally linked' (Larson 1979: 610).

I see professionalization as the process by which producers of special services sought to constitute *and control* a market for their expertise. . . . Professionalization is thus an attempt to

translate one order of scarce resources – special knowledge
and skills – into another – social and economic rewards.

(Larson 1977: xvi, xvii)

The processes that Larson identifies as at work in the creation of a
professional market and the negotiation of cognitive exclusiveness
deserve elaboration.

The creation of professional markets involves three processes.
First, for a professional market to exist, a distinctive commodity
has to be produced and, above all, the commodity or professional
service has to be standardised. In the case of medicine, for
example, it was essential to overcome the pre-modern situation
where consumers, when they changed providers, also changed
medical commodities. This meant eliminating diverse competing
products and establishing one market for medical services.
Second, the producers themselves have to be produced if their
products are to acquire a distinctive uniformity. Third, the attitude
of the state towards education and monopolies of competence is
crucial to the success of the professional project. The tendency
toward monopoly by elimination of competing products led professional entrepreneurs to solicit state sponsorship or state-
enforced penalties against unlicensed practitioners beyond professional control. In the case of medicine, the situation that prevailed
until the nineteenth century was that the market for medical
services was highly competitive and lacked standardisation of
either commodity or producers. At the beginning of the nineteenth century, the most significant axis of competition was
between the lower ranks of the general practitioners or surgeon–
apothecaries and the higher ranks of prestigious physicians. Unification therefore became part of the process of standardisation of
both producer and product. The professional project in medicine
was singularly successful in securing state sponsorship for monopolistic control, argues Larson, partly because medicine operated
in an arena of vital concern for the individual and the community,
and state concern over recurrent epidemics is cited as evidence.

Although Larson defines the professional project as essentially
a market project, her thesis is not exhausted by an analysis of the
market conditions of professional monopoly. She argues that
there are further cognitive conditions, and that market conditions
alone are insufficient to guarantee professional autonomy. In
order to secure market control the profession must unify its

cognitive base and establish cognitive exclusiveness. Its cognitive base must be formalised or codified sufficiently to allow standardisation of the product as well as of the producers. At the same time it must be scientific in Kuhn's sense of a field in which progress is marked, so that its changing nature prevents excessive routinisation at the same time as maintaining relative inaccessibility of expertise. Larson's emphasis on the cognitive conditions of professional monopoly picks up upon Jamous and Peloille's (1970) cognitive definition of a profession as an occupation which maintains a high indetermination/technicality ratio. In this way the production processes particular to 'professional' activities always contain an important margin of indetermination. The I/T ratio expresses the possibility of transmission of mastery of intellectual or material instruments used to achieve a given result. Technicality (T) describes the instrumental means that can be mastered and communicated in the form of rules. Indetermination (I) describes the means that escape rules and, at a specific historical moment, are attributed to the virtualities of producers.

In Larson's thesis the negotiation of cognitive exclusiveness that is essential to the maintenance of professional monopoly is secured in the empirical arena of the modern university, a capitalist institution. Larson specifies the modern means of professionalisation and distinguishes between those that are independent of and those that are dependent upon the professional market. This use of the term 'modern' distinguishes the ancien régime professional, dependent upon aristocratic patronage and élite sponsorship, from professions seeking to devise their own criteria of exclusion–inclusion on the basis of tested competence over a professionally defined body of knowledge. It parallels Elliot's (1972) distinction between 'status' and 'occupational' professions. State backing for the professional project is sought on the grounds of superior competence, rather than association with an élite.

An important distinction between *autonomous* and *heteronomous* means of professionalisation is evolved by Larson. This is a distinction between means which are defined or created to a significant extent by professional groups themselves, which are autonomous means, and those which are chiefly defined or formed through other social groups, which are heteronomous means. This distinction is set out in Table 2.1 and will become a particularly useful one in the analysis of gender and professionalisation.

Larson also identifies the institutional locations through which the means of professionalisation were mobilised. Major institutions were the modern university and professional associations, which provide sites for the mobilisation of autonomous means of closure, and the state, which provided the institutional location for the mobilisation of heteronomous means of closure, particularly state sponsorship of legal monopoly.

Table 2.1 Modern means of professionalisation

Autonomous means	Heteronomous means
Systematic training and testing	Registration and licensing
Institutionally located in professional schools and the modern university	Institutionally located in the state

Adapted from Larson 1977: 68

The work of neo-Marxist writers such as Johnson and Larson, who locate an analysis of the professions within an analysis of capitalist social, economic and political relations reminds us that professionalisation is not simply a process of occupational closure, but is locked into broader sets of structural and historical systems. Johnson's later (1982) work on the relationship between the state and professions is also particularly important in this respect. In fact, the autonomy of professional groups has been somewhat overstated, and Johnson's discussion of the state–profession relation suggests how professions have been crucially dependent upon state sponsorship. There is then a symbiotic relation between professions and the state. So, although neo-Weberian closure concepts may usefully be developed in order to capture the variety of strategies which characterise professional projects and used to unpick their gendered dimensions, it is also essential that these gendered projects are located within the structural and historical parameters of patriarchal capitalism. Nonetheless, despite its valuable insights, the neo-Marxist current of writing on the professions has neglected their gendered dimensions.

Professions and patriarchy

The spectre of the 'semi-profession' has haunted discussion of gender and professionalisation. Indeed, gender was integral to the very definition of a 'semi-profession' which according to Etzioni (1969) has two defining features. It is an occupation located within a bureaucratic organisation and one in which women predominate. The sheer preponderance of women places a brake on the extent to which these occupations can professionalise (Etzioni 1969, Simpson and Simpson 1969). Grist to the mill of this thesis was provided by Simpson and Simpson's reductionist thesis which merely read off the subordinate position of the 'semi-profession' in the occupational pecking order from the attitudes and predispositions of women in these occupations.

Thus it was claimed that 'semi-professions' are not professions because women lack occupational motivation, ambition and any drive toward intellectual mastery (sic.), are incapable of exercising authority over men (due to their own belief in male superiority), or of forming occupational communities and maintaining constructive colleague relations because they are 'less able than men to disagree impersonally, without emotional involvement . . . think in value terms rather than intellectualising a problem' and tend to spend their time comparing notes on clothing styles and child-rearing which 'does not have the same professionalizing effect as the task-related contacts of professionally dedicated workers' (Simpson and Simpson 1969: 241). Consequently, the subordinate position of the (female) semi-profession in relation to the (male) profession is due to the fact that women are willingly compliant and tractable subordinates, ideally suited to the role of 'hand-maidens of a male occupation that has authority over them' (Simpson and Simpson 1969: 231).

In short, because women are not men, 'semi-professions' are not professions. It is paradoxical that the functionalist paradigm of profession within which the semi-professions thesis is located has been largely displaced, but the semi-professions thesis lingers on. Very recently Rueschemeyer (1986) is able to casually suggest that the 'high devotion/low power syndrome' of the social service professions 'articulates well with traditional conceptions of women's role' (1986: 137). The 'semi-profession' thesis is based on an androcentric model of profession, which takes what are in fact the successful professional projects of man at a particular point in history to be the paradigm of profession. It is a 'machismo theory of professionalisation' (Parkin 1979) which is saturated with an 'oversocialised conception of woman' (Hearn 1982). As Parkin, at his most acerbic, points out:

> The implication is of course, that if the semi-professions were staffed mainly by men they would be far more likely to attain professional autonomy and closure – what might be called the machismo theory of professionalisation. It might come as an interesting piece of news to workers in mining, docks, and construction industries that their routine submission to managerial command is a characteristically feminine trait. But perhaps it is only the white-collar version of manhood that is so staunchly resistant to the importunities of authority and all encroachments upon personal autonomy.
>
> (1979:104)

Disappointingly though, Parkin concludes that the emphasis upon the gender composition of an occupation presents the least promising point of departure for an analysis of degrees of professional closure. He is more inclined to argue that it is the semi-professions' location in bureaucracies which precludes the possibility of occupational autonomy. So men have not prized these occupations and exclusionary devices against women have not operated with the same degree of rigour as in the established professions. But it seems to me that Parkin is inadvertently advancing a rather curious argument that the gender of an occupation is important, but *only* when it is a predominantly male occupation. But then, surely, gendered exclusionary practices will operate in occupations 'prized' by men, and so play some role in sustaining professional closure. Paradoxically, Parkin wants to relegate the gender composition of an occupation to a contingent rather than a determining factor in occupational closure, but then suggests that gender will operate as an exclusionary device when an occupation is 'prized by' men.

How, then, do we move onto a less androcentric terrain on which to theorise the relation between gender and professionalisation? Hearn (1982) has offered a radical redefinition of professionalisation as a patriarchal process, where semi-professionalisation indicates a state of partial male dominance of an activity, whilst full professionalisation indicates complete male control:

Full professionalisation comes when the activity is fully dominated by men. . . . Full professionalisation is also signalled
by the monopolisation by men of the particular area of
emotional life, free from competition from other, probably
more female dominated occupations . . . while semi-
professionalisation indicates partial patriarchal domination;
full professionalisation indicates full patriarchal domination.

(Hearn 1982: 195–6)

Professionalisation is a process whereby men socialise and seek to
control activities that relate to emotional experiences, biological
reproduction and the reproduction of labour power. It has also
been a process whereby men have wrested control over these
activities away from women in the private sphere and reconstituted
them as exclusively male activities within the public sphere.

Does Hearn point the way towards theorising the relation
between professions and patriarchy? Although Hearn opens up
the possibility of theorising professionalisation in relation to patriarchal processes, the manner in which he then conflates patriarchal and professional control at a definitional level is problematic.
Professional control is defined *as* patriarchal control, professional
power *as* male power. This raises a number of problems.

First, it precludes by definitional fiat alone the possibility of
women engaging in professional projects because these become,
by definition, male projects. Second, Hearn substantiates his case
with reference to activities associated with the (private) spheres of
reproduction and the emotions. But where does that leave male-
dominated professions such as accountancy, engineering, law,
architecture and company-secretaryship, which do not incorporate such activities but which still claim the status of professions?
Third, Hearn retains the notion of a 'semi-profession' located on
a continuum of states of relative professionalisation. But such an
ideal–typical continuum is problematic (cf Johnson 1972),
because it does retain some notion of what a profession *essentially*
is. Of course, in Hearn's case, professionalism is essentially patriar-
chalism, so relative states of professionalisation are conceptualised
along a continuum of *degrees* of male control over activities. But
professional control is more complex than this as the distinction I
have developed between different stratagems of closure suggests.
Finally, Hearn locates patriarchal domination within the spheres

62

of domestic labour and reproduction and argues that 'Those areas of social life that were not directly under capitalist domination, yet which contributed to reproduction and where emotions were especially likely to be unleashed, became clear targets for male domination through professions' (Hearn 1982: 188). Capitalist domination therefore inhabits the separate sphere of socialised labour and the production of goods and commodities, so patriarchy and capitalism become two independent systems of domination inhabiting different spheres of social life. But to divorce professional power so completely from the sphere of capitalist relations strikes me as incautious, particularly in view of the emphasis placed on the structural and historical interrelationship between professionalisation and capitalism by writers such as Larson and Johnson.

Gamarnikow (1978) has also explored the relation between patriarchal and professional modes of control by examining the sexual division of labour in health care, but looks at the relationship between genderisation, rather than simply masculinisation, and professionalisation. The gendering of the nurse–doctor relation served to de-professionalise this relation, as the subordination of nursing to medicine was secured through the construction of an ideological equivalence between two sets of relations, nurse–doctor and female–male relations. Essentially, it was patriarchal family relations which provided the ideological blue-print for this ideological reconstruction of interprofessional relations and their transformation into male–female relations. The doctor–nurse–patient relationship takes on the ideological resonances of power relations between men, women and children within the patriarchal family and the doctor takes on a position equivalent to the father. Gamarnikow's account of the interrelationship between patriarchal and professional modes of control is therefore a rather limited one, because patriarchal relations structure familial relations, but are ideologically 'reconstructed' in other spheres of social life, such as the labour market. This is to minimise the importance of patriarchal practices operating in the labour market itself, as Hartmann (1979), Cockburn (1983) and Walby (1986, 1990a) insist they do, as well as to read off women's subordination in the labour market from their subordination in the family.

Professional projects and patriarchal structures

It is necessary to map out a less androcentric terrain within which to locate discussions of professions and patriarchy. The generic concept of profession is also a gendered one. It takes what are in fact the successful professional projects of class-privileged, male actors at a particular point in history to be the paradigmatic case of profession. So the first step towards purging analyses of their androcentric bias is to abandon any generic concept of profession and redefine the sociology of professions as the sociological history of occupations as individual, empirical and above all historical cases rather than as specimens of a more general, fixed concept (cf Freidson 1983).

The term 'professional projects' serves to establish the concrete, historically bounded character of professionals as empirical entities 'about which there is little ground for generalising as a homogeneous class or a logically exclusive category' (Freidson 1983: 33). As Freidson suggests, suitable case studies are established on the basis of an occupation's own claim to being or becoming a profession – whether or not this claim is realised. This then opens up the way to bringing female professional projects into view.

To abandon a generic notion of profession, and work with a more historically specific notion of professional projects does not, however, preclude making general statements about what constitute professional projects. Professional projects are strategies of occupational closure which seek to establish a monopoly over the provision of skills and competencies in a market for services. They consist of strategic courses of collective action which take the form of occupational closure strategies *and* which employ distinctive tactical means in pursuit of the strategic aim or goal of closure. As we have seen, Larson (1979) emphasises that the core of the professional projects is the structural linkage it seeks to secure between education and occupation. Thus credentialist tactics, the use of educational certificates and accreditation to monitor and restrict access to occupational positions, are one of the major tactical means of professional closure. Indeed, Freidson (1986) has suggested that the nearest we may get to identifying an 'essence' of profession is that they are occupations which make formal education a prerequisite for employment. Credentialist tactics are also central to Parkin's definition of what constitutes professional closure practices, and are similarly privileged by other writers such as Murphy (1988), Collins (1979), Crompton (1987) and Crompton and Sanderson (1989). But, as Crompton (1987) observes, credentialism has been overlaid by gendered exclusion. Credentialism is not simply a matter of employing individualistic rules of closure, as Murphy (1988) claims, but gendered collectivist criteria of exclusion have been employed by men engaged in professional projects. Exclusion by gender is not an informal credential system, as Freidson (1986) suggests, but gendered exclusion has been embedded in credentialism and formed a key plank of professional projects.

Legalistic tactics have also been central to professional projects. These describe the attempt to gain a legal monopoly through licensure by the state (MacDonald 1985). Again, it is the neo-Weberian view which conceptualises professionalisation as a strategy of closure characterised by the use of legalistic and credentialist tactics (cf Parkin 1979). So professional projects have typically sought to mobilise both credentialist and legalistic tactics of closure. Some writers emphasise credentialism (Freidson 1986, Crompton 1987, Parkin 1979), others stress the importance of registration (MacDonald 1985, Johnson 1982). However, these tactical means of closure have to be mobilised in some way, and, once again, the gender of the agents of professional projects makes a difference to their ability to do so. But in order to understand how this makes a difference, it is necessary to locate gendered professional projects within the structural and historical matrix of patriarchal capitalism.

Professional projects, then, are pursued through legalistic and credentialist tactics – these are their distinguishing features. However, the tactical means of professionalisation strategies have to be mobilised in some way. Legalistic tactics involve the mobilisation of heteronomous means of closure within the institutional arena of the state. The archetypical legalistic tactic was to seek state sponsorship of the professional project. Whereas credentialist tactics entail the mobilisation of autonomous means of closure and are mobilised within the institutional terrain of civil society, within the modern university and occupational collegiate organisations. The necessity for grounding gendered professional projects within the structural parameters of patriarchal capitalism is established by the fact that these institutional sites for the mobilisation of the means of professional closure were simultaneously structured by patriarchy as well as by capitalism.

In the age of professionalism, the late eighteenth and nineteenth centuries, men who engaged in professional projects were able to mobilise both class-based and gender-based power resources in their struggles to secure market power and occupational closure. Autonomous means of professionalisation were institutionally located within civil society, a sphere that was the sovereign sphere of bourgeois male actors. In medicine, medical corporations and associations provided the institutional means for the mobilisation of tactics of closure and were also sites where male power was organised and institutionalised. The modern university, which was an important location for the negotiation of cognitive exclusiveness in the form of systematic education and examination, was patriarchally structured, governed by and admitting only men, in many cases well into the nineteenth and twentieth centuries. It admitted only bourgeois male actors, who used their powers to exclude women.

Larson stresses the structural linkage between education and occupation as lying at the core of the professional project. In nineteenth-century patriarchal capitalism access to secondary and higher education was the exclusive prerogative of bourgeois and aristocratic men, and indeed some of the early campaigns waged by equal rights liberal feminists were to open up channels of access to secondary and higher education for bourgeois women (Dyhouse 1981, Strachey 1935). Bourgeois men were structurally privileged in attempts to secure this linkage between education and occupation, particularly when this was secured within the institutional arena of the modern university.

Similarly, access to the heteronomous means of registration and licensing was an exclusively male prerogative as these means of professionalisation were institutionally located within the state, which was patriarchally structured until into the twentieth century, when franchise was gradually conceded to women from 1918 onwards. It was within these institutional arenas of civil society and the state that professional closure was secured historically as a patriarchal mode of closure.

Equally, and more importantly from the point of view of the discussion of female professional projects, it is necessary to locate the professional projects of women within the structural matrix of nineteenth-century patriarchal capitalism. The patriarchal nature of the institutions which provided the backdrop for professional projects would have placed severe constraints on women's ability to engage in such projects. Civil society was the sovereign sphere of bourgeois male actors, and it was extremely difficult for women to act collectively in this sphere by, for example, forming occupational associations. Consequently, if women did form occupational associations and seek state-sponsored registration they were bound to have to mobilise proxy male power in order to represent their collective interest at the institutional level of the state. Historically, the role of the state has been central to strategies of professionalisation (cf Johnson 1982), and this is equally true of female as it is of male professional projects. But in the nineteenth and early twentieth centuries, when female professional projects were being waged, access to state sponsorship was mediated not only by the class relations of capitalism but also by the gender relations of patriarchy.

Furthermore, if women were to pursue credentialist tactics in order to forge a link between education and occupation, their exclusion from the modern university system meant that they had to utilise other institutional locations for education and training programmes, negotiating cognitive exclusiveness in other arenas. Thus, nurse training evolved within the institutional location of the hospital whilst midwifery training was eventually formalised within the institutional umbrella of a professional association of medical men, the Obstetrical Society. In order to receive medical education, women were eventually forced to open up a separate medical school, the London School of Medicine for Women.

CONCLUSION

An analysis of female professional projects needs, then, to ask the following kinds of questions. How were women to mobilise the means of credentialism when the modern university was an exclusive male preserve that admitted only men, was governed by men and used its powers to exclude women? How were women to lobby the state when it was a patriarchal capitalist state to which women had no access, save by proxy male power? What were the implications for female professional projects of the very fact that they had to rely on the support and intervention of organised groups of men in order to advance their own cause?

It is necessary, then, both to gender the agents of professional projects and to recognise and address the fact that collective actors engaged in such projects are positioned not only within class relations but also within gender relations of dominance and subordination, or the gender relations of patriarchy. Only then can we begin to analyse female professional projects in England in the nineteenth and early twentieth centuries. Part II consists of case studies of gender struggle over the relative positioning of men and women in the emerging medical division of labour between 1850 and 1940. The focus is on the collective efforts of women themselves, who do not simply acquiesce in the face of patriarchal practices, but contest these in a variety of ways. The fact that women have organised collectively and engaged in struggles in the labour market, goes some way towards liberating women from the spectre of the 'semi-profession' concept, as it demonstrates that women have engaged in professional projects, attempting to be mistresses of their own fates, rather than fatefully acquiescing to the role of 'handmaiden' to male professionals.

Nineteenth-century medical professionalisation was a male professional project, whilst the campaigns for state registration of midwives and nurses were female professional projects. The gender of the actors and the broader structures of male dominance made a difference to both the form and the outcome of male and female professional projects. In medicine, professional closure was constructed as a form of patriarchal closure, sustained by the operation of gendered collectivist criteria of exclusion in the institutions of civil society, such as the modern university and the professional corporation (the autonomous means of closure) and sanctioned by the state (the heteronomous means of closure). Women's orchestrated challenge to the male monopoly of legitimate medical practice assumed the form of a usurpationary strategy of inclusion as they sought to be included within a structure of positions from which they were collectively excluded solely on account of their gender. These issues are examined in the following chapter on gender and medical professionalisation.

The remaining chapters demonstrate how the concept of a demarcationary strategy is absolutely vital in understanding how patriarchal practices played a key role in the creation of professional dominance in the emerging medical division of labour. Freidson (1977) and Larkin (1983) are absolutely right to stress the importance of inter-occupational 'imperialist' strategies in the maintenance of the professional dominance of medicine. However, although Larkin (1983) explores in detail the ways in which occupational imperialist, or what I term demarcationary, strategies are contested by groups subject to these, the phenomenon of female professional projects in the jostling for position in the emerging medical division of labour has been neglected. So, by utilising closure concepts and approaching midwives' and nurses' campaigns for state registration in an analytical manner similar to that in which other writers approach male professional projects, I specify the strategical forms and the tactical means which women used in their quest for professional status. The concept of a dual closure strategy is used to unpick the complexities of female professional projects, and I also explore the tactical and institutional means which women had at their disposal. Did women try to use credentialist or legalistic tactics and, if so, upon which did they concentrate and which were more successful?

Finally in Part II the mixed-gender occupation of radiography is examined and, once again, the concept of demarcation is used to explore the gendering of jobs, but this time *within* an occupational labour market. Male radiographers engaged in a strategy of internal demarcation, but this should properly be seen as a form of intra-occupational control, as it was part and parcel of radiographers' own attempts to professionalise their occupation, despite the fact that they had already conceded to medical radiologists' demarcationary strategy of de-skilling.

Part II

GENDER AND PROFESSIONAL PROJECTS IN THE MEDICAL DIVISION OF LABOUR

3

GENDER AND MEDICAL PROFESSIONALISATION

When the 1858 Medical (Registration) Act unified previously disparate orders of medical practitioners into an uneasy alliance between physicians, surgeons, apothecaries and general practitioners, the modern medical profession was born. But from that point onwards only men could engage in legitimate medical practice as a 'legally or duly qualified medical practitioner'. The 1858 Medical Act had set up a male monopoly and had effectively excluded women from access to the ranks of the medical profession. The act's parliamentary sponsor, William Cowper-Temple, had never intended this, and indeed there was nothing in the wording of the act to legally exclude women from becoming registered medical practitioners. In fact, gendered exclusionary mechanisms did not operate at the institutional level of the state, but in the institutions of civil society: the university medical faculties, the various Royal Colleges of Physicians and of Surgeons and other medical corporations, as well as teaching hospitals. Women were excluded from medical education and examination in all of the institutions which made up the nineteen portals of entry onto the medical register.

Medical professionalisation is perhaps one of the best examples of a male professional project. But medicine was not to remain an exclusive male preserve for long. The male monopoly over legitimate medical practice was quickly challenged by aspiring women doctors. It is at the point when women challenged gendered exclusionary practices that the precise mechanisms through which men were able to institutionalise male power within professional projects are thrown into sharp relief, and it becomes possible to identify the institutional arenas within which male power and privilege were most effectively organised and defended. So the following case study of men, women and medical practice in the nineteenth century provides the terrain on which to demonstrate the utility of two of the closure concepts set out in the previous chapter. Professional closure in medicine was historically constructed as a mode of patriarchal closure, and was sustained by gendered strategies of exclusion. Women's challenge to the exclusive male prerogative over medicial practice provides an example of a gendered strategy of inclusion, which I have defined as a countervailing, usurpationary response on the part of an excluded group.

First, though, before detailing the elaborate twists and turns of women's struggle to enter the medical profession and medical men's staunch defence of their male monopoly, it is necessary to set the scene for this episode by surveying the relationship between gender and healing activities in the pre-modern era and identifying broader structural and historical shifts in the transition from pre-modern to modern medical practice.

GENDER AND MEDICAL PROFESSIONALISATION: FROM THE PRE-MODERN TO THE MODERN ERA

The 1858 Medical (Registration) Act was the lynchpin of the formation of the modern medical profession. It gave legal definition to the term 'qualified medical practitioner' by setting up a state-sponsored register of qualified practitioners and delineating the legal as well as the institutional parameters of the modern medical profession (Waddington 1984: 136–7). Drawing on Larson's distinction between heteronomous and autonomous means of closure, the 1858 Medical Act represented the use of heteronomous means, in the form of a monopoly secured through legislative tactics within the institutional arena of the state. Thereafter, the General Medical Council, the statutory body set up under the terms of the 1858 Act, focussed its energies on credentialist tactics by mobilising autonomous means of closure and attempting to consolidate and impose some uniformity on existing, diverse systems of medical education and examination. There were nineteen routes of entry onto the medical register; systems of medical education and examination institutionally located in civil society, in the medical colleges and university medical faculties (cf Stevens 1966). Professional closure in medicine was secured in the twin arenas of the state and civil society and it was this process, together with processes linked to the institutional relocation of medical practice from the domestic to the market arena, that sounded the death knell for women's participation in healing practices.

In previous centuries, health care had been provided by a range of itinerant and community-based healers, many of whom were women, and it was the elimination of these types of healers, together with the control of newly emergent ones, which were processes at the core of medicine's modern evolution (Larkin 1983). By the mid-nineteenth century, however, medical diagnosis and treatment had become the exclusive prerogative of medical men, and women had become restricted to the care of the sick, as nurses, and to the attendance of women during natural labour, as midwives. When the profession formally unified in 1858, male groups of physicians, surgeons and apothecaries were included whilst the female group of midwives was not (Verluysen 1980).

So the history of the transition from the pre-modern to the modern practice of medicine is also the history of the re-structuring of gender divisions in health care as women were excluded from certain spheres of competence and confined to others. The twin concepts of gendered exclusion and demar-cation, set out in the previous chapter, therefore become crucial in charting the complex restructuring of gender divisions in the emerging modern medical division of labour in the nineteenth century. Generally, however, sociological analyses of the rise of the modern medical profession (Waddington 1984, Larson 1977, Freidson 1970a, Berlant 1975, Elliott 1972) have neglected to examine the twin processes of professionalisation and masculin-isation that marked the transition from pre-modern to modern medical practice. This has been left to a small body of feminist analyses (Ehrenreich and English 1973, 1979, Oakley 1976, Verluysen 1980, Chamberlain 1981, Doyal 1986, Pinchbeck 1981, Clark 1919).

Professionalisation and masculinisation of medical practice

What I shall refer to as the 'strong thesis' of the relation between the professionalisation and masculinisation of medical practice sets great store by the fact that, prior to the professionalisation of medicine, the arts of healing were practised throughout history by women. There is indeed a wealth of evidence to suggest this was the case (cf Power 1921, Hurd-Mead 1937, Hughes 1943, Pelling and Webster 1979, Wyman 1984), although the historical evidence is fragmentary and it is often difficult to establish the precise form which female practice took (Pinchbeck 1981), particularly whether healing practices were 'sold' in a market arena, provided *gratis* or in the context of more informal exchange mechanisms by village 'wisewomen'. The strong thesis claims that the Church, the state and the nascent medical profession (largely physicians) were united in the repression of a whole range of female medical practice, particularly that of wisewomen, and it is the witch-hunts in medieval Europe between the fourteenth and seventeenth centuries which are cited as the major means whereby the female monopoly over healing was broken. Indeed the strong thesis stands or falls on the strength of its imputed connection between witchcraft and female healing practices (Verluysen 1980).

The strong thesis is open to criticism on a number of counts. First, it resorts to a highly conspiratorial notion of 'well-organised campaigns' against women healers, and overlooks the fact that men as well as women were engaged in popular healing or 'empirics' and that the Church was a declining force in the regulation of medical practice during this period (Doyal, Rowbotham and Scott 1973). The strong thesis is also weakened by evidence that women continued to engage in healing activities well into the eighteenth century and by the fact that women from all classes, not just wisewomen of the peasant class, practised medicine (Verluysen 1980). Ultimately, its exclusive focus on wisewomen and neglect of skilled educated women weakens – although not entirely invalidates – the strong thesis for, as Verluysen (1980) argues:

Indeed, if skilled educated women had not competed with various categories of medical men, it is unlikely that the denigration of female practice would constitute such a strong theme in past medical writings, or that female healers in England and elsewhere would have been prosecuted for what were seen as infringements on licensed physicians' and surgeons' practices. If, as medical historians have implied, female healers had been primarily religious mystics or illiterate incompetent old wives, they would hardly have constituted any threat to respectable medical practitioners.

(Verluysen 1980: 194)

I think the strong thesis is insufficiently sensitive to the discontinuities between the pre-modern and the modern practice of medicine, and foremost amongst these for an explanation of the demise of women's participation in healing activities must surely be the restructuring of medical markets and the associated rise of 'occupational professionalism' in the modern era, together with the unification of previously competing orders of medical practitioners, and the associated demise of former localised and diverse forms of control over various types of medical practitioners. Prior to unification, guilds of barber-surgeons had operated at the local level, and even the Royal College of Physicians had jurisdiction only within the London area (cf Pelling and Webster 1979). The strong thesis also neglects more general changes in social and economic relations that marked the rise of industrial capitalism, and the impact these had on the participation of women in a whole range of activities, including healing activities. It is nevertheless true that male practitioners had periodically attempted to exclude women from practising physic (from as early as 1421 when London physicians petitioned 'that no woman use the practyse of fisyk' (Power 1921: 23)), although their greatest concern would surely have been with the domestic practice of medicine by upper-class wives, who 'persuade the sick that they have no needs of the Physition' (John of Cotta cited in Chamberlain 1981: 46), or who provided medical aid in the community as 'ladies bountiful', about whom John of Ardenne, a fourteenth-century physician, was particularly scathing (Chamberlain 1981).

In fact, the historical tensions around the gender of the practitioner seemed to be related to the more general tension between the domestic and market modes of providing various healing practices. Although in the pre-modern era women did certainly engage in market provision, charging a fee for their services, (cf Wyman 1984, Pinchbeck 1981, Power 1921), nonetheless women's healing activities were largely undertaken in the non-market domestic or community arenas (cf Pinchbeck 1981, Clark 1919, Chamberlain 1981). Women practised medicine as a domestic art in their capacity as wives and mothers (Clark 1919, Hughes 1943) and on a charitable basis for poor neighbours as 'the unofficial doctor of the village' (Wyman 1984: 23), particularly if they were noble women (Reynolds 1920, Hurd-Mead 1937) or the wives of clergy (Wyman 1984, *British Medical Journal* 1941: 124). The domestic sphere was, then, the main institutional site where women engaged in healing activities. Access to medical knowledge was informal and varied, gained largely by experience and the oral transmission from mother to daughter, as well as from published sources for literate, upper-class women. (Hughes (1943) tells how Sir John Paston copied books of physic for the Paston ladies.)

The evidence that women's healing activities were circumvented by domestic and familial relations in the pre-modern era is important in explaining the demise of female practitioners of healing in the modern era. Both Pinchbeck (1981) and Clark (1919) stress how women enjoyed access to skills and experience which they subsequently lost owing to the reorganisation of production that accompanied the rise of industrial capitalism. Richards (1974) too has argued that in the pre-industrial framework, women were absorbed in a broad range of activity which was subsequently narrowed by the structural changes associated with the industrial revolution. Before discussing the structural changes occurring around the provision of medical services, the fact that women did engage in something more closely approximating 'professional' medical practice in the context of market relations must also be established.

The evidence for this is fragmentary (Pinchbeck 1981), although can be gleaned from the application by women for licences to practice as physicians, surgeons and midwives (cf Hurd-Mead 1937, Wyman 1984), from advertisements placed by women (cf Pinchbeck 1981), and from instances of prosecution of unlicensed women practitioners (cf Pelling and Webster 1979, Clark 1919, Hurd-Mead 1937). But, once again, marriage relations provide an important route of access for women to the knowledge and skills which enabled them to engage in market-oriented medical practice. Marriage amongst the class of independent traders and master craftsmen was very much a business partnership, and so the marriage relation became an important way in which women might acquire their marketable skills and experience. Widowhood also provided women with an important means of access to independent female practice.

> Her marriage to a member of the guild conferred upon a woman her husband's rights and privileges, and as she retained these after his death, she could, as a widow, continue to control and direct the business which she inherited from her husband.
>
> (Clark 1919: 151)

Referring specifically to medical practice, Pinchbeck observes how:

> In some instances, wives and daughters of professional men appear to have been so closely associated with their work, that they were considered almost as partners, and after the death of the husband or father, as the case might be, continued to practise independently.
>
> (Pinchbeck 1981: 302)

In the pre-modern era, then, women's healing activities were circumvented by domestic relations, which provided the institutional context for women's engagement in both domestic and market forms of healing practices. But it is important to recognise the corollary of this, which is that familial relations were also constituted as patriarchal authority relations, and hence provided the pre-modern framework within which women's access to medical skills and practice was regulated as well as facilitated. Once this is established, then the reasons for the demise of female medical practitioners can be more squarely located within the shifting nature of provision of medical services together with the rise of 'occupational professionalism' in the transition to industrial capitalism. The focus then turns not on the imputed historical continuities in the 'exclusion' of women from medical practice, as in the 'strong thesis', but on important structural breaks with the past and discontinuities in means of control over female medical practice.

Men, women and modern medicine

There were two key developments relating to the organisation of medical practice which were at the core of the transition from pre-modern to modern medical practice and are of particular significance in charting the demise of female medical practice. The first has to do with changes in the market for medical services, and the second with changing forms of organisational control over medical practitioners.

Changes in the structure of the market for medical services accompanied the development of industrial capitalism. Franklin (1950, cited in Waddington 1984) argues that the market for medical services was rapidly expanding by the end of the eighteenth century and that this was due to the expansion of the middle class and the growth of their incomes, whereas in the pre-industrial era the services of medical practitioners were sought by only a small section of the population and the market arena was relatively unimportant compared to the domestic arena. Waddington emphasises how, prior to the nineteenth century 'most care of the sick was not even part of the market economy, for it took place within the context of familial and neighbourhood relationships which were outside the realm of market exchange' (1984: 181). There was, therefore a low level of effective demand for market services in pre-industrial England, due to two limiting processes. One was the inability of large sections of the population to pay for medical services; the other was the persistence of traditional attitudes which amounted to a preference for sources of care other than that provided by practitioners in the market arena; in other words, a preference for familial and neighbourhood services (Waddington 1984).

However, what is neglected in accounts of the restructuring of markets for medical services is the significance of the fact that medical care provided in non-market, domestic and neighbourhood arenas was gender-specific. It was provided overwhelmingly by women. Thus, the shifting location of medical care from domestic to market arenas is recognised, but the shift in the gender of the providers is ignored. The preference for alternative sources of care was in fact a preference for medical care provided specifically by women in the context of familial and neighbourhood relations. Equally, the 'strong thesis' of the demise of female medical practice fails to give sufficient credence to these important structural shifts in the nature of the organisation of medical markets.

The development of a large and expanding market for medical services by the beginning of the nineteenth century also provided the context for the development of occupational specialisation, which Waddington (1984) sees as a basic prerequisite for the emergence of modern professional occupations. There were certain elements of this process which impacted on the participation of women in market-oriented medical practices. We have seen how it was the coincidence of household and business activities which facilitated the involvement of women in the provision of market-oriented medical services in the pre-modern era. The craft nature of surgery (Cope 1959) and the trade associations of the apothecary (Wall et al. 1963) facilitated the involvement of family labour. However, the process of occupational specialisation in the nineteenth century entailed the shedding of ancillary 'business' activities and the setting of medical practice on a new, more specialised footing divorced from retailing and business activities. So developments associated with occupational specialisation also contributed to the demise of female medical practice, because they severed gender specific routes of access to and involvement in the market-oriented activities of the family business. The severing of women's involvement in a whole range of 'business' activities as these were divorced from familial sites has, of course, been more widely established by Davidoff and Hall (1987). Clark is surely right when she observes, although somewhat benignly, that 'women were forgotten, and so no attempt was made to adjust their training and social status to the necessities of the new economic organisation' (1919: 299) and how, when women did enter the expanding market arena, they 'entered the labour market as individuals, being henceforward entirely unprotected in the conflict by male relations' (1919: 289–290). Clark also sets great store by the fact that women were excluded from specialised sites of education and training outside the sphere of family relations, and sees this as an important contributing factor in their exclusion from the emergent professions. It was indeed important, and yet often overlooked.

Changing forms of organisational control over medical practice became urgently necessary because the traditional, tripartite system of orders had been de-stabilised and become largely ineffective by the beginning of the nineteenth century (Parry and Parry 1976). A new breed of general practitioner was emerging, who variously combined the practice of medicine, midwifery, surgery and pharmacy, and who therefore defied the tripartite, compartmentalised structure of medical practice (Parry and Parry 1976, Waddington 1984, Wall et al. 1963). Indeed, the movement for medical reform was spearheaded by the new general practitioner (Vaughan 1959, Stevens 1966) as the doctors registration movement from the 1820s onwards represented the attempt to legitimate this new form of general practice. Again, these developments had implications for gender relations around medical care. Medical men possessed the organisational means necessary to forge new controlling mechanisms over medical practice in the market arena and thus were able to institutionalise male power in the market arena as the modern market for medical services was emerging. Women were left out in the cold, and one of the reasons for this was that they had failed to secure the organisational means of controlling and protecting forms of female practice, even though midwives had tried, unsuccessfully, to organise themselves into a college in the seventeenth century.

Summary

In pre-modern medical practice, the bulk of women's healing activities had been circumvented within the domestic arena, whether they were providing health care for family and neighbours or involved in market-oriented provision. The shift in the dominant location of medical services from the private domestic to the public market arena sounded the death knell for women's medical practice. Hearn's (1982) argument that the simultaneous masculinisation and professionalisation of activities revolved around the wresting of these out of the private sphere and relocating them exclusively within the market arena therefore captures a key process in the demise of female medical practice. Medical men themselves were not passive onlookers in the face of some inexorable structural changes, but had always sought to exclude women from lucrative medical practice, and proponents of the 'strong thesis' are right to call attention to this. But they also had to establish the relative inefficacy of women's domestic cures compared to marketed ones, and establish a consumer preference for marketed services over and against the alternative medicines offered by educated, upper- and middle-class women in the domestic sphere. Furthermore, as Hartmann (1979) has argued generally, women did not have access to the organisational forms which enabled men to collectively represent their interests in the public market arena, and these occupationally based organisations were crucial in the doctors' registration movement and unification of medicine in 1858.

In addition, Larson (1977) has emphasised that the core of the professional project is the structural link it secures between education and occupation. The forging of this link in arenas of civil society from which women were excluded sealed the historic construction of the modern medical profession as an exclusively male sphere of occupational specialism. In the next section I focus on the precise ways in which this link was formed in the context of modern medicine and 'occupational professionalism'. I have looked so far at some of the processes whereby gendered forms of medical practice were restructured in the transition from the pre-modern to the modern organisation of medical practice. I now turn to the main focus of this chapter, which is to look at the relation between gender and occupational professionalism, particularly the gendered strategies of exclusion and inclusion which emerged in the mid-nineteenth century as women immediately contested the effective male monopoly over modern medical practice.

EXCLUSIONARY CLOSURE IN NINETEENTH-CENTURY MEDICINE

The 1858 Medical (Registration) Act sealed the fate of women in the modern medical profession. Women found it impossible to gain access to the medical register, despite the fact that 'The Act of 1858 spoke generally of "persons", and did not make any exclusion of female persons as compared with males' (*Hansard* CCXXX 1876). So rules of sexual exclusion were not explicitly codified into the act and William Cowper-Temple, who had framed the 1858 act, later declared that it was not his intention that women should be excluded from medical education (*Hansard* CCXXX 1876). Women were 'practically excluded from the register, though not excluded by the law' (*Hansard* CCXXVI 1875: 268). Gendered exclusionary mechanisms were not directly embedded in the legalistic tactics of professional closure.

Instead, gendered strategies of exclusion were pursued within the orbit of credentialist tactics in the institutional arena of civil society: the British universities and medical corporations that made up the nineteen portals of entry to the medical register for 'although the Statute permitted the registration of women, the conditions imposed by the medical corporations and by the Universities prevented them from being admitted to the register' (*Hansard* CCXXX 1876: 998). The 1858 act had excluded women from registration because it had failed to provide for the compulsory admission of women to universities, medical schools or qualifying examinations (Manton 1965: 64). Women were simply unable to secure the link between education and occupation, the link which Larson (1979) identifies as the core of the professional project.

The name of one woman was entered in the first medical register issued by the General Medical Council of Great Britain and Ireland in 1858. This was Dr Elizabeth Blackwell, who had received her MD from the medical college of the University of Geneva in America in 1849. During a visit to England in 1858 she gave a series of lectures on the importance of women's entrance into the medical profession, and her name was submitted to the General Medical Council for inclusion in the Medical Register (Blackwell 1914: 179). Dr Elizabeth Blackwell was able to register under a special clause permitting those already in possession of a foreign medical degree to register (Stansfeld 1877).

Dr Elizabeth Blackwell recalled that, at one of her lectures in Marylebone Hall in 1859 'the most important listener was the bright, intelligent young lady whose interest in the study of medicine was then aroused – Miss Elizabeth Garrett – who became the pioneer of the medical movement in England' (Blackwell 1914: 176). In 1860 Elizabeth Garrett began her studies in medicine, surreptitiously at the Middlesex Hospital under the pretext of being a surgical nurse, but had to overcome many obstacles on the way to becoming the second woman on the medical register in 1865. It became evident that the exclusion of women from the medical profession may not have been in the spirit of the 1858 Medical Act, at least as far as its parliamentary sponsors were concerned, but it was the intent of members of the medical profession – practitioners, professors and students of medicine alike – who responded in the 1860s to the claim of one woman to study and practise medicine with increasingly explicit anti-feminist sentiments and actions.

The first obstacle encountered by Elizabeth Garrett was the hostility of male medical students to her presence at lectures and on the wards at the Middlesex Hospital, where she was striving to establish herself as an official medical student. A memorial from the male medical students about the admission of female students was presented to the Middlesex Hospital Medical School Committee. It stated that 'the promiscuous assemblage of the sexes in the same class is a dangerous innovation likely to lead to results of an unpleasant character' and called for separate classes to be provided for women who wished to study surgery or medicine on the grounds that:

lecturers are likely (although unconsciously) to feel some restraint through the presence of females in giving explicit and forcible enunciation of some facts . . . the presence of young females in the operating theatre is an outrage on our natural instincts and feelings calculated to destroy those sentiments of respect and admiration with which the opposite sex is regarded by all right-minded men, such feelings being a mark of civilization and refinement.

(Minutes of the Middlesex Hospital Medical School Committee, vol. III 1861: appendix I, cited in Manton 1965: 351–5)

The reference to the inhibiting effect of the presence of women students in previously all-male classes on the use of obscenity is an interesting one. Newman (1957) refers to the widespread and outspoken demand of the right to be obscene in Victorian society, and observes in relation to this that the medical lecturers who were the most vocal in their opposition to the admission of women into courses of medical education were the anatomists 'who wanted to teach indecent mnemonics and were incapable of imagining any other way of implanting meaningless details' and the obstetricians (observes Newman, rather casually) 'who apparently just wanted to be indecent' (Newman 1957: 302). A contributor to the *Oxford Undergraduates' Journal* in 1870 wrote in support of mixed classes in medical education: 'Professors will have to give up amusing their students by improper stories; students will have to give up thinking there is anything amusing in indelicate stories and allusions' (cited in Jex-Blake 1886: 160).

Newman argues that the total disappearance of the use of obscenity in medical education was one result of the entry of women into medical education. Another result was 'an increase of assiduity amongst students' (although he adds in a sexist manner that the superior abilities of women to apply themselves to hard work is an 'excess' for which men are too 'sensible'!).

The second obstacle was the persistent refusal to admit women by medical staff on the committees of medical schools at the Middlesex, Westminster, London and Grosvenor Street hospitals (Blackwell 1914: 185–6) on the grounds that, seeing as the examining bodies were not prepared to admit women, the schools could not be expected to train what were, in effect, illegal practitioners (Blackwell 1914, *Lancet* 1861).

The third obstacle encountered was that of the medical corporations – the examining bodies themselves. The Royal College of Surgeons turned down Elizabeth Garrett's request in 1861 to attend lectures on obstetrics with a view to sitting the examination for their diploma in midwifery. The College took legal advice and the solicitor of the College declared:

> that although there was nothing in the Charter relating to the examination for the certificate of qualification in midwifery showing an intention that such certificates should be confined to male persons, yet that on the whole his impression was that there was quite sufficient doubt as to women having any right to claim to be examined to justify the College refusing to depart from the practice which had hitherto prevailed of admitting only men to examination for the certificate in midwifery, and suggesting that an answer to that effect might be sent to the letters from Miss Garrett and her father.
>
> (Cope 1959: 21)

The Royal College of Surgeons took legal advice on receipt of Elizabeth Garrett's application in 1864 to be admitted to examination for a licence, and was able to declare that 'the language of the Charter and of the Bye-laws precludes the College from granting licences to practise to Females, and also from admitting them to examination for a licence' (Cooke 1972).

The Society of Apothecaries was approached by Elizabeth Garrett. They submitted their charter for legal advice and were informed that the purpose of the charter was to enable them to regulate the sale of drugs so, because there were no legal grounds for refusing to allow women to sell drugs, they could not refuse to admit them to their examination (Manton 1965). However, Elizabeth Garrett had to conform to regulations, one of which required her to be apprenticed to an apothecary for five years and the other to attend three years in a medical school in the UK following prescribed courses of lectures (Letter from E. Garrett to E. Blackwell, 8 May 1862, cited in Blackwell 1914). The first she could comply with, the second 'is more difficult' she wrote in something of an understatement, as what followed was an encounter with the next obstacle which became a familiar and obdurate one to aspiring medical women; the resilience of university medical faculties to the claim of women to be admitted to medical lectures and medical degrees.

Elizabeth Garrett then decided to 'make an attempt at London University' (letter from E. Garrett to E. Blackwell, 8 May 1862, cited in Blackwell 1914). The University Senate declared that it had no power to admit women. Undeterred, Elizabeth Garrett together with Emily Davies submitted that under the terms of its impending new charter provision was made for women to be admitted (Manton 1965). Senate voted against the motion on the casting vote of the chancellor (Jex-Blake 1886) although the particular issue of admitting women to medical degrees had not been raised (Blackwell 1914). The Scottish universities with medical faculties were then approached, first Edinburgh, then St Andrews, but both declined to admit women to medical lectures and examination. However, during her stay at St Andrews, Elizabeth Garrett had received private instruction from a sympathetic Regius professor of medicine and, on the grounds that she had received private instruction, the Society of Apothecaries agreed that she could sit their examination. After arranging further private instruction from a hospital in London, Elizabeth Garrett presented herself for examination and became a licentiate of the Society of Apothecaries in 1865. Her name then went on the medical register.

A woman had slipped through the net of patriarchal closure. But the institutional means of control over the occupational infrastructure of medicine were patriarchally structured and controlled exclusively by medical men, who were able to prevent any more women slipping through the net simply by amending the regulations that governed entry to the examinations of the medical corporations in such a way as to make it impossible for women to comply (*Hansard* CCXXX 1876: 998). The Society of Apothecaries made a new ruling that, henceforth, candidates for their examination could not substitute private instruction for public lectures at a recognised medical school, as Elizabeth Garrett had done, and indeed as all women would have to do given their exclusion from public arenas of medical education.

A GENDERED STRATEGY OF INCLUSION 1869–76

After Elizabeth Garrett's precarious route to the medical register had been negotiated, this was immediately closed to prevent any other women from entering the medical profession. The outcome of one successful attempt by a woman to slip through the net of patriarchal closure was to make the male monopoly even more watertight. How were women to storm the citadel of male monopoly over medical education, examination and registered medical practice? At the end of the 1860s a more sustained, orchestrated campaign began to take shape and a collective usurpationary strategy of inclusion was to emerge.

The overall task confronting women who wished to practise medicine in Britain was to establish the means whereby the link between education and occupation could be made by women as well as by men. The key to the maintenance of professional closure as patriarchal closure in medicine lay in the exclusion of women from the institutional arenas of medical education and examination that made up the nineteen state-approved routes of access to registered medical practice under the terms and conditions of the 1858 Medical Act. Exclusionary mechanisms were embedded in the sphere of civil society, in the medical corporations and modern university. They were only indirectly reinforced within the institutional arena of the state. This suggests that, although legalistic tactics in the form of state sponsored registration have been central to modern professional projects, including that of medicine, patriarchal closure has been primarily sustained through credentialist tactics by controlling access to education and accreditation.

Aspiring women doctors' inclusionary strategy initially concentrated on gaining access to university medical education and examination, through countervailing credentialist tactics. But the universities proved remarkably resilient to women's usurpationary claims, so priority was eventually given to countervailing legalistic tactics of usurpation and the attempt to gain access to medical education and examination by lobbying parliament for an amendment to the 1858 act. But women's struggle to enter the medical profession was not simply a form of occupational politics, but was also a form of gender politics. It is possible to distinguish between credentialist and legalistic tactics of occupational politics, and the equal rights and separatist tactics of gender politics. These four tactics may combine in various ways, as Table 3.1 illustrates.

Women, then, used credentialist and legalistic tactics. They challenged mechanisms of gendered exclusion embedded within credentialism and operating within the autonomous means of professional closure, namely the institutional locations of the modern university and medical corporations. This element of women's usurpationary strategy is described as a countervailing credentialist tactic. Women also challenged the mechanisms of gendered exclusion embedded within the legalistic tactics of

Table 3.1 Tactics of usurpation

	Credentialist	Legalistic
Equal rights	The University of Edinburgh, 1869–74	1. Universities (Scotland) (Degrees to Women) Bill, 1875
		2. Medical (Qualifications) Bill, 1876
Separatist	The London School of Medicine for Women, est. 1874	Medical Act Amendment (Foreign Universities) Bill, 1874 and 1876

professional closure and located within the heteronomous means of professional closure, at the institutional level of the state. This they did by seeking state sponsorship of their usurpationary project (just as medical men had sought state sponsorship for their professional project) in the form of parliamentary bills that sought to amend the 1858 Medical Act. This facet of women's usurpationary strategy is described as a countervailing legalistic tactic.

Along the dimension of gender politics a distinction may be made between an equal rights and a separatist tactic as the specifically gendered tactics of usurpationary struggle. The equal rights tactic describes women's attempts to break the male prerogative over the system of medical education and examination by gaining access to existing, male-dominated systems of medical education and examination, namely the modern universities and medical corporations. In addition, separatist tactics were resorted to, as women attempted to open up separate, gender-specific routes of access to the system of medical education and registration.

The following analysis of women's usurpationary struggle in the 1860s and 1870s examines, first, credentialist tactics pursued on the terrain of civil society and, second, legalistic tactics pursued in the institutional arena of the state legislature.

Credentialist tactics

Between 1869 and 1873 a group of women led by Sophia Jex-Blake struggled to receive medical education and present themselves for medical degrees at the University of Edinburgh. This episode has been well documented (cf Jex-Blake 1886, Thorne 1915, Bell 1953) so the main outline of events is generally familiar. In 1869 Sophia Jex-Blake was refused admission to medical classes by the Senate of Edinburgh University, not on grounds of principle but of expediency. It was not worth making concessions for the convenience of one lady (Jex-Blake 1886: 71–5, Bell 1965). Then four other women – Edith Pechey, Isabel Thorne, Matilda Chaplin and Mrs Evans – joined her and, as there were then five, the university could no longer exclude them on the grounds of expediency alone. The five women were admitted to be matriculated and study medicine, although in separate classes from male students. The women paid medical lecturers three times the fee that the male students did for the privilege.

However, in 1870 the opponents of medical women attempted to prevent them from completing their medical education by putting pressure on medical lecturers who were providing separate classes. The women switched to the Edinburgh Extra-Mural School, where three doctors admitted them to classes. The gathering opposition to the women students was led by Professor Christison of the Medical Faculty, who was also a manager of the Royal Edinburgh Infirmary, which had accepted the women for clinical instruction. Christison then managed to reverse this decision on constitutional grounds. Male undergraduates then began to take an active part in the struggle against the women. This was fuelled, suggests Bell (1953) by the glowing academic achievements of the women at the end of the winter session (1869–70) when four of them gained honours and one of them, Edith Pechey, came first in the chemistry examination, an achievement which merited a Hope Scholarship. However, this was awarded to the man immediately below her on the class list (Jex-Blake 1886: 81–3, Bell 1953: 72).

In November 1870 the 'indignities' (Lutzker 1974) and 'petty annoyances' (Thorne 1915) to which the women were increasingly subject came to a head in the riot at Surgeon's Hall, where the women were to sit an examination. A dense crowd had gathered outside the hall and the gates were slammed in their faces by a number of young men 'who stood within, smoking and passing about bottles of whisky, while they abused us in the foulest possible language' (Jex-Blake 1886: 92). One of the medical students already in Surgeon's Hall came to their aid and opened the gate for them. During the examination a sheep was pushed in by the rioters. When the examination was over, the women left protected against the rioters by a bodyguard (armed with osteological specimens, recalled Isabel Thorne) of some of their fellow students (Jex-Blake 1886: 93, Thorne 1915: 14).

This incident of public and collective male violence, both physical and verbal, against women who openly transgressed the bounds set for them within patriarchal relations is evocative of the violence and sexual assault meted out to a deputation of suffragettes on 'Black Friday', 18 November 1910 (cf Morrell 1981). In 1913 Christabel Pankhurst was to argue that the manners of chivalry can only be maintained while women willingly abide by the restrictive rules men have imposed upon them, but that, once women challenge these rules, chivalry is dead (cf Spender 1982, Sarah 1983). Indeed, Sophia Jex-Blake referred somewhat ironically to the rioters outside Surgeons Hall as 'chivalrous foes' (1886: 93).

However, male power in the institutional sphere of civil society is not routinely exercised as force or physical and verbal intimidation, but simply by changing the rules. By July 1873 the University of Edinburgh, by a series of elaborate twists and turns, had succeeded in restoring the patriarchal status quo ante by declaring that, although the women medical students could continue to receive medical instruction in separate classes, this did not imply any right to obtain medical degrees (Jex-Blake 1866: 138). 'The majority of medical men in the University . . . were adverse to them; and the doors of the Scotch University were shut against admission of ladies' (*Hansard* CCXXX 1876: 998).

The struggle at Edinburgh demonstrated that the modern university system provided a key site for the institutionalisation of gendered credentialist tactics. It was a countervailing credentialist tactic because it sought to replace gendered collectivist criteria of exclusion with non-gendered criteria of inclusion. It was also an equal rights tactic because it sought to secure the admission of women to an existing, traditionally male-dominated institution of medical education.

Following the defeat at Edinburgh, legalistic tactics were employed by presenting bills to parliament annually between 1874 and 1876, but credentialist tactics were pursued further. The next move was to open the London School of Medicine for Women in 1874 (cf Jex-Blake 1886: 176–84, Thorne 1915). This provided women with a gender-specific route of access to medical education, so women could establish the link between education and occupation in an empirical arena independent of the patriarchally structured institution of the modern university. This is why it can be called a separatist tactic, for if women were not to be admitted to existing male-dominated routes of access to medical education, then they would have to devise their own system of medical education.

Once the London School of Medicine for Women was opened, women could at least receive a medical education. However, there were further obstacles to be overcome before they could sit medical examinations. First, the school had to be officially recognised by at least one of the nineteen examining boards, which had to agree to admit women students from the London School of Medicine for Women to their examinations. Second, the women students had to be admitted to clinical instruction in a hospital with at least one hundred beds (Thorne 1915). All of the examining boards flatly refused to admit women to their examinations. The Royal Free Hospital was approached to provide clinical instruction because it had no male medical students but its medical staff objected to admitting women students (Thorne 1915: 362).

So the ultimate success of this credentialist tactic depended upon the parallel pursuit of legalistic tactics. These concentrated on securing state sponsorship for the women's cause as 'the school could not continue to exist if the way to examination were long barred to women'. Further progress was blocked unless parliament could 'repudiate their supposed disability of sex' and 'practically remove that disability' (Stansfeld 1877: 891–2).

Legalistic tactics

Between 1874 and 1876 women turned their attention to countervailing legalistic tactics. These describe their attempts to break the male monopoly over medical education, examination and registration by means of an act of parliament. But women had no access to the state and could not voice their collective interests except by enlisting the patronage of men, so proxy male power was mobilised by enlisting the support of influential members of the dominant group.

In relation to the issue of mobilising proxy male power, Parkin (1979) makes two perceptive observations about effective feminist struggles of usurpation. They have frequently grounded their usurpationary claims in moral appeals and, in addition, they may gain support from a sector of the dominant group committed to liberal ideology. It was indeed the proponents of radical liberalism who championed the women's cause, although Sophia Jex-Blake recalls how they 'always found excellent friends and bitter foes in both camps' (1886). Among the parliamentary champions of the women's cause were James Stansfeld, the radical liberal MP who was also active in championing the radical midwives' cause when he was governor of the Poor Law Board, James Bright MP, Russell Gurney MP and Recorder of London, and William Cowper-Temple MP, who had introduced the 1858 Medical (Registration) Act.

James Stansfeld highlighted the double claim involved in women's fight to enter the medical profession. There was both a liberal, equal rights claim of women to have the right to study and practise medicine, and there was a moral claim of women to be medically attended by women doctors, if they chose (Stansfeld 1877). The claim of women to be treated by members of their own sex carried strong moral appeal and Dr Elizabeth Blackwell (1860) argued that it was not a natural arrangement that women and children seeking medical treatment should have recourse entirely to men. Women's claim to practise medicine in order to safeguard the modesty as well as the health of their own sex cast some considerable doubt on the legitimacy of an exclusive male prerogative over medical practice. However, women's struggle to enter the medical profession was not to be won on the moral strength of their claim, but through the persistent pursuit of legislative changes that would expose chinks in the armour of patriarchal closure in the medical profession. This was no simple task.

Two legalistic tactics were pursued in tandem between 1874 and 1876. The first, a separatist tactic, attempted to create a separate, gender-specific route of access to the medical register for women. The second, an equal rights tactic, sought to include women within the existing systems of medical education and examination, thus opening up a route to the medical register on the same terms as men.

Under the terms of the 1858 Medical Act women were not legally excluded from registered medical practice, so the separatist, legalistic tactic sought to capitalise on two factors. By the early 1870s women could gain medical degrees from a number of European universities such as Paris, Berne, Berlin, Leipzig, Vienna and Zurich (*Hansard* CCXXX 1876: 999; Stansfeld 1877) and, under schedule A of the 1858 Medical Act anyone already possessing a degree of MD from a foreign university and practising in Britain before 1 October 1858 was eligible for registration (Stansfeld 1877).

In 1875 and again in 1876 William Cowper-Temple introduced the Medical Act Amendment (Foreign Universities) Bill into parliament. This bill aimed to secure women's access to the medical register by proposing that foreign degrees were to be recognised once again, but this time only when they were held by women. The objective, then, was to bypass those patriarchally structured institutions which blocked women's access to the credentials necessary for registration and to set up a further gender-specific, twentieth portal of entry to the medical profession in Britain.

Cowper-Temple's bill amounted to an attempt to secure for women a right denied to men, who could not gain admission to the medical register by possessing a foreign degree. It therefore aimed to give special treatment to women and sat rather uneasily within the parameters of a liberal ideology. Of course, it was opposed precisely on these grounds; that it sought to treat women and men differently, letting women slip into the profession by a side door, legally forced open for them (*Hansard* CCXXX 1876: 1005). Even the General Medical Council could safely hide behind the cloak of liberalism and decry the injustice of a proposal which called upon them to grant to women a privilege denied to men (Minutes of the General Medical Council 25 June 1875: 90; 3 June 1876: 235–6). This they declared was 'subversive of the main principle of the Medical Act'. The government also declared its unwillingness to admit the principle of enabling foreign degrees to be a route of access to the practice of medicine in England (*Hansard* CCXXX 1876: 1018).

Cowper-Temple's bill stood on far shakier ground than the legalistic, equal rights tactic that was being pursued in tandem. This was the Medical Act (Qualifications) Bill of 1876 'for enabling Examining Bodies to treat their charters and statutes as not being limited to one sex, but as applying to both' (*Hansard* CCXXX 1876: 1003). At its second reading in August 1876, Cowper-Temple's bill was withdrawn in favour of this more 'moderate' enabling Bill, which was also preferred by the government. Cowper-Temple warned of its limitations though:

This also was good as far as it went, the weak part of it being that it was only an enabling Act, and did not compel anyone to act upon it. After the experience they had of the way in which the medical bodies had treated women candidates, he was afraid that the Bill, if passed, would not have the effects of securing the objects which its promoters desired . . . [due to] a silent, dogged, obtuse refusal on the part of the medical men in the country to allow women to enter the Profession of Medicine.

(*Hansard* CCXXX 1876: 1003–1004)

He also pointed to the 'no-win' situation of women when they seek equality with men, who defend their advantages on the grounds that 'There is no equality at all between men and women, and women are not to have the advantages which are given to men by the corporations or universities' (*Hansard* CCXXX 1876: 1001). But the irony was that when women asked for special treatment (what we would now call 'positive discrimination') they were met with loud and indignant calls for equality of treatment.

Between 1874 and 1876 bills which aimed to secure women's access to the system of medical education were introduced annually into parliament. The first, the Scottish Universities Bill, was introduced by Cowper-Temple in 1874 and again in 1875. It was a direct attempt to pull the rug out from under the feet of the university court of Edinburgh which had prevented women medical students from continuing there on the grounds that, in admitting them in the first place, it had exceeded its powers (*Hansard* CCXIX 1874: 1530). The bill simply proposed to give the universities of Scotland the powers to admit women if they so wished, not to force them to use that power.

Supporters of this bill sought to give women equal access to the university system of medical education and examination, which would then enable women to comply with the conditions for registration (*Hansard* CCXIX 1874: 1537). Opponents of the bill came up with a number of desperate, ingenious arguments. Why should the universities of Scotland be singled out to be granted powers to admit women and not all British universities (*Hansard* CCXIX 1874: 1541)? Anyway, what was the use of conferring powers on Scottish universities when they did not want to exercise these even if they did possess them? And, in any case, they did not have the necessary resources to provide the extra buildings and lecture programmes for women to be educated separately from men (*Hansard* CCXXII 1875: 1160). The bill aimed to remove doubts about the legal position of the university with respect to the admission of women, but there *were* no doubts, for 'Women were now, and always had been, excluded altogether from the Universities' (*Hansard* CCXXII 1875: 1132) – and long may they continue to be, was the prevailing sentiment! After all, it was claimed, 'The universities, colleges and medical schools have been built by men for men, and have been paid for by men' (*British Medical Journal* 1876: 202).

In 1876 the Medical Act (Qualifications) Bill was introduced into parliament by Russell Gurney MP, and received Royal Assent that same year. This extended the powers of every examining body empowered under the terms of the 1858 Medical Act to grant qualifications for registration, to all persons without distinction of sex. It was an enabling bill, so was permissive rather than compulsory. Why, then, did this legalistic, equal rights tactic of usurpation succeed where others had failed?

In 1875 the General Medical Council was asked by the government to consider the general question of 'whether women ought to be able to look to medical practice, or certain branches of it, as open to them equally with men as a profession and means of livelihood' (Minutes of the General Medical Council 1875: 89). The General Medical Council then felt bound to consider the whole question of the admission of women to the medical profession (Minutes of the General Medical Council 1875) whereas up until that point it had been able to rely on the resilience of gendered exclusionary mechanisms operating within the university system and medical corporations. The General Medical Council drew attention to the 'almost insuperable hindrances, moral, as well as physical, to the efficient Education and successful pursuit of Medicine by women' (Minutes of the General Medical Council 26 June 1875: 140) and declared 'The Medical Council are of opinion that the study and practice of medicine and surgery, instead of affording a field of exertion well fitted for women, do, on the contrary present special difficulties which cannot be safely disregarded' (Minutes of the General Medical Council 1875: 94). At this point, however, the question arose as to the precise meaning of the phrase 'cannot be safely disregarded' and whether this should be taken to imply the necessity for the legal exclusion of women from the medical profession (Stansfeld 1877).

It was at this point, argued Stansfeld perceptively, that 'the position of the opponents of medical women became untenable and the legalised admission of women to the ranks of the profession only a matter of time' (Stansfeld 1877). This was because, when pressed on this matter, the General Medical Council conceded 'That the words "which cannot be safely disregarded" be left out and the following words inserted in their place "but the Council are not prepared to say that women ought to be excluded from the profession"' (Minutes of the General Medical Council 25 June 1875: 94).

The General Medical Council had thus declared that it was unwilling to declare that women should be excluded de jure from the medical profession. At the same time the General Medical Council's reluctance to adopt such a legalistic tactic of exclusion in relation to the general question of women's admission to the medical profession was matched by their unwillingness to sanction any real challenge to the credentialist mechanisms of gendered exclusion which operated in the institutional context of civil society, in the modern university and medical corporations. Their response to Russell Gurney's bill 'to remove restrictions on the granting of qualifications for registration under the Medical Act on the ground of sex' was that, as long as such measures were discretionary rather than compulsory, did not interfere with the 'free action' of universities and medical colleges, and did not grant women any right in the government of examining bodies, they could see no grounds for opposition (Minutes of the General Medical Council 1876, Stansfeld 1877).

The resilience of patriarchal closure

To what extent, then, had the successful pursuit of a strategy of inclusion by means of a legalistic, equal rights tactic destabilised patriarchal forms of exclusionary closure within medicine? Strachey rather optimistically concludes that 'the struggle was at an end. . . . After this everything suddenly became easier' (Strachey 1935: 255). However, the success of a legalistic, equal rights tactic represented but a minor threat to the citadel of male monopoly which did not collapse, but crumbled only slowly.

The 1876 Enabling Act had no real teeth, and was permissive rather than mandatory. The University of Edinburgh persisted in its refusal to allow the women who had studied medicine there to present themselves for medical degrees (Thorne 1915) and remained obdurate in its refusal. Only the Kings and Queens College of Physicians in Ireland agreed to admit women to their examination immediately after the 1876 Act and to recognise the London School of Medicine for Women (Bell 1953). Five women – Sophia Jex-Blake, Eliza Dunbar, Frances Hoggan, Louisa Atkins and Edith Pechey, all of whom had received clinical training during their time at Edinburgh and studied at Edinburgh and the London School of Medicine for Women – presented themselves for examination in Dublin and added their names to the medical register in 1877 (Jex-Blake 1886: 204, Note NN: 95). By 1877 thirty-four women had completed the initial three years' curriculum at the London School of Medicine for Women, but the problem of clinical training had still not been resolved (Thorne 1915). Largely due to the efforts of James Stansfeld, Honorary Treasurer of the London School of Medicine for Women, the Royal Free hospital agreed to admit students from the London School of Medicine for Women in 1877 for an experimental period of five years (Bell 1953).

Elsewhere, the medical profession's resistance to women's claim to study and practice medicine was still strong. In 1877 the Convocation of the University of London agreed to admit Edith Shove to its medical examinations, but the Medical Faculty immediately presented a petition signed by 250 male medical graduates protesting against Senate's decision and proposed 'that it is inadvisable to admit women to degrees in medicine before it shall have considered the general question of their admission to the degrees of all faculties' (Jex-Blake 1886: 216–8). It then proved necessary to lay before Convocation a new charter admitting women to all degrees of London University and, much to the dismay of the Medical Faculty, this was done successfully in January 1878. The University of London became the first British university to admit women to degrees (Pratt 1897: 86). In view of the fact that the university had declined by one vote sixteen years previously to admit women to its degrees, Sophia Jex-Blake commented wryly 'Strange to think if one man had voted differently, the result would have been anticipated by sixteen years, and almost the whole condition of the intervening period have been changed!' (Jex-Blake 1886: 215).

The university was an autonomous institution of civil society and the site of credentialist tactics, but not as autonomous as the medical profession's own corporations and colleges, and it was the latter that proved especially resilient to the claims of medical women. Gendered credentialism was successfully sustained for a considerable period by the medical corporations. By a series of elaborate twists and turns most of the institutions that made up the nineteen portals of entry to the medical profession resisted the claims of women to medical education and examination.

The Society of Apothecaries did not admit women to its examinations until 1888 (Thorne 1915). The British Medical Association passed a resolution as late as 1878 excluding women from membership and this was not rescinded until 1892 (Thorne 1915). But it was the prestigious Royal Colleges of Surgeons and of Physicians that proved the most resilient to the claims of women. In 1861 the Royal College of Surgeons had taken legal advice and declined Elizabeth Garrett's request to sit their examination in midwifery. In December 1875 Sophia Jex-Blake, Edith Pechey and Isabel Thorne has applied for admission to the Examination for Midwifery Certificate of the College (Minutes of the General Medical Council XIII 1876: 27, Jex-Blake 1886: 194). This certificate had been introduced in 1852 and inadvertently recognised as sufficient for registration under the 1858 Medical Act (Parry and Parry 1976, Minutes of the General Medical Council XIV 1877). The Council of the Royal College of Surgeons took legal advice on whether they had the power to admit women to the examination in midwifery and, if so, whether they could be compelled to admit them. The verdict was affirmative on both counts (Minutes of the General Medical Council XIII 1876: 27–8). The Royal College of Surgeons wrote to the General Medical Council drawing attention to 'the difficulty in which the College is placed' but was offered a way out of their predicament when the three examiners, all of the Obstetrical Society, resigned.

In 1877 the Royal College of Surgeons again expressed their concern to the General Medical Council about what they were to do about women knocking at their door after the 1876 Enabling Act had been passed (Minutes of the General Medical Council XIV 1877). Immediately, an Extraordinary Meeting of the Council of the Royal College of Surgeons was called and resolved that 'women are not eligible to become Members or Fellows of the College, and [that the College] is therefore not prepared to admit them to be examined for those qualifications (Minutes of the General Medical Council XIV 1877: 104). In 1895 the Dean of the London School of Medicine, Dr Elizabeth Garrett Anderson, again asked if students of the school could be admitted to their examination, but the Council passed a resolution that 'it is not expedient that the College should admit women to the examinations for its diploma of Member' (Cope 1959: 124).

By 1906, when the number of qualified women doctors stood at 750 and 169 students were enrolled at the London School of Medicine for Women, the Royal College of Surgeons reconsidered the question of the admission of women at its annual meeting. A poll of members on the issue revealed substantial majorities against the admission of women to membership (415) and to fellowship (1,182). Meanwhile, however, the council itself decided 'that it is desirable to admit women to the examination for the Diploma of Member' (Cope 1959: 126), and women were admitted in 1908.

The Royal College of Physicians provided another institutional location for the dogged pursuit of gendered credentialist tactics. The college had taken legal advice as early as 1864 when Elizabeth Garrett had sought admission. She was rejected on the grounds that 'the language of the Charter and of the Bye-laws precludes the College from granting licences to practise to Females, and also from admitting them to examination for a licence' (cited in Cooke 1972). After the passage of the Enabling Act in 1876, the Royal College of Physicians resolved in 1878 'that the College do steadily adhere to the terms of its charter and do not grant its licence to practise physic to women' (cited in Cooke 1972). Again in 1875, following a petition from the London School of Medicine and the Royal Free Hospital to admit their women students to its examination, the college declined once more. But by 1907 the Royal College of Physicians was pressed by the Royal College of Surgeons to consider admitting women, as it was (largely because of the question of women's admission to the Conjoint Diplomas of the two colleges). In 1909 the Royal College of Physicians reluctantly followed suit, but like the Royal College of Surgeons, introduced bye-laws prohibiting women from taking part in the government of the college. In 1909 Ivy Woodward became the first woman member of the Royal College of Physicians, but it was not until 1925 that the bye-law prohibiting women from fellowship was amended, and in 1934 Dr Helen Mackay, a paediatrician, was elected fellow (Cooke 1972).

CONCLUSION

This chapter has drawn upon closure concepts in order to analyse some of the ways in which a male monopoly over medical practice was sustained, and the ways in which a group of aspiring women doctors challenged this monopoly. It has been argued that the male professional project in medicine took the form of a gendered exclusionary strategy sustained by credentialist and legalistic tactics, whilst women's challenge took the form of an inclusionary strategy of usurpation, which describes their attempts to gain access to a structure of occupational positions from which they were excluded solely on account of their gender.

A closer analysis of women's struggle to enter the medical profession revealed that a variety of different tactics were used. These were the credentialist and legalistic tactics of occupational politics, and the equal rights and separatist tactics of gender politics. Countervailing credentialist tactics described the attempts by women to gain access to some form of medical education and examination. The attempt by women to gain medical instruction and degrees at the University of Edinburgh between 1869 and 1873 was an equal rights, credentialist tactic and sought to secure women's access to existing male-dominated systems of medical education. The setting up of the London School of Medicine for Women in 1874 was a separatist, credentialist tactic. This sought to by-pass the institutional locations of male power which were proving so unassailable and to set up a separate route of access for women to medical education and the credentials necessary for registration as a qualified doctor.

Women also employed countervailing legalistic tactics by seeking state sponsorship of their usurpationary project. The Universities (Scotland) (Degrees to Women) Bill of 1875 and the ultimately successful Medical Act (Amendment) Bill of 1876 were equal rights, legalistic tactics which aimed to secure women's access to the medical register on the same terms and conditions as men. The Medical Act Amendment (Foreign Universities) Bill of 1876 was a separatist, legalistic tactic because it tried to open up for women a separate route of access to the medical register, by recognising foreign medical degrees as well as British ones. It was the former, the equal rights tactic, which was eventually successful, culminating in the passage of the 1876 Enabling Bill. But it was to prove a Pyrrhic victory, as the resilience of gendered credentialist mechanisms in the universities and medical corporations demonstrated.

The twists and turns of the women's struggle, their hollow victories and resounding defeats in the face of the remarkable resilience of the medical profession to the women's claims to practise medicine, reveal just how male power and privilege were sustained within the orbit of professional control. An analysis of the struggles between medical men and aspiring women doctors underscores a number of points I have already made about the necessity of moving the sociology of professions onto a less androcentric terrain, the importance of gendering the agents of professional projects and of structurally locating these projects within the parameters of patriarchal capitalism.

Professional projects employed both autonomous and heteronomous means of closure. Credentialist tactics of systematic training and testing depended upon the mobilisation of autonomous means located in the sphere of civil society: the modern university and the professional corporations. Legalistic tactics of registration and licensing depended upon the mobilisation of heteronomous means, institutionally located in the state. The necessity for grounding professional projects within the structural and historical parameters of patriarchal capitalism is suggested by the fact that these institutional sites for the mobilisation of the means of professional closure were simultaneously structured by patriarchy and capitalism. They were sites within which male power was already institutionalised and organised.

Patriarchal closure in the modern medical profession proved extremely resilient in the face of women's usurpationary claims when these were pursued through countervailing credentialist tactics, as the unsuccessful chapter at the University of Edinburgh proved. Male power was therefore institutionalised far more effectively through credentialism, mobilised through autonomous means in the sphere of civil society. It was here that gendered exclusionary mechanisms proved most obdurate and resilient. Patriarchal closure was also sanctioned by the state in its sponsorship of medical men's professional projects, and so indirectly sustained by heteronomous means. However, because state sponsorship of professional projects represents the use of heteronomous means of closure, then professional control may be weakest at this point. Indeed, patriarchal closure in medicine proved most susceptible to women's challenge when this took the form of a countervailing legalistic tactic, and concentrated on amending the 1858 Medical Act.

The institutions of civil society therefore assume central importance in explaining women's exclusion from the profession of medicine, as women's usurpationary project was more effective when pursued at the level of the central state. This suggests that the resources of male power were most effectively institutionalised within the modern university and professional corporations, whilst the nineteenth-century patriarchal capitalist state was the weakest link in the chain of patriarchal closure.

4

MEDICAL MEN AND MIDWIVES

This chapter examines the troubled inter-occupational relations between doctors and midwives through an analysis of the debate about midwives' registration. The twin concepts of exclusionary closure and inclusionary usurpation used in the previous chapter only capture some of the complex and varied processes of occupational closure in the emerging medical division of labour. In Chapter 2 I outlined another set of strategies which relate to processes of inter- rather than intra-occupational control. These were demarcationary and dual closure strategies. Demarcationary strategies are mechanisms of inter-occupational control of related or adjacent occupations in a division of labour. Dual closure strategies describe the countervailing responses of occupational groups hit by the demarcationary strategies of a dominant social and occupational group.

A paradigmatic case of gendered demarcationary strategies in the emerging medical division of labour is found in the troubled relations between medical men and midwives in the latter half of the nineteenth century (cf Donnison 1977, Verluysen 1980). Medical men's demarcationary strategies describe their intervention in the affairs of midwives, an adjacent but unregulated occupation in the provision of medical services. The protracted debate about midwives' registration reveals that medical men were intimately concerned with defining and controlling the inter-occupational boundaries between medical and midwifery practice.

In the following account, I distinguish between two responses of medical men to the problem of the unresolved boundary definitions between medicine and midwifery. On the one hand, medical men engaged in a demarcation strategy of de-skilling which centred around the distinction between normal and abnormal labour, but sought to ossify this division of labour by constructing the inter-occupational relations whereby the medical profession could supervise, contain and control midwifery practice. Medical advocates of the de-skilling strategy advocated the education and registration of midwives as a means of controlling both the knowledge base and the sphere of competence of midwifery, as well as its occupational infrastructure. The other response of medical men was a demarcation strategy of incorporation which aimed to incorporate virtually the whole gamut of tasks associated with the occupational role of midwife within the exclusive sphere of competence and control of the medical profession. This latter strategy, if successful, would have signalled the demise of the independent midwifery practitioner.

Medical men's demarcation strategies represented one side of a gender struggle in which midwives were also engaged, defending the female prerogative over midwifery practice. Midwives' responses to their insecure and tenuous position in the nineteenth-century medical division of labour are analysed here as female professional projects, using the concept of dual closure. As projects of dual closure, they exhibited both usurpationary and exclusionary aims. Midwives' professional projects were constrained by the gendered demarcationary strategies of medical men and along their usurpationary dimensions they were countervailing strategies in the face of these. But midwives in their turn also strove to secure a degree of exclusionary occupational closure as they sought to restrict access to the occupation of midwifery to a limited circle of eligibles.

Just as it is possible to distinguish between different types of demarcationary strategy pursued by medical men, so too it is possible to distinguish between different types of dual closure strategy adopted by midwives. The first, a revolutionary strategy, sought to radically redefine the inter-occupational relations between midwives and medical men by re-skilling the midwife and securing for midwifery a position parallel to that of medical men. The second, an accommodative strategy, conceded to a more de-skilled role for midwives, who would be clearly subordinated to medical men in the emerging medical division of labour. In addition, first, I examine the tactics employed and ask whether these were credentialist or legalistic, and second, I discuss the means of closure that were mobilised and ask whether these were autonomous or heteronomous. I demonstrate how midwives' professional projects of dual closure were importantly constrained by the gendered demarcationary strategies of medical men and by the patriarchal structuring of the state and civil society, which together constitute the institutional locations within which the heteronomous and autonomous means of closure are mobilised.

MIDWIVES AND MEDICAL MEN

The spheres of female midwifery and male medical practice had been a focus of struggle since the seventeenth century (Donnison 1977, Oakley 1976, Ehrenreich and English 1973a,b, 1979, Verluysen 1980). In the pre-modern provision of medical services vast numbers of women earned their living from midwifery (Clark 1919). Most midwives were unlicensed practitioners and, although ecclesiastical licensing of midwives had operated in the sixteenth and seventeenth centuries, it was never rigorously enforced and licensed midwifery was only the tip of the iceberg (Forbes 1964).

Midwives had made various attempts to organise themselves in the seventeenth century. In 1616 they petitioned King James I for a Royal Charter (Clark 1964, Donnison 1977). Their petition was referred to the Royal College of Physicians, who objected because, as the official historian of the college noted, 'It expressed the disconcerting doctrine that what was sauce for the gander was sauce for the goose' (Clark 1964: 236). Further attempts were made to organise midwives in 1633 and in 1687 (cf Clark 1919, Hurd-Mead 1937, Donnison 1977, Aveling 1872). The Chamberlen family, who had invented the short forceps for delivery in childbirth, allegedly masterminded the 1616 and 1633 attempts to incorporate midwives, which were intended to grant monopolies to Peter Chamberlen and later his son rather than to midwives. But is was a London midwife, Mrs Cellier, who petitioned King James II for a Royal Charter in 1687, stressing the need to educate and regulate midwives.

Moves to educate and regulate midwives were necessary because of the emergence of 'men-midwives' who were encroaching on a traditionally female sphere and gradually expropriating midwifery skills by observing the practices of midwives (often difficult because of the taboo on men being present in lying-in rooms). As early as the seventeenth century men-midwives were seeking to de-skill the midwife by restricting her role to 'attending' and not 'intervening' during labour. Dr Willughby, a seventeenth-century man-midwife, declared:

> The midwife's duty in a natural birth is not more but to attend and wait on Nature, and to receive the child, and (if needs require) to help to fetch the after-birth, and her best care will be to see that the woman and child be fittingly and decently ordered with necessary conveniences. And let midwives know that they be Nature's servants.
>
> (cited in Aveling 1872: 40)

Intervention was to be left to the men-midwives with their instruments.

London midwives attempted in various ways to protect female midwifery from the encroachments of men-midwives. They re-asserted that midwifery was a female sphere, attempted to improve the education and skill of midwives, and to demonstrate the irreparable harm that could be done through the use of instruments in childbirth by clumsy and incompetent men-midwives (cf Aveling 1872, Donnison 1977, Hurd-Mead 1937). In the eighteenth century Mrs Margaret Stephen, a royal midwife, lectured midwives on anatomy and the use of forceps (Aveling 1872) and Mrs Elizabeth Nihil was well aware of the danger that men-midwives and their instruments were de-skilling and fragmenting midwifery:

> I cannot comprehend why women are not capable of completing this business when begun, without calling in men to their assistance, who are often sent for when the work is near finished, and then the midwife, who has taken all the pains, is counted of little value, and the young men command all the praise.
>
> (quoted in Aveling 1872: 109)

In the eighteenth century male practice in midwifery grew unabated (Donnison 1977) and in the nineteenth century medical men were struggling to establish 'obstetrics' as a specialism within the medical profession. The occupational boundaries between midwifery and medicine continued to be contested in the nineteenth century, but the historical and institutional arena within which the struggle was played out had changed by then. The tripartite division of labour between physicians, surgeons and apothecaries had, following a period of deregulation in the eighteenth and early nineteenth centuries (cf Waddington 1984), uneasily resolved itself into a unified medical profession by means of the 1858 Medical Registration Act. However, female midwifery remained in a highly ambiguous position having been, as it were, left out in the cold (cf Verluysen 1980). And a new form of medical practitioner had emerged by the mid-nineteenth century – the general practitioner who defied the compartmentalised structure of the three orders of physicians, surgeons and apothecaries (Parry and Parry 1976: 104) and incorporated functions of diagnosis and prescription (formerly the physician's prerogative), dispensing (formerly the apothecary's prerogative) and midwifery.

By the early 1870s, sexually segregated spheres of competence within the emerging medical division of labour were clearly in evidence, with women engaging in the four spheres of midwifery, nursing, dispensing and the management of medical institutions, all of which were considered by the General Medical Council as 'services for which women are specially adapted' (Minutes of the General Council X 1873: 171). However, what was unclear at this point in time was the precise nature of the inter-occupational relations between these occupations and the medical profession. In the latter half of the nineteenth century medical men were to find themselves simultaneously defending patriarchal forms of exclusionary closure within the medical profession and, as the following account of the troubled relations between medical men and midwives demonstrates, constructing patriarchal forms of demarcationary closure.

The protracted debate around proposals for a state-sponsored system of midwives' registration spanned the years between the 1860s and the passage of the Midwives Act in 1902. It was during this period that the division of labour between midwives and doctors, the inter-occupational relations of control between medicine and midwifery, and the occupational infrastructure of midwifery were openly contested. The following does not attempt to be an exhaustive account of the many twists and turns in the events that eventually culminated in the passage of the Midwives Act in 1902, as Jean Donnison (1977) has already provided such an account. Instead it focuses on the different strategic responses of medical men and midwives to the task of establishing and maintaining boundaries between medical and midwifery practice in the modern medical division of labour, and uses concepts of demarcationary and dual closure to sociologically unpick these strategies.

108

'THE SPIDER LEGISLATING FOR THE FLY': MEDICAL MEN AND MIDWIVES' REGISTRATION

The nineteenth-century medical profession did not speak with one voice when it came to the issue of midwives' registration, but were divided over this issue. On the one side there were medical men, predominantly provincial general practitioners who formed a vocal, minority section of the British Medical Association, and who opposed any form of registration for midwives. Essentially, they sought to incorporate the 'medical' core of midwifery skills within the exclusive sphere of competence of medical men, to abolish female midwifery as a distinct occupational role and to destroy the independent midwifery practitioner with her own clients. On the other side were medical men, amongst the most prominent of whom were obstetricians of the London Obstetrical Society, who advocated the registration of midwives and sought to preserve the independent, female midwifery practitioner but with a rigidly demarcated and de-skilled sphere of competence.

The central issue was one of occupational demarcation. Anti-registrationist medical men advocated a demarcation strategy of incorporation. Pro-registrationist medical men advocated a demarcation strategy of de-skilling. The crucial difference between these two strategies was that: the de-skilling strategy sought to preserve the role of midwife as an independent practitioner who had her own clients and who was therefore called out to attend women in the first instance; whereas the incorporatist strategy sought to dissolve the independent midwifery role into the obstetric or monthly nurse role directly supervised by medical men, who were called upon by the client in the first instance. It is salutary to remember that a similar debate occurred in the United States between 1908 and 1918, and the outcome was the complete demise of the midwife and the triumph of a single standard of obstetrics wholly encompassed within the medical profession's sphere of competence (Donegan 1978, Kobrin 1966).

The division of labour between midwives and medical men had been a focus of struggle since the seventeenth century. By the mid-nineteenth century it had been constructed as a division between assistance and intervention in the process of labour. This corresponded with the construction of a division in the very process of labour itself into 'normal' and 'abnormal' conditions. 'Normal' labour was discursively constructed as a 'natural' process which required attendance or assistance. 'Abnormal' labour was constructed as those conditions requiring intervention, frequently by means of instruments, and it was these conditions that were becoming 'medicalised'. The major problem facing medical men in the nineteenth century was how to ensure that midwives did not transgress into the 'medicalised' portions of parturition. 'Everything must be done to limit the midwife severely to the simple duties of a natural case'(*Lancet* May 1890). 'The question of restricting the action of midwives is an important one. Their function is to attend natural labour and to know in what cases it is their duty to send for medical men' (*British Medical Journal* 22 March 1890).

Further, there was the thorny problem that labour was, for the most part, 'normal' up until the point when it could be construed as 'abnormal' in so far as it deviated from the normal and required intervention. This meant that, if a midwife was called upon in the first instance to attend labour, it was the midwife herself who had to decide when a labour qualified as 'abnormal' and therefore when a doctor's presence was required.

A demarcationary strategy of incorporation

One solution to this problem of defining and policing occupational boundaries was a demarcationary strategy of incorporation. It was simply impossible to draw a hard and fast line between natural and unnatural labour, so midwives could not be restricted to attendance upon normal or natural labour and were to be abolished altogether, it was argued (HMSO 1892: 129). The solution was for medical men to incorporate normal as well as abnormal labour within their exclusive sphere of competence. Henceforth, medical men would superintend the whole process of labour and simply delegate certain tasks to 'obstetric nurses' who would act only under the supervision of a medical man. Medical advocates of the incorporatist strategy opposed midwives' registration and instead aimed to replace the independent practitioner role of midwife by the dependent, ancillary role of 'monthly' or 'obstetric' nurse who was to act only under the charge and supervision of a medical man.

The obstetric nurse is a nurse who, under the charge and supervision of a medical man, carries out that portion of attendance which is more suitable to a mere women, the changing of sheets and the attending of the patient, and attentions of that kind.

(HMSO 1892: 133)

Midwifery or obstetric nurses were to exercise no discretion at the level of execution in their daily practice, but were to attend women during natural labour under medical control and supervision (*British Medical Journal* 1899: 690).

The most vociferous opposition to midwives' registration came from a section of the British Medical Association, mainly provincial general practitioners from urban centres and rural districts (*Nursing Notes* 1896: 56, 1902: 111). General practitioners enjoyed a relatively tenuous monopoly over medical practice and were envious of monopolies over hospital practice enjoyed by members of the Royal College of Physicians. They complained 'we have to go to the open market to get our work' (HMSO 1892: 56). Midwives' registration would legitimate a new state-sponsored order of independent practitioners, who would pose a competitive threat to general medical practitioners and threaten their precarious monopoly (HMSO 1892: 45, 46, 57, *Hansard* XXXIII 1895: 1136, *British Medical Journal* 1898: 639, 659). By creating a new order of trained and registered midwives 'the bread would be snatched out of the mouths of medical men' and 'the profits of hard-working practitioners diminished' (*British Medical Journal* 1873: 354). But busy general practitioners, especially those in country districts, would welcome the assistance of midwifery or obstetric nurses (*British Medical Journal* 1899: 351).

Midwives' registration would create not just a new but also an inferior class of midwifery practitioners (*British Medical Journal* 1902: 1173). It would permit midwives with only a few months' training to assume responsibilities for which they were insufficiently trained, compared to medical men (HMSO 1892: 128). But to be safely competent to attend obstetric cases, a complete education in medicine and surgery as well as midwifery was necessary (HMSO 1892: 128). In fact the 1886 Medical Act declared proficiency in medicine, surgery *and* midwifery as a pre-requisite of medical qualification and registration, so midwifery had been formally incorporated into the corpus of knowledge of the medical profession. So, central to the abolitionists' case was the argument that the practice of midwifery should only be undertaken by those fully qualified in medicine and surgery as well as midwifery.

A demarcationary strategy of de-skilling

The other solution to the problem of boundary definition between midwifery and medical practice was a demarcationary strategy of de-skilling. The de-skilling strategy entailed the devolution of tasks associated with attendance on normal or natural labour onto the midwife, thus preserving female midwifery as a distinct occupational role within the medical division of labour. Medical men were to enjoy an exclusive prerogative over those conditions defined as 'abnormal' or 'unnatural' and therefore 'medical'. But how were medical men to ensure that midwives did not encroach on the 'medicalised' portions of childbirth and called upon the assistance of doctors in the event of abnormal labour? The solution was to control midwifery practice through a state-sponsored system of registration. Medical advocates of the de-skilling strategy therefore championed the cause of midwives registration and sought to ensure that any proposed legislation was framed in such a way as to ensure medical control over the occupational infrastructure of midwifery. So 'the boards to which the duty of regulating the registration and examination of midwives is assigned are to consist of medical men of standing who will be likely to impress this limitation on those registered' (*Lancet* 26 May 1890). In order to 'police' the boundaries between midwifery and medical practice, it was imperative that the medical profession had supremacy (*British Medical Journal* 1873: 354).

The resolution of this problem of *control* over the division of labour between midwives and doctors lay at the nub of the Obstetrical Society's proposals for the education and registration of midwives. The Obstetrical Society of London (which was founded in 1857 and by 1873 composed of around 600 fellows, including many eminent obstetricians (*British Medical Journal* 1873: 676)) took the initiative by prescribing and monitoring the knowledge base of midwifery. It instituted its own diploma for midwives in 1872 and produced a comprehensive scheme for the education and registration of midwives. The midwife was defined as 'A respectable woman able to read, write and calculate, understanding the management of natural labour, and capable of recognising any conditions requiring the aid of a medical practitioner' (*British*

Medical Journal 1874: 186, HMSO 1892: 83, Minutes of the General Council XIV 1877 Appendix: 51–5). The midwife's role was to be attending women in natural labour and nursing the woman and baby during the week after childbirth. They were not to use instruments, perform operations or prescribe medicines.

The knowledge base of midwifery was to be kept as minimal as possible for 'What you want to educate midwives for is for them to know their own ignorance. That is really the one great object in educating midwives' (HMSO 1892: 101). Midwifery education was to be 'kept necessarily and designedly limited' (HMSO 1892: 121). Midwives were to be instructed by medical men, examined and licensed by a body appointed by the General Medical Council, and subject to both compulsory registration and the possibility of 'erasure from the register on the grounds of misconduct' (Minutes of the General Council XIV 1877 Appendix: 51–5, *British Medical Journal* 1874: 186). Obviously, the most serious misconduct of midwives would be that of 'exceeding their duties' (*British Medical Journal* 1874: 186) by transgressing occupational boundaries through, for example, failing to call on medical assistance when necessary or administering anything that could be construed as 'medical treatment' to their clients.

The de-skilling strategy aimed to preserve midwifery as a distinct female occupational role in the medical division of labour, permitting the midwife independence in the daily provision of midwifery services and legitimating an independent practitioner–client relationship between a woman and her client. Two questions need to be posed. First, why did a section of the medical profession champion the cause of midwives rather than hasten their demise? Second, why did the de-skilling rather than the incorporatist strategy ultimately prevail?

The evidence suggests that the majority of births in England and Wales were already attended by midwives, whether trained or untrained. Dr Aveling estimated that there were around 10,000 midwives in England and regarded it probable that seven out of every nine births were attended by midwives (*Nursing Notes* 1888 Supplement: 7). Although the unregulated nature of midwifery practice meant that it was difficult to estimate the precise number of midwives in England and Wales, it was conceded that 'On the whole, it may be safely assumed that from one half to three quarters of the confinements in England and Wales are attended by midwives and not by doctors' (Cullingworth 1878: 394). The demand for midwives varied from locality to locality, as the Obstetrical Society enquiry of the 1860s showed. It was estimated that in small towns midwives attended only between five and ten per cent of confinements; in large provincial towns and in villages this could be anywhere between thirty and ninety per cent of confinements (Cullingworth 1878).

The midwife question, argued advocates of the de-skilling thesis and of midwives' registration, was purely one of supply and demand. It was claimed that 'There is, and will continue to be a demand for the services of midwives, for this, if for no other reason, that they can be obtained more cheaply' (Cullingworth 1878: 394) and that 'Midwives exist and will exist in spite of anything we may do, and the question is whether they are to exist without proper training or supervision' (HMSO 1892: 101).

There was, in short, a demand for midwifery services from the poor who could not afford the doctor's fee and, it was admitted, may even have preferred to be attended by a local midwife than a doctor.

The crux of the de-skilling strategy was that, given the high proportion of confinements attended by midwives, doctors could not have met the total demand for midwifery services.

> There are not sufficient medical practitioners in this country to enable every poor woman to avail herself of their assistance in time of need, and if there were, it is perfectly obvious that it would be out of their power to incur the expense of employing them.
>
> (*Hansard* CCCXLIV 1890: 1541)

In view of the evident demand for midwives, particularly from the poor, the preservation of midwives was advocated on the grounds of expediency. Dr Aveling, a member of the Obstetrical Society and ceaseless campaigner for the education and registration of midwives, was absolutely clear on this matter.

> If it were possible, I would have every women attended by a duly qualified medical man, but as this cannot be, public safety and humanity demand legislative action to enable 'poor' women to know whether those who call themselves midwives are 'safely competent'.
>
> (*Nursing Notes* 1891: 8)

For their part, medical men opposed to midwives' registration insisted that the fact that poor women needed the services of midwives demonstrated that there was no demand for female midwifery as such, but simply a demand for cheap labour (HMSO 1892: 46, *British Medical Journal* 1902: 408). They also doubted whether educated and registered midwives would be content to serve the poor, suggesting that they would aim for a better class of patient and eat into the general practitioner's midwifery practice (HMSO 1892: 46–7).

The de-skilling rather than the incorporatist strategy prevailed because of the impracticability of doctors meeting the total demand for midwifery services. The evidence also suggests that medical men were reluctant to place themselves in a position where they would be called upon to meet the total demand for midwifery services. There were two reasons for this. The first had to do with the nature of the work, whilst the second was related to the social class of the client.

Midwifery practice was excessively time-consuming from the general practitioner's point of view. This, of course, had much to do with the essentially unpredictable duration of labour. Consequently it was argued that:

> it would be of great advantage to the profession that midwives should be properly instructed, so as to relieve them from the necessity of attending parturient women for hours, and waiting for nature to complete a process which they could neither assist nor prevent. . . . Nothing was more injurious to health and professional enjoyment in rural districts than the compulsory attendance on midwifery practice . . . it would be a great blessing to be relieved of this duty.
>
> (*British Medical Journal* 1873: 406)

The devolution of tasks defined as those of attendance and assistance during labour onto midwives therefore served to relieve reluctant medical men of what they regarded as 'tiresome and unremunerative work' (HMSO 1892: 22).

All women, regardless of their social class, were potentially clients for midwifery services. If doctors had made it incumbent upon themselves to meet this demand by securing a monopoly over the provision of midwifery services, they would have been providing midwifery services for rich and poor alike. But most of this demand for midwives came from working-class women (*Nursing Notes* 1896: 56).

> The richer classes are already provided for in the matter, and have thoroughly well qualified practitioners to attend to their wants. The poorer classes, however, have constantly to have recourse to the assistance of midwives, instead of calling in highly qualified medical men.
>
> (*Hansard* CCCXLIV 1890: 1541)

The preservation of midwives as a distinct occupational group, would effectively stratify both the demand for and the supply of midwifery services; the rich would employ the services of doctors whilst the poor would employ those of midwives. Properly educated midwives could continue to relieve medical men of unremunerative and time-consuming midwifery practice among the poor.

Summary

The demarcationary strategy of incorporation would have signalled the abolition of midwives as a distinct female occupational role in the provision of medical services. It would have achieved this by incorporating virtually the whole gamut of midwifery skills into the sphere of competence of the medical practitioner, who would simply delegate a portion of attendance deemed 'more suitable to a mere women' (HMSO 1892: 133) onto an obstetric nurse. The obstetric nurse was to enjoy no discretion at the level of execution and attend the mother and baby only under the direct supervision of a doctor.

The demarcationary strategy of de-skilling, on the other hand, sought to preserve the female occupational role of midwife, who was to enjoy discretion at the level of execution in her daily practice as an independent practitioner with her own clients, but within a sphere of competence prescribed by the medical profession and restricted to attendance on normal labour. Thus, there was internal dissent within the ranks of medical men, but it was the de-skilling strategy which eventually won through with the passage of the 1902 Midwives Act. Some reasons for this have been suggested. First, it was a strategy of expediency. Second, the prospect of competition from a new class of practitioners was precluded by segmenting the market for midwifery services – midwives for the poor, doctors for the rich.

MIDWIVES' PROFESSIONAL PROJECTS

Trained midwives of the nineteenth century engaged in 'female professional projects' which took the form of strategies of dual closure. These incorporated usurpationary and exclusionary aims, and made use of credentialist and legalistic tactics. Midwives professional projects were exclusionary strategies because they strove to secure a link between education and occupation and to restrict access to the occupation of midwifery to a limited circle of educated and registered women. They were usurpationary in so far as they were countervailing actions in the face of the demarcationary strategies of medical men. But midwives responded to these in two ways. One may be termed a revolutionary response, which sought to radically redefine the status of midwifery, whilst the other may be termed accommodative as this broadly accepted the limited and restricted role envisaged for midwives by medical advocates of the de-skilling strategy of demarcation.

Midwives' professional projects were pursued within a division of labour increasingly the subject of the professional domination or 'occupational imperialism' (Larkin 1983) of the newly unified medical profession and were therefore importantly constrained by the gendered strategies of demarcation of medical men as well as by the patriarchal structuring of the institutional locations of the means of professionalisation. As professional projects they took different forms because they sought to utilise autonomous and heteronomous means of closure in different ways. Midwives' revolutionary strategy of dual closure was associated with the Female Medical Society and Obstetrical Association of Midwives in the 1860s and early 1870s, the period immediately following the 1858 Medical Act. They strove to secure the autonomy of midwives from medical men, and resisted both the limited sphere of competence and the professional subordination of midwifery to the medical profession. The accommodative strategy of dual closure was associated with the Midwives' Institute which emerged later in the 1880s. The Midwives' Institute agitated for a system of midwives' registration that was broadly compatible with that envisaged by the Obstetrical Society of medical men. They accepted the limited sphere of competence and subordinate professional status envisaged for midwives by this section of the medical profession.

A revolutionary dual closure project

The key elements of the radical midwives' revolutionary dual closure project may be identified as: a broad definition of the knowledge base of midwifery; an enlarged sphere of competence that was to include not only normal but also abnormal labour (including the use of instruments in childbirth); and a system of registration that gave midwives a professional status independent of but equal to other medical practitioners in the spheres of surgery, physic and general practice. In short, it asserted the autonomy of female midwives from male medical practitioners; it resisted the professional subordination of midwifery to the medical profession.

The Female Medical Society was formed in the early 1860s with the aims of establishing an obstetrical college for women and of campaigning for midwives' registration (HMSO 1892: 106–7). Credentialist tactics were prioritised and autonomous means of closure – midwives' own Female Medical Society – were utilised. The Female Medical College was concerned to rectify the fact that there was no system of education and examination of midwives in Britain, who were 'only acquainted with a routine and comparatively empirical practice' and incapable of dealing with emergencies in childbirth (Edmunds 1864: 22). Although it prioritised the need for midwives' education, it also aimed to pave the way for women to enter the medical profession as fully qualified medical practitioners.

The Obstetrical College was set up by the Female Medical Society in 1864 (*Nursing Notes* 1888: 10, Edmunds 1864) and provided midwives with a far more extensive medical education than that which was to be offered by the Obstetrical Society of Medical Men which instituted its diploma in midwifery in 1872 (Aveling 1872: 160). Fourteen women enrolled for the first session in 1864 (Prospectus of the Female Medical Society 1864). In 1865, twenty women were attending the Obstetrical College of the Female Medical Society (Donnison 1976: 75). It provided instruction not only in the theory and practice of midwifery but also in 'those branches of medicine which are ancillary to the practice of midwifery' (HMSO 1892: 107) and was also to include 'surgery of the organs with which they have to deal' (HMSO 1892: 107).

Crucially, midwives were to be provided with a medical education that would enable them to perform obstetric surgery. Dr

James Edmunds, Honorary Secretary of the Society, claimed that he thought women could perform obstetrical operations as well as men, providing that they had been properly educated (HMSO 1892: 115). The Female Medical Society's proposals resisted the de-skilling of midwifery and reasserted the right of midwives to use instruments and deal with those aspects of parturition that were being 'medicalised' and incorporated within the sphere of competence of medical men. It sought to re-skill the midwife.

By opening a college to educate midwives, those associated with the Female Medical Society were using credentialist tactics in the pursuit of their professional project. They also used legalistic tactics, but these were not given such priority. They campaigned for an amendment to the medical acts that would give women access to a registrable diploma as midwives so that they could 'occupy the position of educated specialists precisely analogous to that which dentists now occupy, in relation to the general practice of medicine' (HMSO 1892: 106–7). It was envisaged that midwifery would become a specialist branch of medicine but separate from the general practice of medicine and surgery. The broad educational programme of the Female Medical College and their enlarged sphere of competence would enable midwives to 'supersede medical men as an ordinary rule in the general practice of midwifery' (HMSO 1892: 108).

The society eventually closed through lack of funds, probably because the opening of the London School of Medicine for Women in 1874 with its goal of providing women with a complete medical education overshadowed and conflicted with the aim of securing a partial education in midwifery (Donnison 1977). Nonetheless, Dr James Edmunds was still advocating a revolutionary professional project for midwives in 1892, when he recalled in his evidence to the Select Committee on Midwives' Registration:

> the idea that we had in view was not to make midwives merely the servants of medical men, but rather to put them in the same position as a dentist who does not send for a doctor to draw out a tooth. . . . I do not advocate making them small jackals to medical men.
>
> (HMSO 1892: 107, 109)

An accommodative dual closure project

In contrast to the revolutionary dual closure strategy of the Female Medical Society, midwives' accommodative strategy involved: a limited definition of the knowledge base of midwifery; a narrow and relatively de-skilled sphere of competence that restricted the midwife to attending normal labour only (and precluded the use of instruments); and a system of registration that would place effective control over the education, examination and registration of midwives in the hands of the medical profession.

This more accommodative dual closure strategy was pursued by the Midwives' Institute and Trained Nurses Club, founded in 1882 with the chief object of protecting the title of midwife by raising the efficiency and improving the status of midwives, and by petitioning parliament for their recognition (*Nursing Notes* 1887: 1–2). From the outset, the emphasis was on legalistic tactics of dual closure, unlike the earlier Female Medical Society which had concentrated on credentialist tactics. The Midwives' Institute accepted the narrow knowledge base and the limited, de-skilled sphere of competence prescribed for midwives by medical men of the Obstetrical Society. Indeed, the condition for full membership of the Midwives' Institute was the possession of the Obstetrical Society's diploma in midwifery. They broadly accepted the Obstetrical Society's scheme for the education and registration of midwives and complied with medical men's construction of the occupational boundaries between midwifery and medical practice. In other words, they acceded to medical men's demarcationary strategy of de-skilling.

Unlike the midwife who described the Obstetrical Society's diploma in midwifery as 'practically good for nothing' (Minutes of the General Medical Council 1873: 197), midwives of the Institute accepted the limited knowledge base and restricted sphere of competence for midwives advocated by the Obstetrical Society. They saw the value of midwifery training in similar terms to medical men of the Obstetrical Society, stressing that the properly trained midwife would know when to send for the assistance of a doctor. The properly trained midwife would be less likely to stray from her restricted role, defined as attendance upon natural labour:

A trained midwife is always taught what natural labour means: she is not supposed to undertake anything else, and she is also instructed to send for medical advice if the case is

120

difficult. . . . A trained midwife would certainly be more likely to call in medical assistance, when necessary, than an untrained one.

(*Nursing Notes* 1892, Supplement: 6–7)

The properly trained midwife would be able 'to recognise at once those difficulties that require the presence of a medical man' (*Nursing Notes* 1888, No. 1, Supplement).

At the 1892 Select Committee on Midwives' Registration, representatives of the Midwives' Institute were questioned closely about the possible temptation for midwives to use instruments. Zepherina Smith of the Midwives' Institute reassured the committee that the Midwives' Institute, like the Obstetrical Society, believed that midwives should be trained to deal with only natural labour, so training in the use of instruments in childbirth would be out of the question (HMSO 1893: 103). However, Rosalind Paget, also of the Midwives' Institute, did add the rider that she was 'of the opinion that midwives should be able to meet certain emergencies if the doctor is not at hand' (*Nursing Notes* 1892, Supplement: 2).

Why did trained midwives pursue such an accommodative strategy of dual closure? The real nub of the Midwives' Institute's compliance with the Obstetrical Society's limited definition of the midwives' sphere of competence was that it also preserved for midwives a degree of *autonomy* in the practice of midwifery. Midwives would 'undertake the care of a case of "natural labour" unaided by any medical man' (*Nursing Notes* 1888, No.7, Supplement: 65). The daily practical accomplishment of midwives' tasks would not be supervised by medical men:

A midwife is a woman who undertakes to attend cases of natural labour without the direct supervision of a doctor. It is therefore desirable that her knowledge, though limited in extent, should be complete. The most important part of her training consists in being able to recognise early those conditions that require medical aid. It is also absolutely necessary (in order sometimes to save life), that she should be able to deal promptly with those urgent midwifery emergencies, that may at any time arise so suddenly that medical help (in rural districts), though sent for, may not have had time to arrive.

(*Nursing Notes* 1896: 30)

It was the degree of autonomy to be enjoyed by midwives in their attendance upon natural labour that would distinguish them from obstetric or monthly nurses, who were not qualified to attend instead of a doctor, but trained only to nurse the woman and baby 'under the direction of a medical man' (*Nursing Notes* 1888, No.7, Supplement: 65).

> A monthly nurse undertakes to nurse women in their confinements, and take charge of the infant under the orders of a doctor. She has not been trained in the complications and emergencies of labour, and should never take cases on her own responsibility.
>
> (*Nursing Notes* 1896: 30)

Along its usurpationary dimensions, then, the accommodative strategy of dual closure describes both compliance on the part of midwives with some medical men's de-skilling strategy (that had the merit of preserving for the midwife a degree of autonomy) and, by implication, opposition to other medical men's strategy of incorporation, which would have rendered obsolete the distinct occupational role of midwife.

However, despite the broad areas of agreement between midwives of the Institute and medical men of the Obstetrical Society, the fragile nature of the alliance became evident during the course of debates around the specific proposals for midwives' registration in the form of midwives' registration bills before parliament between 1890 and 1902. Institute midwives accepted a de-skilled sphere of competence and the subordination of midwifery to the medical profession. But they were never to accept the medical profession's intentions to stratify the supply of midwifery services and create a class of midwives who would be content to serve the poor, although they did acknowledge that midwives were needed and employed largely by working-class women (*Nursing Notes* 1896: 29).

The Midwives' Institute believed that parliamentary recognition of midwives would raise the status of midwifery practice, which would then become an 'occupation for educated, refined gentlewomen' (*Nursing Notes* 1888: 90) and 'women of the educated classes' (*Nursing Notes* 1888: 11). Professional projects are class-divisive projects. 'When the status of the midwife is improved, which it will be when they are recognised by Parliament, there will be no difficulty in inducing the class of women we should like to see, to enter the profession' (*Nursing Notes* 1888: 11). That they should settle for a life of 'cheap midwifery' was certainly not what Institute midwives had in mind.

In 1890 the Midwives' Institute promoted the first midwives' bill to be introduced into parliament (*Nursing Notes* 1899: 93) and the issue of midwives' registration was promptly referred to a select committee. During the years intervening the 1893 Report of the Select Committee on Midwives' Registration, which agreed that legislative provision for the improvement and regulation of midwives was desirable, and the Midwives' Act of 1902, there were repeated attempts to secure the passage of a midwives' bill. This chapter in the history of the struggle for midwives' registration has been discussed in detail by Donnison (1977). During this period, cracks in the pro-registrationist alliance between midwives and medical men emerged most clearly in relation to the issue of *control* of the profession of midwifery itself. Medical men who advocated midwives' registration were prepared to concede midwives a limited sphere of competence, together with a limited degree of autonomy in the daily practice of midwifery. They were nevertheless reluctant to concede any control over the education and registration of midwives to midwives themselves. Whilst it was also true that Institute midwives conceded the necessity for both a limited sphere of competence and a degree of autonomy, they were never entirely happy about conceding absolute control over the occupational infrastructure of midwifery to the medical profession. Their resistance, weak though this was, centred around the composition of the central midwives' board, the body that would control the profession after the passing of state legislation.

An earlier draft bill drawn up by the Obstetrical Society in 1872 had proposed that the midwifery board should exclusively consist of eleven medical men and that the local boards, appointed by the central board to examine and register midwives, should similarly consist of five medical men. Although the Midwives' Institute was quick to realise that these proposals would place absolute control in the hands of the medical profession, nevertheless their stand on this issue amounted to an immediate concession of effective, if not absolute, control to the medical profession. They never took a determined stand to have one midwife on the central board, let alone to have a midwives' board actually composed of midwives themselves. Their concession amounted to foregoing *direct* representation and settling for indirect representation of midwives. 'If a representation of midwives is absolutely impossible, the midwives consider that a special member of the Midwifery Board should be elected by them to see after their interests only, and be their voice on the Board' (*Nursing Notes* 1888: 93).

A scheme for the regulation of midwives drawn up in 1894 by the Midwives' Registration Association, a body made up entirely of medical men, was greeted favourably by the Midwives' Institute because representation of midwives' interests was allowed for despite the fact that the interests of the medical profession were 'predominantly considered'(*Nursing Notes* 1894: 93). The proposed central midwives' board was to consist entirely of medical men, one of whom was to be nominated by the Midwives' Institute. The Midwives' Institute concurred with this despite the fact that the medical profession had blatantly ensured that they were 'to govern and control a body of women whose interests have been said to clash with their own; it is a little as if the spider undertook to legislate for the fly' (*Nursing Notes* 1894: 95).

Another midwives' bill was drawn up by the same committee in 1897 and described by the Midwives' Institute as 'the best Midwives' Bill we have seen' (*Nursing Notes* 1897: 34–5). There were to be six lay members of the board appointed by the Privy Council and twelve medical practitioners, six appointed by the Royal Colleges of Physicians and of Surgeons, three by the Society of Apothecaries, and three by the Incorporated Midwives' Institute. So midwives' representation had increased to three, but they were to be medical practitioners rather than midwives (*Nursing Notes* 1898: 78). Eventually clause three of the 1902 Midwives Act gave midwives only one elected representative – a medical practitioner, not a midwife – on a central board of nine persons.

Other organisations sympathetic to midwives' struggle for registration had adopted far more uncompromising stands than the Midwives' Institute. The Women's Liberal Federation urged that at least half of the members of the proposed midwives' board should be women, either medical women or trained midwives. The Midwives' Institute argued that this was both impracticable and misguided (*Nursing Notes* 1897: 81). Opposition to the campaigning stance of the Midwives' Institute also came from Florence Fenwick Miller, an ex-pupil of the Female Medical College and editor of the feminist magazine, *Woman's Signal*, who objected to the fact that midwives would be at the mercy of their professional rivals – general practitioners (Donnison 1976: 148). Mrs Bedford-Fenwick, a ceaseless campaigner for nurses' registration, was scornful of the Midwives' Institute's concession of effective control to medical men. A group of midwives who formed the Manchester Midwives' Society in 1896 opposed the 1898 bill on the grounds that it placed control over the registration of midwives in the hands of medical men (Donnison 1976: 150–1). But the Midwives' Institute referred to the radical stance of the Manchester Midwives' Society as 'pretentious' (*Nursing Notes* 1897: 162).

GENDER AND PROFESSIONALISATION

Both these female professional projects contained exclusionary aims and sought to restrict access to midwifery to middle-class gentlewomen. The earlier, more radical Female Medical Society and the later, more accommodative Midwives' Institute both looked forward to the day when midwifery would provide lucrative employment for unoccupied women of the middle classes (HMSO 1892: 113, Edmunds 1864). But there any similarity between these two female professional projects ends.

The dual closure strategy associated with the Female Medical Society and the Obstetrical Association of Midwives in the 1860s and early 1870s mobilised autonomous means of closure – the Female Medical Society – located within the sphere of civil society. They concentrated on the pursuit of credentialist tactics of closure and their main objective was to establish a cognitive base for the practice of independent, re-skilled midwifery. They did not place much emphasis on pursuing legalistic tactics and mobilising the heteronomous means of state registration.

The Midwives' Institute that emerged later in the 1880s put most of its energies into campaigning for a state-sponsored system of registration. They did not engage in credentialist tactics but conceded to the pre-emptive credentialism of the Obstetrical Society, happy to accept the society's diploma for midwives. Instead, they mobilised heteronomous means of closure by turning to the state and pursuing legalistic tactics. Midwives' compliance with medical men's de-skilling strategy hinged upon the necessity for women to mobilise proxy male power to represent their interests in the institutional arena of the state legislature. Midwives found their male sponsors in a section of the medical profession engaged in their own intra-professional struggle to gain a respectable and specialised status for obstetrics within the medical profession. It should come as no surprise then that this female professional project was importantly constrained by the self-interest of a sponsoring group of medical men.

Historically the role of the state has been central in professional projects. Johnson (1982) challenges the notion that there is a simple inverse relation between professional autonomy and state intervention, i.e. the more state intervention, the less professional autonomy. Instead, professionalisation is necessarily a partial development towards autonomy which arises out of the complex articulation of the relation between state and occupation. In particular, areas of independent action are defined *through* an occupation's relation to the state. The accommodative dual closure strategy of midwives sought to establish attendance upon normal labour as an area of independent action defined through their relation to the state. But the state–profession relation of midwives was mediated by the medical profession, and midwives' area of independent action was defined through its relation to another occupation – a dominant, male profession. But at this historical juncture, women's relation to the patriarchal capitalist state had *necessarily* to be mediated by men, and therefore indirect.

Finally, I want to establish that the gender of occupational groups embroiled in inter-occupational, demarcationary struggles, both as architects and as targets of demarcationary practices, is not a fortuitous or contingent but a necessary factor in explaining both the form and the outcome of such strategies.

Gender politics were pressed into the service of inter-occupational politics at critical stages in the emergence of the medical division of labour. The debate about midwives' registration reveals a gendered discourse of inter-occupational relations. Indeed, medical men's demarcationary strategy of incorporation was crucially informed by a discursive strategy of power with gendered subject and object positions. The reconstruction of the division of labour entailed by this strategy was only feasible because of the availability of a discursive construct of 'nursing' which was gendered 'female'. Thus it became possible to propose a dissociation of the 'routinised' portion of midwifery practice from the 'interventionist' portion. It was the presence of 'nursing' functions within this routinised portion that presented medical men with the possibility of so radically reconstructing the medical division of labour by discursively deploying the equivalence of 'nursing' as 'that portion of attendance which is more suitable to a mere woman' (HMSO 1892). In a vain attempt to destroy the

1895 Midwives' Bill it was suggested that the word 'person' be substituted for 'woman', a proposal met with ridicule. Midwives attended labour and nursed the woman afterwards, but it was declared preposterous to 'propose that latter function for men' (*Nursing Notes* 1895: 96).

But if nurses were discursively represented as gendered female, then so too were midwives. Medical men's de-skilling strategy was also informed by a gendered discourse. The boundary between de-skilled midwifery practice, on the one hand, and medical practice, on the other, was constructed as a gendered boundary. Women provided midwifery and men medical services. For example, the surgical demands of obstetrics were discursively equated with masculinity. 'It required all the courage of a man, much less of a lady, and I do not think they would attempt it; if they were trained properly they would not' (HMSO 1892: 128). In addition, the vision of a stratified market in midwifery services was informed by the assumption that men could not 'settle down for life to practice cheap midwifery' (*British Medical Journal* 1873: 354) and that 'The fees which a midwife gets, from 2s 6d to 10s, is a sum quite inadequate to remunerate the services of an educated gentleman' (HMSO 1892: 257).

Thus, gendered discursive as well as gendered closure strategies were used in the construction of sexually segregated spheres of competence in the emerging medical division of labour. Gendered discourses with subjects and objects positioned in patriarchal power relations, as well as patriarchal structures within which male power was institutionalised within the spheres of civil society and the state, facilitated the gendered demarcationary strategies of medical men and constrained the female professional projects of midwives.

5

THE OCCUPATIONAL POLITICS OF NURSE REGISTRATION

In this chapter the notion of a female professional project is further developed through analysing nurses' campaign for a state-sponsored system of registration. The concept of a dual closure strategy is used to sociologically unpick the aims and objectives of this campaign. The long and bitter campaign for a state-sponsored system of nurse registration spanned the years between 1888, when the British Nurses Association formed with the aim of obtaining the legal status of a profession, and 1919, when the Nurse Registration Act was passed. It has been described as 'the thirty years war' by Abel-Smith (1960). The campaign was spearheaded by the redoubtable ex-Matron of St Batholomew's Hospital, Mrs Bedford-Fenwick, who was to use her position as editor of the *British Journal of Nursing* to pen a vast number of pro-registrationist editorials and pursue her cause doggedly.

Pro-registrationist nurses looked to the state to sponsor their professional project and provide nurses with the machinery of self-government, thereby granting nurses the autonomy to determine the standard and duration of nurse education, to control entry into the ranks of nurses, and to improve their pay and conditions. The core of pro-registrationist nurses' professional project was the demand for 'self-government' and this was posed as an alternative to the 'subjugation' of nurses. I shall argue that the campaign for nurse registration was a female professional project; a strategy of dual closure with strongly usurpationary and strongly exclusionary aims, employing legalistic and credentialist tactics.

Along its usurpationary dimension this campaign posed a strong challenge to three sets of power relations. The first of these was the employment relation between hospitals and nurses within

128

which hospitals controlled both the standard and length of nurse training, as well as the pay and conditions of nursing labour. The second of these sets of power relations was the inter-occupational relation of control between medical men and nurses, particularly the power of the élite medical corporations such as the Royal Colleges of Physicians and of Surgeons to gain a controlling foothold in any proposed statutory nursing body. The third set of power relations to be contested were gender relations as Mrs Bedford-Fenwick's advocacy of 'self-government' for nurses was linked to her broader commitment to the autonomous organisation of women in the labour market and to women's suffrage (cf Hector 1973).

Nurses' professional project also contained exclusionary aims. These were three-fold. First, to set up a centralised means of control over the occupational infrastructure of nursing (Bellaby and Oribabor 1980). This was to be a central board or council of nurses, a statutory body set up by act of parliament, and would provide the institutional means of regulating the supply of nursing labour, thereby creating an occupational monopoly. But it would not necessarily follow that this would be under the control of nurses themselves. And so the second key exclusionary dimension of nurses' professional project was the demand of self-government for nurses, which meant majority and direct representation of nurses on any central body set up to control the affairs of the nursing profession. Mrs Bedford-Fenwick persistently and stubbornly sought to ensure that any central body was composed of a clear majority of nurses and that these nurse representatives were elected by registered nurses themselves. The third exclusionary dimension was the demand for a one-portal system of entry into nursing. This hinged around centralised control over the curriculum, as well as the duration and standard of nurse education, and a single register. This one portal was to be 'the uniform examination of the Central Council' (*British Journal of Nursing* 1905: 252).

The reason why it took thirty long years to get a nurse registration act onto the statute book was that it provoked so much opposition. The main opposition came from the expanding voluntary hospital sector, who were to prove powerful opponents of registration. The opposition of the medical profession is, in my view, generally overstated. Whilst some doctors opposed nurse registration out of a confused mixture of motives (cf Baly 1980),

129

others proved staunch supporters – in particular a section of medical men led by Mrs Bedford-Fenwick's husband, Dr Bedford-Fenwick. But there was also opposition from within the ranks of nurses themselves, opposition led covertly and surreptiously by Florence Nightingale, who did not believe that registration was the way for nurses to consolidate their modern, reformed role in the emerging medical division of labour and expanding system of hospital care. Nurses, then, were divided over the issue of nurse registration. It is essential to approach this division within the ranks of nurses as different strategic responses to the task of consolidating the changing role and status of modern, reformed nursing and to the task of constructing a power base for the female occupation of nursing.

Unfortunately, the struggle for registration has been given rather short shrift in some of the major accounts of nursing history. In his seminal history of the nursing profession Abel-Smith somewhat dismissively describes the struggle for registration as 'a battle for status conducted against a background of rampant snobbery and militant feminism' (1960: 67). Mrs Bedford-Fenwick is described as 'uncompromising' and 'opinionated', whilst Florence Nightingale, aided by her 'charm' and 'social influence', is credited with having played 'the major role in transforming the recruitment, training and practice of the new profession' (1960: 20). Similarly, in the sociological literature, there is a tendency to resort to the 'rampant snobbery' explanation of the campaign for nurse registration. Parry and Parry (1976), for example, treat the professional project of the humble general practitioner with due analytical reverance, but then go on to refer somewhat dismissively to the search for professionalism amongst nurses as:

> more an expression of the antipathy felt by the status con-
> scious lady-nurses towards those recruited from the working
> class than it was an effort to establish a self-governing pro-
> fession of nursing. The leaders of the nurses' Registration
> Movement continued to have more in common with doctors
> who came from a similar class background to themselves
> than they had with the mass of ordinary nurses.
>
> (Parry and Parry 1976: 181)

But professional projects are by their very nature divisive. Class prejudice did indeed divide the ranks of nurses but it would be mistaken to attribute class prejudice solely to the pro-registrationist nurses (cf Vicinus 1985).

In the following account, I propose a less value-laden and pejorative explanation which seeks to sociologically unpick the aims and objectives of the nurses' registration movement in so far as it represented a professional project for nurses. I dwell not upon the personalities of prominent nursing leaders, but upon the occupational politics they espoused, sharing Davies's (1980a) dismay at the myopic focus of some nursing historians on personalities and their consequent neglect of issues relating to the institutional arrangements of nurse training and practice. I hope that my approach is more in line with the rewriting of nursing history pioneered by Celia Davies and the new commitment to develop 'diverse approaches' and question 'an orthodox history of nursing' (Davies 1980a: 9). Radical approaches to conventional themes are emerging (Maggs 1987), including a reassessment of the myth and reality of the Nightingale reform and its legacy for nursing (cf Baly 1987). Nonetheless, some historians persist in the myopic focus on personality deplored by Davies. For example, Smith's (1982) wholesale debunking of the Nightingale myth pivots around discrediting Nightingale, the woman, in what can best be described as a vicious misogynous tirade.

A biography of Mrs Bedford-Fenwick by Hector (1973) has done much to rehabilitate Mrs Bedford-Fenwick and force a reassessment of her contribution to nursing. Hector challenges Abel-Smith's unsympathetic portrayal of Mrs Bedford-Fenwick as an advocate of a divided nursing profession, of lady pupils and of snobbery, as well as his more sympathetic portrayal of Florence Nightingale as champion of the cause of the ordinary woman to train as a nurse. Concentrating instead on their different conceptions of the nursing role, Hector contrasts Nightingale's vision of nursing as a dedicated calling more akin to a religion with little importance attached to status and reward, and Mrs Bedford-Fenwick's vision of occupational professionalism, where occupational expertise brought with it the deserved trappings of status and economic rewards.

THE CAMPAIGN FOR NURSE REGISTRATION: AN OVERVIEW

Nurse registration had been an issue as early as 1872 when the General Medical Council appointed a special Committee on the

Medical Qualification of Women to consider the possibility of drawing up regulations for the education and registration of nurses and midwives (Minutes of the General Medical Council 1873). In 1874 Dr Henry Acland wrote in the preface to Florence Lees' *A Handbook of Hospital Sisters* that, although the Medical Act of 1858 allowed women to be registered as medical practitioners (a statement contradicted in practice) 'It made no provision for the registration of trained nurses, however complete their education and however great their skills, whether as midwives or nurses' (*Nursing Record* 1893: 97). Ironically, the book was dedicated to Florence Nightingale. The author alluded to the possibility of nurses being registered by the General Medical Council. More than a decade was to pass before the subject of nurse registration emerged as a campaigning issue with the formation of the British Nurses Association (BNA) in 1887 (*Nursing Record* I 1888: 2).

The BNA formed as a breakaway body from the Hospitals' Association, which had been set up in 1886 by Henry Burdett although he and others associated with the Hospitals' Association were to become staunch opponents of nurse registration. A meeting of the Hospitals' Association in 1887 declared the registration of nurses to be one of its major objectives (*Nursing Notes* 1887: 8) and a Nursing Sub-Committee of the Hospitals' Association was duly set up to formulate a scheme for registration. It proposed that the condition for registration should be not less than three years' training, but the Council of the Hospitals' Association subsequently overturned this decision and substituted a period of one year's training. In one of her many retrospective accounts of the struggle for nurse registration, Mrs Bedford-Fenwick records how:

> the leaders of the Nursing profession . . . retired in a body from the Hospitals' Association, and . . . they formed the British Nurses' Association for the primary objects of bringing about the Registration of nurses who had gone through not less than three years' Hospital training, and of keeping the control of the Nursing Profession solely and altogether in professional hands.
>
> (*Nursing Record* 1892: 570)

Mrs Bedford-Fenwick, a member of the sub-committee, promptly resigned from the Hospitals' Association and set up the BNA (*British Journal of Nursing* 1905: 102). At this juncture, the appropriate length of nurses' training was the issue which opened up the rift between pro-registrationist nurses and the hospitals together with their training schools. The lines of opposition had been drawn between the lay employers of nurses and a section of the nurses led by Mrs Bedford-Fenwick.

The issue of nurse training threw into sharp relief the issue of the balance of power between nursing employers and nurses themselves. Pro-registrationist nurses challenged the autonomy of hospital training schools in deciding the appropriate length of training for nurses. In due course, they were to increasingly challenge the autonomy of hospitals in deciding the content and standard of nurse training, as well as the conditions of employment of nursing labour. We see here a nascent credentialist tactic in the pro-registrationist stance.

> The BNA declared that its objective was to obtain the legal status of a profession, and a charter to enable them to register properly trained nurses . . . [and of] . . . placing nursing upon a proper footing, and making it a recognised profession, and securing a royal charter to enable really trained nurses to be legally registered as such, and so distinguished from women who are not found worthy of the name.
>
> (*Nursing Record* 1888: 5, 13)

The BNA became the Royal British Nurses Association (RBNA) in 1893 when it was granted a Royal Charter. Nursing became the first female occupation ever to be granted one (*Nursing Record* I 1895: 130). Registration, it was argued, would 'form nursing into a distinct profession [and] clearly define who are and who are not real members of the profession'. Nurses' work would become recognised 'as a skilled and scientific calling' and suitably rewarded (*Nursing Record* 1888: 26).

From the outset, the quest for professional status by means of registration was articulated as a project of social closure aiming to restructure the class base of nursing (*Nursing Record* 1888: 86). It was envisaged that 'larger numbers of educated women' would be attracted to nursing, which in time would become 'a profession for cultured women' (*British Journal of Nursing* 1904: 492). It is precisely this class-divisive nature of pro-registrationist occupational politics that lies at the heart of the charges of 'rampant snobbery' levelled against the pro-registrationists by commentators such as Abel-Smith (1960) and Parry and Parry (1976).

The significance of these early years of the campaign for nurses' registration lies primarily in the emergence of a clear line of demarcation between those in favour of and those against registration. Pro-registrationists were represented by the RBNA led by Mrs Bedford-Fenwick and composed of nurses described by Abel-Smith as 'those lady nurses who were not influenced by Florence Nightingale' (Abel-Smith 1960: 70). The anti-registrationists were represented by the larger London Hospitals, their training schools and matrons, together with Florence Nightingale herself. The lines of opposition were seen by Mrs Bedford-Fenwick to be drawn as follows:

> On the one side, this Association, supported by the leaders and the rank and file of the medical and nursing professions, attempting to protect the sick against ignorant and untrustworthy, and even dangerous, women, who term themselves Nurses. On the other, the authorities of a few Hospitals, who have for years privately attempted to hinder and thwart the efforts of the Association, because the protection of the public will involve a diminuition in their receipts.
>
> (*Nursing Record* 1892: 270)

The Hospitals' Association, spearheaded by Henry Burdett, and the Nightingale Fund, whose secretary was Henry Bonham-Carter, emerged as the major platform for the opposition to the RBNA's campaign for nurses' registration (*British Journal of Nursing* 1905: 102). By 1889, the nurse training schools attached to some larger London hospitals had publicly declared their opposition to nurse registration which, they argued 'would (1) lower the position of the best trained nurses, (2) be detrimental to the advancement of the teaching of nursing, (3) be disadvantageous to the public, and (4) be injurious to the medical practitioner' (*Nursing Notes* 1889: 79). Florence Nightingale was strongly opposed to registration, and although her opposition was covert, it was nevertheless effective (Abel-Smith 1960: 71–2). Under the terms of its charter the RBNA were empowered only to maintain and publish a 'list' of trained nurses rather than the 'register' it had hoped for. It was Nightingale and her allies who were largely responsible for this, and she declared triumphantly in a letter to *The Times* in 1893 that 'the list will have nothing in common with legal registers of the medical or other profession, but will simply be a list of names published by the Association' (cited in Abel-Smith 1960: 72).

The formation of the RBNA also marked the beginnings of an interesting alliance between nurses and medical men around the issue of nurse registration. The RBNA admitted only medical men and nurses to membership and, as its charter was granted to an equal number of representatives from the medical and nursing professions, it was managed by both medical men and nurses (*Nursing Record* 1888: 298, 1893: 229). In 1895 the British Medical Association at its annual meeting adopted a motion put to it by Dr Bedford-Fenwick supporting nurse registration (*British Journal of Nursing* 1904: 48). However, when the motion was referred to the Parliamentary Bills Committtee of the BMA another one declaring a legal system of registration of nurses to be inexpedient in principle was put to the meeting and carried. Carried by six votes to five, it was voted for by both the Medical Honorary Secretary and the delegate of the Executive Committee of the RBNA itself. So the RBNA was now controlled by medical and nursing interests opposed to registration. It had renegued, for the time being, on its commitment to nurses' registration, and quickly abolished its Register of Trained Nurses. This meant that Mrs Bedford-Fenwick and her supporters had been ousted from their power base.

The pro-registrationists eventually regrouped around the Society for the State Registration of Trained Nurses (SSRTN) which formed in 1902 with the declared aim of securing the registration of trained nurses by means of an act of parliament. But the waters of registration were to be muddied again when the drafting of a nurses' registration bill by the newly formed SSRTN in 1903 was promptly matched by the drafting of another bill by the – ostensibly anti-registrationist – RBNA a few months later.

In 1905 a Parliamentary Select Committee agreed 'that it is desirable that a Register of Nurses should be kept by a Central Body appointed by the State [and] that this Central Body should by set up by Act of Parliament' (HMSO 1905, *British Journal of Nursing* 1905: 107–8). Between 1904 and 1914 there was a nurses' registration bill before parliament annually (Morley 1914, Abel-Smith 1960). In 1908 the bill reached a third reading in the House of Commons, before meeting with opposition in the House of Lords (Morley 1914). After three different bills had been put before parliament by three different organisations in 1909, the Central Committee for the State Registration of Nurses (CCSRN) was formed in 1910 (*British Journal of Nursing* 1910: 88) 'for the purpose of securing united action in regard to State Registration, until a satisfactory law has been passed by parliament' (*British Journal of Nursing* 1916: 231).

The formation of the CCSRN drew together into one parliamentary pressure group a number of associations, including by now the RBNA as well as Mrs Bedford-Fenwick's campaigning base, the SSRTN, and the BMA, which sought some form of state registration for nurses. Mrs Bedford-Fenwick and Dr Goodell, Honorary Secretary of the Metropolitan Counties Branch of the British Medical Association, were joint honorary secretaries. Between 1910 and 1914, the CCSRN put its nurses' registration bill before parliament each year (*British Journal of Nursing* 1916: 451) but without success. It was the escalating challenge posed by such a strategy to hospital employers which proved the major obstacle to success in the campaign for a state-sponsored system of registration.

THE POLITICS OF OPPOSITION TO NURSE REGISTRATION

I have already suggested that the two key elements of the opposition to nurse registration were the voluntary hospitals and Florence Nightingale, together with her allies such as Henry Bonham-Carter, Secretary of the Nightingale Fund, and matrons and nurses influenced by the Nightingale philosophy of nursing. It is only by recognising the symbiotic relationship between the Nightingale reform of nursing and its institutional framework, the voluntary hospital, that the politics of opposition to nurse registration begin to make sense.

The opposition of the voluntary hospitals

Voluntary hospitals were privately funded, operated quite independently of the Poor Law with its workhouse infirmaries, and were governed by lay committees of hospital governors (Abel-Smith 1964). By setting up nurse training schools in large voluntary hospitals such as St Thomas's Hospital in London, where Nightingale located her school of nursing in 1860, Nightingale and her followers believed that they would have the greatest impact on nursing by transforming it from above (Vicinus 1985). It was the voluntary hospital, then, which provided the institutional shell for the modernisation and reform of nursing. The

Nightingale system of nurse training made political and economic sense in the hospitals and it was essentially a compromise based on the existing institutional framework of the hospital (cf Davies 1980b, 1982). Nightingale's conception of the nurse as a devoted, disciplined and selfless worker together with her strategy of on-the-job training meant that hospitals were staffed with a cheap, disciplined and compliant labour force of probationers. There was no physical school of nursing as such, so the hospital did not have to bear the expense of teaching staff. Its major outlay was to provide living quarters for nurses, but it gained from this arrangement because a smaller stipend could be paid and its nursing labour was constantly available.

The inception of a campaign for nurse registration in the 1880s coincided with the period when the hospital sector began to expand. Hospital nursing grew alongside the expansion of the hospital sector (Maggs 1983: 6). By 1905 it was estimated that just over 11,000 nurses were employed in voluntary hospitals (HMSO 1905) with a further 5,000 employed in Poor Law service (Abel-Smith 1960). Three-quarters of those working in hospitals were probationers (nurses in training) (Maggs 1983) so probationers undoubtedly provided a valuable source of cheap nursing labour for hospitals. In addition, hospitals controlled nursing labour in ways other than through the employment relationship. Institutes were attached to hospitals which acted as agencies, placing nurses in private work and providing them with board and lodging in between cases (Morley 1914). The clients' fees were paid to the institute which then paid the nurse a fixed annual salary. It was claimed that half of the general hospitals in England and Wales had private nursing staff available for hire (HMSO 1905: 79). Hospitals, then, functioned not only as direct employers of nursing labour but also as indirect employers, mediating between the client and nurses in private, home nursing. Up until 1914, private duty nurses made up nearly three-quarters of the nursing labour market (Maggs 1983: 131). Of course, it was private duty nursing and its individual contractual relations with patients that Mrs Bedford-Fenwick was really interested in reorganising in a comparable way to the medical profession (Dingwall, Rafferty and Webster 1988: 79). It was private duty nursing which was to provide the high status occupation suitable for middle-class women.

State registration with its more stringent regulations for examination and registration would stay progress in hospitals by exacerbating the problem of supply of nurses. As the demand for nurses was increasing along with the expansion of the hospital sector, hospital governors argued that nurses were not being trained in sufficient numbers to meet demand and, if only trained nurses were to be registered, then there would not be enough nurses to fill posts (HMSO 1904: 32). Already, by 1904, the demand for hospital nurses was outstripping the supply of trained nurses. Furthermore, if nurses, like other trainee professionals, were required to pay for their education and training, then it would be impossible to recruit enough nurses. Upper-class women who could afford to pay for their training comprised a comparatively small proportion of nurses and, after the initial period of influx from the 1860s, it was becoming increasingly difficult to attract them into nursing. In addition, a uniform standard of nurse training was said to be an 'illusory goal' in the face of the diversity of training facilities that existed in the voluntary hospitals. Diversity of practice was justified on the grounds that variety of nursing knowledge and experience was needed, depending upon the hospital (HMSO 1904: 28–59 and Appendix 2).

A key element of any professional project is the attempt to gain control over the education, training and practice of an occupational group by the members of that occupation themselves, thus securing a link between education and occupation, the link which Larson (1977) claims is the essence of the professional project. The campaign for nurse registration threatened to disrupt the symbiotic relation between reformed nurse training and practice, on the one hand, and the staffing needs of the expanding voluntary hospital sector, on the other, and to diminish the autonomy enjoyed by voluntary hospitals in relation to both nurse training and employment. In short, the claim to occupational autonomy on the part of pro-registrationist nurses threatened to undermine the balance of power in the employment relation between hospitals and nursing labour, where hospitals were the stronger partner, exercising considerable employer control over modern nursing. A major plank of the opposition to nurse registration, then, was made up of 'the authorities of some hospitals . . . keenly jealous of their rights and privileges, and openly fearful of any infringement of, or interference with, their power over their nursing subordinates' (Breay 1897: 501). As Dingwall, Rafferty and Webster accurately surmise:

If the hospitals allowed the occupation to organize itself and create a more homogeneous market, they recognized that their influence would be matched by that of a monopolistic supplier of nursing labour. Instead of nurses working on terms set by the hospitals, the hospitals would have to employ nurses on terms set by the occupation.

(Dingwall, Rafferty and Webster 1988: 81)

But what of the opposition of matrons and nurses themselves?

The opposition of matrons and nurses

The nub of matrons' and nurses' opposition to nurse registration was that it threatened to undermine some of the real gains for nurses that resulted from the Nightingale reform. It is now generally agreed that the Nightingale reform had very little impact on nursing practice (cf Davies 1982, Gamarnikow 1978) but had a lasting impact in the sphere of nurse management (cf Carpenter 1977, Bellaby and Oribabor 1980, Vicinus 1985, Davies 1982, Gamarnikow 1978). The Nightingale reform ultimately had a far greater impact upon the occupational role and institutional position of the hospital matron than it did upon the ordinary nurse. Its major achievement was to enhance the managerial role of the matron, setting up a female chain of command in the hospital hierarchy. It was this that was being defended by matrons and nurses opposed to registration.

Largely due to the Nightingale reform, there was a dramatic transition in the occupational role of the hospital matron from little more than a domestic manager and housekeeper to the manager of an independent nursing staff (Carpenter 1977, Abel-Smith 1960, Davies 1982). On taking up her post as Matron of Guy's Hospital in the 1880s, Miss Burt declared that she was not about to follow in the footsteps of her predecessor, who had been content to perform housekeeping duties and exercised no control of the nursing staff (Cameron 1954: 206). By centralising all matters to do with nursing in the office of the matron, the office of matron was enhanced at the expense of the position and authority of the ward sister (Williams 1980, Cameron 1954). This transition from housekeeper to the manager of an independent staff by matrons was not necessarily a smooth one. At Guy's Hospital, Miss Burt had the support of the hospital governors, but met with opposition from medical staff (Cameron 1954) because the diminution in the role of ward sister undermined the ability of the ward physician to control the everyday accomplishment of nursing tasks on the wards (Williams 1980). At a Lowestoft hospital, when the new matron appointed in 1890 was put in sole charge of the nursing department and promptly attempted to dismiss one of the ward sisters, she resigned following an outcry from the medical staff and the committee of governors itself (*Nursing Record* 1899: 389–91).

By 1880 the matron in the voluntary hospital had become established as the head of an independent nursing department and controlled her own nursing staff without interference from lay administrators, frequently by-passing them and reporting direct to the hospital committee of governors (Abel-Smith 1960). The changing authority relations in the voluntary hospital are succinctly summarised by Abel-Smith:

> To put it baldly, if the matron was to undertake what she considered to be her duties, she had to carve out an empire of her own. She had to take over some of the responsibilities of the medical staff and some of the responsibilities of the lay administration. In addition she had to centralize the administration of nursing affairs, lowering thereby the prestige of her sisters. . . . In a remarkably short time the matrons got their way and took over positions of undisputed authority between the medical staff and the lay adminstrators. A system of tripartite administration replaced bipartite administration. By 1880 the change had occurred in most of the leading voluntary hospitals of London.
>
> (Abel-Smith 1964: 68)

Thus, the most distinctive contribution of Nightingale to the structure of modern nursing was to set up a chain of command which by-passed lay administrative and medical staff and which centred around the expanded role of the hospital matron. One of the distinguishing features of this chain of command was that it was an exclusively female one, which was precisely what Nightingale herself had intended:

> The whole reform in nursing both at home and abroad has consisted in this; to take all power over the Nursing out of the hands of the men, and put it into the hands of *one female*

trained head and make her responsible for everything (regarding internal management and discipline) being carried out. Usually it is the medical staff who have injudiciously interfered as 'Master'. How much worse it is when it is the Chaplain. Don't let the Chaplain want to make himself matron. Don't let the Doctor make himself Head Nurse. *There is no worse matron than a chaplain.*
(1867 letter from Miss Nightingale to Mary Jones, cited in Abel-Smith 1960: 25)

The disagreements between nurses themselves around the issue of nurse registration revealed fundamental disagreements as to how nursing should go about the task of establishing itself as an autonomous female occupational sphere in the emerging division of labour and in the expanding hospital sector of health care. The main axis of disagreement centred around where the locus of control over nursing should lie. Should this be located within the expanded occupational role of the matron in what was essentially a decentralised female authority structure operating at the institutional level of the hospital, or should it be located within a central controlling body of nurses at the supra-institutional level along the lines of male professions such as medicine? Anti-registrationist nurses favoured the former, pro-registrationists the latter arrangement. The opposition of matrons to the campaign for nurse registration had much to do with the fact that they imagined it would lessen or even destroy their newly found authority over their nurses (*Nursing Record* 1888: 86).

The goal of registration was seen by Nightingale to subvert the high ideal of nursing as a calling and moreover a calling through which a secularised and this-wordly form of religious satisfaction could be found by women (Cook 1914). Nightingale deplored the 'mercantile spirit . . . of forcing up wages' and 'mere money making on the part of Nurses and their societies', as these sullied the higher ideal of nursing as a dedicated, selfless calling (Cook 1914: 360, 363). This introduces the third key element of the opposition's stand against registration, which is the radically divergent discursive constructions of the nurse which informed those opposed to and those advocating registration. In a manner reminiscent of Pringle's analysis of the different discursive constructions of the secretarial role in the twentieth century (cf Pringle 1989), we can discern two different and opposing discursive definitions of 'the nurse' that coexisted by the end of the nineteenth century.

The Nightingale philosophy had constructed a discourse of nursing that was a gendered discourse which placed the unique moral qualities of the woman-as-nurse at the centre of this discourse. This is revealed in Nightingale's conception of nursing as dedicated service and as a profession for single women of impeccable moral standards (Vicinus 1985) and in the stress on an intimate link between character and femininity (Gamarnikow 1978). Nurse training was largely concerned with the development of moral character – 'character, character, character. All the influences of the training and the organization must be to form or develop her character' (Nightingale Papers cited in Hector 1973).

The discursive construction of the nurse by the champions of the Nightingale philosophy pivoted around what the nurse *was*, rather than what she did. Discursively, the nurse and the woman were one and the same, whilst the qualities of the good nurse were those of the good woman – 'sympathy', 'cheerfulness', 'self-control', 'unselfishness' (HMSO 1905: 30, appendix: 98–105), 'kindness', 'patience', 'trust-worthiness', 'self-control' and 'discretion' (*Nursing Record* II 1888: 301). The opposition's case against registration rested on the assertion that registration does not touch character:

> Inasmuch as any system of registration must be based on the results of testing by examination the technical capabilities of a nurse, it of necessity raises to a predominant position this side of her work, and leaves entirely unconsidered those personal qualities upon which her main value depends, such as good temper, manner, tact, discretion, patience and unselfish womanliness. It is these characteristics which cannot be ascertained by examination, and which no system of registration can include.
>
> (HMSO 1904 appendix: 98)

The Nightingale regime of training had instituted major themes in the discourse of nursing: gender, subservience, vocation, discipline, and morality (Chua and Clegg 1990). Chua and Clegg, in their otherwise excellent attempt to analyse the history of nurse professionalism within a framework which combines concepts of closure and discursive strategies, nonetheless overstate the continuity in the discursive construct of the nurse over time. For there was not one, but two competing discursive constructions of the nurse by the end of the nineteenth century. The registrationist campaign was informed by a discourse of professionalism which pivoted around the discursive construction of the nurse in terms of what she *did*, foregrounding her technical competence and skill, rather than allegedly intangible moral qualities so talked about by the anti-registrationists.

Summary

The politics of opposition to nurse registration pivoted around a defence of the gains for both hospitals and nurses of the Nightingale reform. In particular, the campaign for registration threatened to undo the symbiotic relation between the voluntary hospitals and reformed nursing. The Nightingale reform had secured for women a sphere of autonomy in the form of a female occupational hierarchy at the apex of which sat the hospital matron with her expanded managerial role. The hospitals for their part had benefited from the Nightingale reform by having a cheap and flexible supply of nursing labour, particularly probationer nurses. But the campaign for registration aimed to create a centralised, supra-institutional control mechanism for the occupation of nursing. This was to be external to the two interlocking internal systems of control located within the institutional framework of the hospital. One of these was the overall controlling mechanism of the employment relationship, within which hospitals exercised considerable control and autonomy in relation to both the conditions of nursing labour and the content of nurse training. The other was the impressive measure of internal control exercised by the matron over her nursing staff.

For nurses themselves, the debate about nurse registration revealed fundamental disagreements about how nursing should go about consolidating itself as an autonomous, female occupation within the emerging male-dominated medical division of labour and expanding system of health care. The central point of disagreement was where the locus of power should lie. Should this be located in the expanded occupational role of the matron in what was an essentially decentralised female authority structure operating at the institutional level of the hospital? Or should this be located in a central controlling body of nurses at the supra-institutional level along the lines of male professions, such as medicine?

THE CAMPAIGN FOR REGISTRATION: A FEMALE PROFESSIONAL PROJECT

I now examine in detail the campaign for registration spearheaded by Mrs Bedford-Fenwick. As I have already signalled, the concept of dual closure can be fruitfully used to sociologically unpick the aims and objectives of the campaign which, I argue, was a 'female professional project'.

As a project of dual closure Mrs Bedford-Fenwick's campaign contained usurpationary and exclusionary dimensions and used legalistic and credentialist tactics of closure. The three key demands of the campaign were: a centralised means of control over nursing in the form of a statutory body; the direct and majority representation of nurses on this statutory controlling body; and a one-portal system of entry into nursing. These aims were exclusionary because they were clearly aimed at restricting access to the ranks of nursing, regulating the supply of nurses and restructuring its class base. They were also usurpationary because they posed a strong challenge to existing sets of control relations within which nursing was embedded. They challenged inter-occupational relations of control of medicine over nursing because they sought to pre-empt the possibility of the medical profession gaining a controlling foothold in any professional organisation of nurses and, because they threatened to dislocate the symbiotic relation between hospitals and reformed nursing, they also challenged existing institutional relations of control of hospitals over nursing labour. And finally they sought to pre-empt the possibility of male professionals and employers controlling a female occupation, as Mrs Bedford-Fenwick was acutely aware that the interests of nurses were also the interests of women.

Legalistic and credentialist tactics

Legalistic and credentialist tactics of closure both figured prominently. The increasing emphasis placed by Mrs Bedford-Fenwick on state registration as distinct from a voluntary system represented the use of legalistic tactics. A legal, compulsory system of registration rather than a voluntary one could only be secured through mobilising heteronomous means of state sponsorship. A state-sponsored system of nurse registration was viewed as an integral element of nurses' professional project. 'An adequate form of •

144

legal status meant professional enfranchisement' (*British Journal of Nursing* 1916: 252). Registrationist nurses viewed state sponsorship of their professional project as 'the foundation stone in the erection of the edifice of their profession' (*Nursing Record* I 1893: 302). Indeed, a state-sponsored system of registration established by act of parliament soon came to be viewed as the only effective means of obtaining a system of professional control (*British Journal of Nursing* 1904: 47, 1905: 104).

Credentialist tactics also figured prominently. In the early years of the campaign these had been more embedded and revolved around the issue of the length rather than the content or standard of nurse training. But they came to figure far more prominently in the later years of the campaign. Initially credentialism was articulated mainly in relation to the supply of nurses. In 1889, arguing the case that nurses should pass a preliminary examination in literacy and basic education prior to entering nurse training schools, it was said of such an examination that 'Not only would it ensure that Nursing, like the other professions, would only be open to educated people, but it would immediately and largely diminish the excessive crowding into the ranks which is now prevalent' (*Nursing Record* I 1891: 21).

Occupational closure by means of credentialist tactics was also explicitly linked to social closure. Restricting entry to educated gentlewomen was an aim of pro-registrationists and this was seen as simply continuing a trend already in evidence:

> The fact is, that during the last decade and a half, a continually increasing number of gentlewomen have adopted nursing as a profession; have raised the whole status of Nurses; have crowded out the old workers of the Sairey Gamp class; have, because well educated and enthusiastic, introduced numerous niceties and improvements into their work; have paid for their education at hospitals.
>
> (*Nursing Record* 1892: 569)

Until the Crimean War, it was argued, nursing had been in the hands of women of the servant class, but after this point in time a better class of women had been entering nursing (HMSO 1904: 2). Occupational and social closure would consolidate this trend.

It was hoped that credentialist tactics would restrict entry to educated gentlewomen. By 1906 Mrs Bedford-Fenwick was to describe the movement for state registration as primarily 'an educational movement' (*British Journal of Nursing* 1906: 267) and this was linked to an increasing emphasis upon a one-portal system of entry into nursing (*British Journal of Nursing* 1905: 252).

Credentialist and legalistic tactics went hand in hand, as Mrs Bedford-Fenwick believed that 'The registration of Nurses by Act of Parliament is the only means by which a general standard of education and a definite system of professional control can be obtained' (*British Journal of Nursing* 1904: 47) and that 'Without registration it is impossible to maintain adequate standards of education, or to enforce efficient discipline throughout the nursing profession' (*British Journal of Nursing* 1916: 232). One of the tasks of the central board or council was to be to decide upon the curriculum of education (*Nursing Record and Hospital World* 1895: 122). A central board was needed to bring about uniformity in both the length and content of nurse education and training as well as to set and monitor the standard of nurse education (*British Journal of Nursing* 1910). The role of the central board was to be crucial if nursing was to unify its cognitive base by setting up a common programme of nurse education and a single qualifying examination.

Legalistic tactics pivoted around securing access to heteronomous means of closure in the form of state sponsorship of a professional project. So nurses, like midwives and aspiring women doctors, depended upon the mobilisation of proxy male power in the pursuit of their female professional project. Like midwives, nurses depended in particular upon the support of a section of the medical profession. Mrs Bedford-Fenwick, herself an ardent women's rights supporter, was only too aware of the fact that female nurses depended so absolutely on medical men to find a voice in the public sphere. In 1914 when the Nurses' Registration Bill was being debated in the House of Commons, Mrs Bedford-Fenwick reports how, in her capacity as editor of the *British Journal of Nursing*, she was '(much as she resents it) a prisoner behind the *grille* in the ladies' gallery' and how, as a passive and powerless spectator, she wondered 'would these men with absolute power over our conditions of life file to the right or to the left?' (*British Journal of Nursing* 1914: 201).

Credentialist tactics depend upon the mobilisation of autonomous means of closure, such as occupational associations. These too were absent in nursing, although Mrs Bedford-Fenwick was an advocate of women's autonomous organisation. Unlike the medical profession with its royal colleges, 'The Nursing Profession has . . . no College in which its own interests are gathered up and centred, although no doubt the establishment of such a college would be one outcome of the establishment of Registration by the State' (*British Journal of Nursing* 1905: 252).

The paradox, then, was that nurses did not possess these autonomous means of closure and furthermore that, historically, nurse training had already come to be located within the institutional location of the hospital. Moreover, the knowledge base of nursing was evolving as derivative of that of medicine, and this precluded nurses from negotiating a sphere of cognitive exclusiveness. It is important, then, to recognise the legacy of the Nightingale reform of the system of nurse training and particularly the fact that, due to its institutional location within hospitals, it placed a severe constraint on nurses' pursuit of credentialist tactics. It is almost tempting to conclude that credentialist tactics would have been doomed from the outset were it not for the fact that Mrs Bedford-Fenwick and her supporters persistently sought to dislocate the symbiosis between nurse training and its institutional location, the hospital, by relocating control over the content and standard of nurse training – i.e. its knowledge base – in a central, controlling body of nurses.

A strategy of dual closure: exclusionary dimensions

There were three key exclusionary elements of the registrationists' dual closure strategy. These were, first, a centralised system of control over the occupational infrastructure of nursing; second, self-government for nurses in the form of majority and direct representation of nurses on the central statutory body empowered to regulate nursing; and, third, a one-portal system of entry into nursing.

First, there was the demand for a centralised means of control over the affairs of nursing. The major outcome of state sponsorship of nurse registration would be the creation of a central board or council to function as a centralised means of control over the occupational infrastructure of nursing. This controlling mechanism would be external to and independent of the existing internal systems of control located within the institutional framework of the hospital. By establishing a central body to regulate the machinery of registration, an act of parliament would provide the statutory means of regulating nursing practice. In other words, a state-sponsored system of registration would provide the institutional means of regulating the supply of nursing labour and of ensuring something approaching a monopoly of practice. But whilst a central body would provide the mechanism of control, it would not necessarily ensure that this lay in the hands of nurses themselves. It was the policy of direct and majority representation of nurses, expressed as 'self-government' for nurses, that would ensure the occupational autonomy of nurses within the medical division of labour and system of hospital medical care.

So the second demand of pro-registrationist nurses was for self-government for nurses, which meant direct and majority representation on any central body set up to govern nursing. Mrs Bedford-Fenwick adopted an uncompromising stand for the necessity for nurses' self-government as distinct from what she saw as their possible subjugation to other sets of interests. Mrs Bedford-Fenwick's advocacy of nurses' self-government represented an attempt to ensure that the mechanisms of closure were under the control of nurses themselves as distinct from lay hospital administrators or medical men. This element of Mrs Bedford-Fenwick's strategy is revealed through her combined tactics of ensuring that the central controlling body was composed of a clear majority of nurses and that nurse representatives were directly elected by registered nurses themselves. It was a bid for autonomy, and may be contrasted to the midwives' strategy of voluntary subordination, where they quickly conceded both the principle of direct representation of midwives and that of a controlling majority of midwives on the Central Midwives' Board.

The objective of nurses' self-government through majority and direct representation was embodied in the nurses' registration bill drawn up by the Society for the State Registration of Trained Nurses (SSRTN) in 1904, and lay at the heart of the critical stance adopted by the SSRTN in relation to the Royal British Nurses' Association's (RBNA) alternative bill. Mrs Bedford-Fenwick's comments (cf *British Journal of Nursing* 1904, 1905) on the competing draft bills of the RBNA and the SSRTN reveal one of the central planks of the pro-registrationist closure strategy to be the principle of self-government of nurses.

Under the terms of the RBNA draft bill, to which Mrs Bedford-Fenwick objected:

the conditions of nursing labour would be absolutely dic-
tated by a combined oligarchy of medical and lay employers
of nursing labour [and so] the same men are in power who
have repeatedly betrayed our interests . . . for their policy is
quite consistent, and deprives nurses of all responsibility and
power in their own professional matters; it is the policy of
subjugation of, instead of self-government for, nurses.

(British Journal of Nursing 1904: 1–2)

The issue of 'subjugation or self-government' revolved ultimately
around the composition of the central board 'which was to govern
the nursing profession' (*British Journal of Nursing* 1904: 2). Mrs
Bedford-Fenwick aimed to ensure self-government for nurses
through *direct* representation on the central board. This, combined with a resistance to a clear medical or lay majority on the
proposed nurses' central board, represented their means of ensuring self-government for nurses and of countering the prospect of
medical or lay employer control over the occupational infrastructure of nursing. Although both the RBNA and SSRTN bills
embodied the principle of registration, nevertheless Mrs Bedford-
Fenwick was to object to the RBNA Bill on the following grounds:

When we come to the provisions of the two Bills we find the
essential difference is that the one drafted by the nurses –
while providing the due representation of the medical profession and of hospital committees as nursing educational
authorities – places a just measure of control on the Governing Body in the hands of the Matrons and nurses themselves,
selected and elected by the thousands of registered nurses
whose life and work will be affected by the Act. . . . On the
other hand, the Bill of the Exectuive Committee of the Royal
British Nurses' Association, while nominally giving the larger
number of votes to nurses, in reality places the balance of
power in medical and lay hands, as the nine Matrons whom
it suggests shall be placed on the Board take their seats, not
as the elect of their colleagues or of the Registered Nurses,
but as the nominees of the lay Committees of Training-
schools, thereby ranging them at once as representing the
interests of the employers of nurses, not necessarily those of
the members of their own profession.

(British Journal of Nursing 1904: 21)

The crux of Mrs Bedford-Fenwick's discontent with the proposed composition of the central board in the draft RBNA bill of 1903 was that it only allowed for six direct representatives of nurses elected by nurses. Six direct representatives for a potential electorate of 50,000 trained, registered nurses was considered insufficient by Bedford-Fenwick (*British Journal of Nursing* 1904: 81). She also argued that because the nine matrons on the central board were to be nominated by lay hospital boards they 'could not in any way be considered representative of the interests of registered nurses at large' (*British Journal of Nursing* 1904: 46).

At a special general meeting of the RBNA, this was amended due to the intervention of pro-registrationists from the SSRTN so that matrons rather than hospital boards elected their representatives. Mrs Bedford-Fenwick also seconded another successful amendment which increased the number of matrons from nine to ten, on the grounds that it had been agreed at the same meeting to increase the number of nominated medical practitioners from nine to ten. She also argued that medical representatives should be drawn from those members of the medical profession who were closely associated with the education of nurses through nurse training schools, rather than from 'academic bodies, who never have taken, and who cannot take, any practical part in the education and discipline of nurses' (*British Journal of Nursing* 1904: 81).

Mrs Bedford Fenwick's opposition to the original RBNA draft bill revolved around the fact that it placed control over the occupational infrastructure of nursing in the hands of the medical profession and the employers of nurses (*British Journal of Nursing* 1904: 21, 81) and, furthermore, that it did not specify the length of nurse training necessary for registration and called for a 'roll' rather than a register of nurses (*British Journal of Nursing* 1904: 81-2). The SSRTN's own proposed Bill, by contrast, incorporated an altogether different view of the composition of the central board (cf *British Journal of Nursing* 1905: 25). It ensured that effective control of the nursing profession was placed in the hands of nurses and matrons, who were to form a clear majority on the board. The medical profession but not the training schools were represented. Out of a proposed general nursing council of thirty-one persons, fourteen were to be nurses (ten of whom were to be elected representatives of registered nurses), eight were to be matrons, and only six were to be medical practitioners. The remaining three members were to be one medical practitioner and one nurse appointed by the Privy Council, and either a medical practitioner or a nurse appointed by the Asylum Worker's Association.

Thus, it was plainly intended to ensure that control over the occupational infrastructure of nursing lay with nurses themselves, either as directly elected nurses or as hospital matrons appointed by matrons as distinct from hospital committees. In this way neither the interests of the medical profession nor those of the lay hospital employers of nursing labour could predominate. There was the sheer numerical preponderance of directly elected nurses or matrons, who were to number twenty-two out of a board of thirty-one. In addition, there was no representation at all for hospital committees as lay employers of nursing labour. Furthermore, there was clearly an attempt to prevent medical practitioners from the élite controlling bodies of the medical profession such as the Royal Colleges of Surgeons and of Physicians from gaining a foothold in the controlling body of the nursing profession. The five medical practitioners to be appointed by the General Medical Council were to be lecturers or teachers of nurses in nurse training schools attached to general hospitals (*British Journal of Nursing* 1905: 250). The only professional association of doctors to gain any representation was the BMA, which in any event only gained one representative.

Self-government for nurses, then, was to be ensured through the composition of the central body and Mrs Bedford-Fenwick insisted that directly elected or appointed matrons and nurses should be the majority and controlling interest group. The possibility of lay employers of nursing labour gaining a foothold in the affairs of nurses was precluded by ensuring, firstly, that hospital matrons were appointed by matrons rather than members of hospital committees and, secondly, that hospital training schools were represented by medical staff rather than by the lay administrators of the hospitals to which the schools were attached. Furthermore, by restricting representation of the medical profession to medical practitioners in their capacity as educators of nurses in training schools, the possibility of the vested interests of organised surgeons, physicians and general practitioners being represented on the nurses' general council through their colleges, society, and association was also precluded.

These principles of direct and majority representation for nurses sought to preclude the possibility that the interests of either the medical profession or hospital employers would represent the *controlling* interests in the machinery for governing the affairs of nurses, thereby precluding the possibility of the 'subjugation' of nurses in the context of both the interoccupational relations of the medical division of labour between medical men and nurses, and the employment relations that bound hospital employers and significant sections of nursing labour.

Finally, there was the demand for a one-portal system of entry to nursing which was a key element of the pro-registrationists' closure strategy. This revolved around the use of credentialist tactics and assumed an increasingly central role in their campaign. It also invited the most opposition. In its nurses' registration bill drawn up in 1904, the SSRTN advocated that the central council should have powers not only to regulate the issuing of certificates and the conditions of admission to the register but also to regulate nurse training and examination (*British Journal of Nursing* 1905: 251). The one-portal system of entry to nursing hinged around centralised control over the curriculum of nurse education as well as the length and standard of nurse education and training 'For to nurses who are promoting the State Registration movement, it is a matter of primary importance that there should be one portal to their profession – namely, the uniform examinations of the Central Council' (*British Journal of Nursing* 1905: 252).

At the third conference of the Central Committee for the State Registration of Nurses in 1910 two resolutions were adopted and regarded as fundamental to any scheme for state registration. Both these resolutions stressed the necessity of a one-portal system for the effective working of a system of state registration:

(1) That this Conference is of opinion that State Registration can only be satisfactorily carried out by a single-portal system for the United Kingdom . . . (2) That under a single-portal system nurses should be admitted to the Register only after (a) a three years' course of training with a definite curriculum prescribed by a Central Nursing Council, conducted in recognised hospitals and nursing schools, and (b) having passed a uniform State examination conducted by examiners appointed by, and under the supervision of the Central Nursing Council at suitable centres throughout the Kingdom.
(*British Journal of Nursing* 1916: 293)

All these three elements of the campaign – a central body, direct and majority representation and a one-portal system of entry – can be described as 'exclusionary' in their aims. But the campaign also presented a strong challenge to existing sets of power relations, so also contained 'usurpationary' dimensions.

A strategy of dual closure: usurpationary dimensions

The usurpationary dimensions of nurses' dual closure strategy challenged three existing sets of power relations. First, they challenged the balance of power in the employment relation between hospitals and nursing labour, and I have already stressed how nurses' dual closure strategy threatened to dislocate the symbiotic relation between voluntary hospitals and modern nursing.

Second, it had implications for the balance of power in the inter-occupational relations between medicine and nursing in the medical division of labour. Mrs Bedford-Fenwick's views on the inter-occupational relationship between doctors and nursing may be characterised as a reluctance to translate the principle of medical supervision over the practical accomplishment of nursing work into the principle of medical dominance over the occupational infrastructure of nursing. At the inception of the British Nurses Association Mrs Bedford-Fenwick stated that, beyond its primary object of seeking a Royal Charter to legalise the registration of nurses 'it was intended to ensure that members of the Nursing Profession of the future should remain under the supervision of medical men' (*Nursing Record* 1888: 249). The doctor's role in the medical division of labour was that of treatment and diagnosis, whilst nurses acted only under the directions of doctors (*British Journal of Nursing* 1904: 445). In the daily accomplishment of nursing work nurses were not 'self-acting', to use Mrs Bedford-Fenwick's phrase. They did not, in other words, enjoy discretion at the level of execution. Nonetheless, Mrs Bedford-Fenwick was increasingly reluctant to translate this lack of discretion at the level of execution that characterised the daily accomplishment of nursing tasks into the principle of medical dominance over the occupational infrastructure of nursing. "That it is the duty of nurses to carry out the directions of medical staff in relation to the treatment of the sick is unquestionable; but there the authority of the medical practitioner ends' (*British Journal of Nursing* 1905: 10).

Nurses' usurpationary strategy rendered a third set of power relations explicit and problematic, and this was patriarchal relations in the medical division of labour. The principle of nurses' self-government was articulated explicitly as the right of women to self-government independent of male control, be this exercised by lay employers or by medical men. The relation between nursing and medicine was articulated as a gendered relation. It was not simply the case that nurses as an occupational group strove for a measure of independence from medicine, but it was also the case that they articulated their common interests as women in the medical division of labour.

The demand of male workers for reasonable independence in the management of their own affairs, for just conditions of work and life, is now realised in most civilised countries, and by all the laws of evolution the same right will be conceded to women workers sooner or later.

(*British Journal of Nursing* 1904: 21)

Thus, it was not only inter-occupational and employment relations that were being contested, but also the gender order of broader sets of patriarchal relations of male dominance and female subordination which were structuring the health division of labour.

The usurpationary and exclusionary elements of Mrs Bedford-Fenwick's gendered strategy of dual closure were strongly linked. The exclusionary aim of autonomous control by nurses over the conditions of nursing labour was also strongly usurpationary because it resisted the subjugation of a woman's sphere of competence to male control, whether this was exercised within the context of inter-occupational or employment relations. Mrs Bedford-Fenwick also attributed the reform of nurse training and practice in hospitals to 'social movement on the part of women' (*Nursing Record* 1892: 570) and argued that women should carve out for themselves a wider sphere of influence within the hospital, advocating that they sit on hospital committees (*Nursing Record* II 1893: 82). Her advocacy of the autonomous organisation of women in the labour market is reflected in her involvement in the British National Council of Women, of which she herself was honorary secretary and which was set up to promote the better cooperation and organisation of women's work and 'To encourage the formation of societies of women engaged in trades, professions, and in social and political work, in connection with which no organised union at present exists' (*Nursing Record* 1895: 445–6).

MEDICAL MEN AND NURSE REGISTRATION

I have already suggested that the opposition of medical men to nurse registration has generally been overstated. In reality, the stance of doctors on this issue was confused and complicated. Baly (1980) suggests that some doctors with fashionable practices catering for middle-class clientele supported registration because they saw the value of being able to ask for a trained nurse, whereas others with less lucrative practices saw registered nurses as a threat and a potential source of competition. As in the case of midwives' registration, there were fears about the creation of a new, independent order of medical practitioners (cf *British Medical Journal* 1908: 472, 1904: 125, HMSO 1904: 43–6). Once again it was general practitioners who were most likely to fear a competitive threat to their precarious professional monopoly. It was claimed that nurse registration would encourage families to consult nurses rather than general practitioners (*British Medical Journal* 1908: 472) and that nurses would begin to encroach on general practitioners' sphere of competence by practising minor surgery and giving medical advice to patients (*British Medical Journal* 1908: 493). It was best that nurses got their work through the doctor, who was the best judge of a nurse's competence (HMSO 1904: 44).

The support of a section of medical men for nurse registration proves far more interesting. I have already argued in the case of midwives seeking registration that, because women had to mobilise proxy male power in their pursuit of legalistic tactics, they were forced to depend upon the support of a section of the medical profession. Pro-registrationist nurses in their turn found this support in general practitioners, whose association, the British Medical Association, resolved in 1895 to support nurse registration, and repeatedly approved in principle the registration of nurses. It was medical men of the British Medical Association who forced the issue into the arena of debate of the General Medical Council during the latter half of the 1890s, a period when the BMA secured a stronger foothold in the affairs of the General Medical Council. Paradoxically, it was this same group of general practitioners who were simultaneously opposing midwife registration (cf Donnison 1977). The two issues were, however, intimately related, and this is discussed more fully in the final chapter. For the moment I want to focus on medical men's support of nurse registration.

General practitioners' involvement in the campaign for nurse registration was Janus-headed, involving a medical politics which was simultaneously directed outward at the problem of potential competitors in the medical division of labour and inward at intra-professional rivalries within the medical profession itself. The humbler general practitioner felt himself to be most vulnerable to competition and the vagaries of the open market for medical services, and insufficiently represented within the state-sponsored controlling body of the medical profession, the General Medical Council. The prestige and power of the élite medical corporations, the Royal Colleges of Physicians and of Surgeons, was resented, along with the privileged and protected position of their members. General practitioners through the British Medical Association were engaged in what may be termed 'occupational populism', challenging the vested interests of élite members of the medical profession. The concept of occupational populism provides the key to understanding the link between the occupational politics of general practitioners' demarcationary strategy and nurses' dual closure strategy.

Mrs Bedford-Fenwick's professional project of dual closure for nurses was underscored by the principle of occupational populism. This, as I have demonstrated, advocated direct and majority representation of nurses on the state-sponsored central board of nursing and persistently opposed any weighty or majority representation of powerful vested interests such as lay hospital employers or élite bodies of the medical profession – or even, for that matter, matrons, of whose tendency towards autocracy Mrs Bedford-Fenwick was sometimes critical (although it is difficult not to suspect that here was the pot calling the kettle black!). The demand for a one-portal system of entry and uniform standard of education had been a goal for the medical profession advocated by the rank and file of general practitioners throughout the nine-teenth and early twentieth centuries, but they were thwarted by the vested interests of élite sections of physicians and surgeons defend-ing a multi-portal and inequitable system of medical credentialism.

Occupational populism, then, proved to be the common ground between pro-registrationist nurses and a section of medical men. Advocating the principle of direct and majority represen-tation of nurses on a general nursing council, Mrs Bedford-

Fenwick draws an analogy between a general nursing council and the General Medical Council, but adds that the 1858 Medical Act 'constituted the General Medical Council solely of members elected by the Corporations and nominated by the Privy Council – the principle of direct representation of the profession not being recognised at all' (*Nursing Record and Hospital World* 1895: 81). Even the reconstitution of the General Medical Council under the 1886 Medical Act Amendment Bill did not increase direct representation sufficiently for the advocates of occupational populism, a section of the British Medical Association. Dr Rentoul (a leading opponent of midwife registration) proposed a motion to a general meeting of the BMA in 1895 that:

> As at present constituted the General Medical Council does not adequately represent the Medical Profession. It is mainly composed of the representatives of what may be called the privileged classes of the profession and falls far short of what is needed as a central governing body.
>
> (*Nursing Record and Hospital World* 1895: 81)

Nursing, argued Mrs Bedford-Fenwick, should learn from the experiences of medicine:

> Now the moral which we desire to draw from this historical review of the constitution of the General Medical Council is that NO NURSING COUNCIL IS LIKELY TO PROVE PERMANENTLY ACCEPTABLE TO THE NURSING PROFESSION UNLESS IT IS CHIEFLY COMPOSED OF MEMBERS DIRECTLY ELECTED BY THE NURSES THEMSELVES. There can be no valid reason – there are many obvious reasons against it – why the mistake made in the Medical Act of 1858, partly remedied in the Medical Act of 1886, and further amendment of which is now demanded, should be made in the case of Nursing legislation.
>
> (*Nursing Record and Hospital World* 1895: 82)

The interests of occupational populism that united pro-registrationist nurses and medical men were further cemented by the proposed composition of the central board or council of nursing outlined in the SSRTN draft bill of 1902, which allowed for representation of the BMA but not of the élite bodies of the medical profession, the Royal Colleges of Physicians and of Surgeons. Dr Cox, representing the BMA and speaking in support of

157

nurse registration in 1916, again articulates the sentiments of occupational populism which coalesced also around the issue of the one-portal system of entry into nursing, by then a central plank of pro-registrationist politics:

> The medical profession has been through the mill, and had serious difficulties with vested interests. It recognised years ago the undesirability of having so many entrances to the profession and reformers had urged a one-portal system. The chief obstacle to this was the vested interests of the various corporations, and nurses would be unwise if they allowed themselves to get into a similar position, when by the exercise of a little foresight and resolution they might prevent it. The British Medical Association therefore wished to get the shortest cut for the ancillary profession of nursing.
>
> (*British Medical Journal* 1916: 252)

Medical practitioners of the BMA claimed that they wished not only to help the occupation of nursing on its road to occupational closure, but also to ensure that medical interests were directly represented on the central nursing council, but by medical practitioners of the BMA rather than the élite medical corporations. Sir Victor Horsley, representing the BMA at a deputation to the Prime Minister, Mr Asquith, in support of the state registration of nurses, protested 'that the British Medical Association was the only organization which represented the whole medical profession'. Moreover, he claimed, the BMA was the only democratic organisation of medical men, as resolutions were discussed at open meetings (*British Medical Journal* 1913: 944).

Draft nurse registration bills of both the SSRTN and the CCSRN ensured that medical practitioners were directly represented on the proposed central nursing council, and not indirectly by means of representatives appointed by the General Medical Council. So, for example, the Nurse Registration Bill of 1908 differed from the midwives' bill because it did not allow for any weighty direct representation of the General Medical Council (only one representative in fact). Neither did it require the rules drawn up by a central nursing council to be submitted to the General Medical Council before approval by the Privy Council (*British Journal of Nursing* 1908: 472). In 1906 the British Medical Association adopted the following resolution by ninety votes to three:

The meeting approves of the recommendation of the Parliamentary Select Committee that there should be State registration of nurses, and is of opinion that on any central council or board appointed the medical profession and the nursing profession should be adequately and directly represented, and that the representation of the medical profession on the Central Nursing Board should be at least one-half of the number of the members of that body.

(British Medical Journal 1916: 259)

By 1910, when the CCSRN introduced its bill into the House of Commons for the first time, the rank and file of medical practitioners had ensured that they were adequately represented on the body that was to regulate the nursing profession. The proposed council was to consist of twenty-one persons: three (one a woman) appointed by the Privy Council; eight medical practitioners, appointed by the British Medical Association, Local Government Boards, the Medico-Psychological Association and the fever hospitals but *not* by the General Medical Council; and eight directly elected registered women nurses (the remaining two members were to consist of either a medical practitioner or a male nurse to represent male nurses, and one mental nurse). The British Medical Association took a foremost part in the drafting of the Nurses' Registration Bill that was to appear annually before parliament between 1910 and 1916 (*British Medical Journal* 1916: 259).

THE STATE AND NURSE REGISTRATION 1916–19

Opposition to the campaign for nurses' registration persisted, and in 1916 there was a significant regrouping of the opposition when Sir Arthur Stanley, Chairman of the Joint War Committee, took the initiative in the formation of a college of nursing by canvassing the nurse training schools of large hospitals urging the need for a voluntary scheme of cooperation. Abel-Smith (1960) argues that the initiative taken by Stanley was largely responsible for the passage of the 1919 Nurse Registration Act and that Stanley achieved much more than Mrs Bedford-Fenwick as he pushed events that had divided the nursing community towards a resolution.

The reasons why Stanley achieved so much more are three-fold, argues Abel-Smith. First, the initiative was taken by a lay person. Second, an organisation on a par with the royal colleges of the

159

medical profession was proposed. And third, he offered initial control to nurse training schools (Abel-Smith 1960: 88). Abel-Smith also notes that the balance of political interests had shifted during the first world war. Widespread public admiration for war-time nurses, evoking sympathy for their struggle for registration, and the fact that women earned the vote, are both identified as precipitating factors in the eventual success of nurse registration. Abel-Smith sets great store by the unprecedented demand for nurses during the war, a demand that was satisfied by recruiting untrained Voluntary Aid Detachments (VADs), organised in 1909 by a Joint Committee of the British Red Cross Society and Order of St John of Jerusalem. There were 80,000 VADs at the outbreak of war and 120,000 by the end of the war (Abel-Smith 1960: 85). The presence of untrained VADs was disruptive and provoked disorder amongst the nursing hierarchy. Their influx convinced many trained nurses of the need for some system of registration.

> It was therefore not surprising that the British Red Cross Society became keen to develop some order in the nursing profession. The matrons and hospital managements were facing similar problems, and were therefore less opposed to some form of organization. And the regular nurses, fearing competition from the VADs, were more anxious than before that their superior status should be given formal recognition.
>
> (Abel-Smith 1960: 87)

Although Abel-Smith provides a valuable account of the events surrounding the eventual passage of the Nurses' Registration Bill, and is undoubtedly correct in identifying the precipitating role of the influx of untrained nurses during war-time, he is wrong to suggest that Stanley and the College of Nursing 'achieved so much more' than Mrs Bedford-Fenwick.

The crux of Stanley's initiative was that it provided the hospitals and their nurse training schools with the means of successfully pre-empting a nurses' professional project that would have undermined the symbiotic relationship between hospitals and nurse training and labour. The College of Nursing may have been pushing for a resolution of the disorder in nursing provoked by the influx of untrained nurses during war-time, but at the same time the fundamental schism between those who wanted a centralised, autonomous occupational infrastructure for nursing and those who wanted a de-centralised institutionally controlled one was still there. Stanley's initiative provided hospitals with the means to ensure that the lay interests of hospitals predominated in the framing of any legislation now deemed expedient, thus pulling the rug out from under the feet of the pro-registrationists' professional project of dual closure.

The initiative to form a college of nursing was taken by the medical superintendent and ex-matron of Guy's Hospital as well as Sir Arthur Stanley (Abel-Smith 1960: 87) and consisted of a circular letter to hospitals with nurse training schools attached drawing attention to the need, not for registration, but for a vaguely specified voluntary scheme of cooperation between nurse training schools (*British Journal of Nursing* 1916: 230–1). The pro-registrationist CCSRN was not consulted, and at a meeting with the protagonists objected that 'we have the anomaly of a voluntary scheme put forward without consultation with the Central Committee for the State Registration of Nurses, and are asked seriously to accept it in substitution for legal registration' (*British Journal of Nursing* 1916: 231).

This was a correct assessment, and the bills subsequently proposed by the College of Nursing were criticised by Mrs Bedford-Fenwick for giving nurses no power at all over nurse training, instead placing this in the hands of hospital committees. They were also criticised by the BMA for not giving the medical profession a part in the machinery that would regulate nurse registration. A voluntary scheme of registration was no substitute for a State Register, argued Mrs Bedford-Fenwick (*British Journal of Nursing* 1916: 300). Moreover, pronounced Mrs Bedford-Fenwick in characteristic style, 'The Nursing College Scheme is set up entirely by lay male authority. . . . No more insolent assumption of authority over a body of professional women has ever been propounded' (*British Journal of Nursing* 1916: 239, 454).

Apart from contesting what she saw as the subjugation of nurses' interests to those of lay employers and of women to men, Mrs Bedford-Fenwick also persistently criticised the College of Nursing proposals on the grounds that they would cut away the principal plank in the policy of state registration – the one-portal system – by including supplementary registers for asylum nurses.

After temporary hiccups in the line up of opposing forces when the pro-registrationist RBNA was for a time being courted by the College of Nursing, the opposing forces were once again lined up as before when in 1919 two nurses' registration bills were before parliament. The RBNA allied with the BMA had its bill before the House of Commons and trusted that the medical profession would allow no compromise over nursing standards whilst the BMA were seeking to ensure weighty medical representation on the regulating machinery of nursing. The College of Nursing had its bill before parliament in the House of Lords, where support was forthcoming from the peerage for a bill which respectfully bowed to pressure from hospitals to take into account hospital staffing needs when setting standards for nurse training (Abel-Smith 1960: 94). The College of Nursing bill was dubbed a 'hospital governors' and matrons' bill' (*British Journal of Nursing* 1919: 404) and a 'private Bill, promoted by a limited company' (*Hansard* CXVII 1919: 574) by various of its opponents.

It was due to the intervention of the newly appointed Minister of Health, Dr Addison, that a Nurse Registration Bill eventually came onto the statute book in 1919 (Abel-Smith 1960, Dingwall, Rafferty and Webster 1988). Faced with two bills of nurse registration, one before the Commons and one before the Lords, Dr Addison tried to secure some measure of agreement between the two interested parties. Although there was by now general agreement that nurse registration was desirable and necessary, there was no agreement on what registration implied in practice, concluded Dr Addison (*Hansard* CXVII 1919: 557).

Pro-registrationist campaigners hoped, as we have seen, to secure control over both the content and standard of nurse education, and over conditions of employment, thus challenging the autonomy of hospital employers in both these areas. Dr Addison was not convinced that the Nursing Council should perform these functions and, finding that the differences between the two camps were so great on these and other issues, introduced his own nurse registration bill which, he claimed, would take public interests into account. Importantly, Dr Addison separated the issue of registration off from the issues of the organisation and education of nurses (*Hansard* CXVII 1919: 560). The Nurse Registration Act went onto the statute book in December 1919.

However, the key question in relation to state intervention in the framing of the 1919 Nurses Registration Act are whose interests were prominent. Abel-Smith's (1960) assessment of the eventual outcome of the long and bitter battle around the issue of nurse registration is that the nursing profession 'came to power' when the Nurses Registration Act went onto the statute book in

1919. This assessment must be seriously challenged. On the contrary, Mrs Bedford-Fenwick's professional project was never realised. This alternative assessment is in accord with those of Davies (1982), Bellaby and Oribabor (1980), and Dingwall, Rafferty and Webster (1988).

Davies (1982) argues that state recognition did not translate into practitioner autonomy. Nursing work continued to be controlled and regulated by the operation of the marketplace and the hospitals. Bellaby and Oribabor (1980) argue that the degree of external autonomy and control achieved by nurses has to be questioned. They identify three internal contradictions that beset professionalism in nursing. First, registration did not unify nursing because the College of Nursing failed to organise nursing under the leadership of trained nurses. This was largely due to the contradiction between the precept of 'unity' and the practice of 'diversity' in the actual circumstances of employment in voluntary hospitals and the public sector. Second, there was the internal contradiction of claiming professional status for nursing which acted within the framework of another profession, medicine. And third, the state, which had apparently granted a monopoly of practice to registered nurses, more or less surreptitiously ensured that no such monopoly was exercised. However, this does assume that producer monopoly characteristic of professional control operates independently of the state, whilst Johnson (1982) suggests that the state–profession relationship is rather more complex than this. Nonetheless, the role of the state in relation to the nurses' professional project is of the utmost importance in assessing the reasons for its failure. Carpenter (1977) has also emphasised the peculiar nature of the state–profession relationship in nursing. Nurses were struggling to utilise their state-sponsored machinery in order to maintain some form of autonomy and control over nursing in the 1920s, a period when the state was not only assuming even greater responsibility for health care but also cutting back on its cost.

Further insights into the state–profession relationship are provided by White (1976) in her assessment of the political influences surrounding the 1919 Nurses Registration Act. White observes that:

> The reasons commonly accepted for the delay in achieving a
> statutory registration of nurses were the lack of agreement in
> the profession over the details of registration, disagreement

over the principle of registration (in which the part played by Florence Nightingale, who was strongly opposed to it, is well known) and the practical problem of defining 'a nurse'. But in the light of the spate of legislation and other legitimizing processes by which other professions had achieved their status earlier in the nineteenth century this delay for the nurses is extraordinary and merits further examination.

White's explanation for this delay is that the campaign for registration was led by an occupational élite of nurses associated with the voluntary hospitals, but it was the Poor Law hospitals which provided the bulk of hospital medical care, treating seventy-five per cent of hospital cases by the end of the nineteenth century. The Poor Law was administered by the local state until 1919 when the minister of health took overall responsibility for its administration. However, despite the fact that the Poor Law nursing service was a major section of British nursing, some members of the medical and nursing professions, particularly the occupational élite of voluntary nurses, regarded it with disdain. Following the 1905 Select Committee on Nurse Registration, the Poor Law authorities, who were not even called upon to give evidence, became increasingly concerned about the prospect of marginalisation of Poor Law nursing under the proposed system of nurse registration (White 1976).

The reorganisation of Poor Law administration in 1919 under the new Minister of Health goes some considerable way towards explaining why the occupational élite of voluntary sector nurses did not in fact secure the degree of occupational closure they sought, and why the state, through the Minister of Health, assumed tight control over the regulatory machinery of nursing. White (1976) suggests that this was part and parcel of the vigilance of the Minister of Health in protecting the interests of the Poor Law hospitals who solved their staffing needs by running a two-tier system of nursing for certificated and assistant nurses. The prospect of a one-portal system of entry with one universal standard of nurse education would have meant the loss of assistant nurses upon whom the smaller and rural Poor Law infirmaries relied in particular (White 1976).

The state, then, assumed the role of the stronger partner in the state–profession relationship in nursing, and this was largely due to the increasing involvement of the state in the provision of hospital medical care through its administration of the Poor Law. But it was also due to the fact that hospitals continued to form a powerful lobby, which conceded the need for some form of registration, but persisted in opposing the prospect of an autonomous and self-governing nursing profession. The passage of the Nurses Registration Act in 1919 did not represent a victory for pro-registrationist nurses. The nursing profession had not come to power. Instead nurses were henceforth to be tightly constrained within a state–profession relation within which they were the weaker partner, as well as within the employment relation between hospitals and nurses and the inter-professional relation between doctors and nurses.

CONCLUSION: THE FAILURE OF A FEMALE PROFESSIONAL PROJECT

The stance of the pro-registrationists has been declared a female professional project of dual closure, which contained both usurpationary and exclusionary dimensions. It had three major exclusionary dimensions. First, it aimed for a centralised system of control over the occupational infrastructure of nursing. Second, it sought to ensure nurses' self-government by means of the principle of direct and majority representation of nurses on the controlling body of the nursing profession. Third, it advocated the principle of a one-portal system of entry into the nursing profession, and demanded that a central body control the education and examination of nurses.

Nurses' dual closure strategy was pursued by means of both legalistic and credentialist tactics. By seeking state sponsorship of a system of nurse registration, nurses employed a legalistic tactic, which entailed the mobilisation of the heteronomous means of closure institutionally located in the state. Credentialism came to figure prominently in the nurses' project of exclusionary closure, which was increasingly defined as an educational project, centering around the one-portal system of entry and seeking to invest considerable powers over the content and standard of nurse education in the central nursing council. Ironically, though, nurse training was already institutionalised within the voluntary hospitals, and neither did nurses possess the autonomous means for mobilising credentialist tactics.

165

Nurses' project of dual closure also contained usurpationary dimensions, which threatened to destabilise the employment relation between hospital employers and nurses, through its challenge to the autonomy enjoyed by voluntary hospitals in defining the content and standard of nurse training, as well as the pay and conditions of nurses. I have argued that it threatened to undermine the symbiotic relation between hospitals and nursing labour established by the Nightingale reform, and that this explains why the major opposition to nurse registration came, not from the medical profession, but from voluntary hospitals and their matrons. It also sought to formalise an inter-occupational relation between medicine and nursing which granted nurses a considerable degree of intra-occupational autonomy. It was surprising, therefore, that a section of the medical profession championed the cause of nurse registration. I have suggested that occupational populism provided the common ground for an alliance between medical men and pro-registrationist nurses, and in the final chapter I shall suggest a rather more devious motivation for this alliance.

Despite the eventual passage of the Nurses Registration Act in 1919, nurses' professional project had failed. Dingwall, Rafferty and Webster (1988), in their recent social history of nursing, draw the same conclusion, and argue that registration was, paradoxically, a significant defeat for the registrationists. It was true that one of the elements of Mrs Bedford-Fenwick's dual closure strategy was embodied in the 1919 Nurses Registration Act. This was the setting up of a supra-institutional central statutory body, the General Nursing Council, to regulate nursing. However this statutory machinery did not provide the institutional location for autonomous control over the occupational infrastructure of nursing by nurses themselves. On the face of it, nurses had secured direct and majority representation, as sixteen of the twenty-five strong General Nursing Council were to be directly elected nurses or former nurses. However, any rules framed by this council had to be approved by the Minister of Health and laid before parliament, which had the power to annul or modify them. The General Nursing Council could not be said to enjoy even 'partial autonomy' from the state, by which it was hamstrung. Direct and majority representation had been granted for nurses, but on a body which had few powers. The council had no powers over questions of pay and conditions of nurses. As regards the system of

166

nurse education, the General Nursing Council was given powers relating to the conduct of examinations, but not to their content. The aim of a one-portal system of entry was also subverted. The register of nurses was to consist of a general register plus supplementary registers for asylum nurses, male nurses and children's nurses, as well as 'any other prescribed part'. Mrs Bedford-Fenwick was eventually defeated in the first council election in 1923, after she had fought unsuccessfully to introduce a broad generalist approach to nursing in the council's first statement of its educational policy objectives (Dingwall, Rafferty and Webster 1988).

Credentialist tactics, which pivoted around the one-portal system of entry, were subverted and legalistic tactics of state sponsorship backfired on nurses. At this critical historical juncture, nurses' professional project had failed.

6

GENDER AND RADIOGRAPHY

This chapter focuses on the feminisation of the new occupation of radiography during the 1920s and 1930s and looks at attempts by male radiographers to forestall this process. Radiography had never been an exclusively male occupation but had a mixed gender composition from the very early days of the application of X-ray techniques in medical diagnosis and treatment. Nonetheless, male radiographers had assumed that the formalisation of routes of access to radiography practice through the setting up of a diploma in radiography in 1921 would keep women out of radiography. They were proved wrong and, by the mid-1920s, radiography had become a predominantly female occupation.

The occupation of radiography provides an interesting case study of a new occupation in the emerging medical division of labour, one which underwent a rapid and inexorable process of feminisation at the same time as members of the occupation sought to regulate entry into their ranks through the use of credentialist tactics. And yet, as we have seen in the case of the nineteenth-century medical profession, the exclusion of women from an occupation engaged in a professional project of closure and seeking to restrict entry into its ranks was most effectively secured through their exclusion from the credentialing process of education, training and examination. So why did the use of credentialist tactics in radiography fail to exclude women or to stem the tide of feminisation? Why were women able to enter the ranks of radiography and avail themselves of radiography training with such relative ease?

But when exclusion fails, there are other ways and means of male power. Gendered strategies of exclusionary and demarcationary closure generate broad sweeping patterns of horizontal and vertical occupational sex segregation respectively. That is, the boundaries between occupations are constructed as gendered boundaries. However, the active engagement of male employees which, as Cockburn (1988) insists, sustains segregation, is not only directed towards maintaining gendered boundaries between occupations. Once women have gained access to the ranks of an occupation, men may continue to be actively engaged in a gendering process through what I shall refer to as gendered strategies of internal demarcation.

A strategy of internal demarcation is a form of intra-occupational control and, in the case of radiography, describes the attempt by male radiographers to distinguish between different types of radiography skills, to gender these skills and to differentially evaluate these gendered bundles of skills. I shall argue that male radiographers engaged in the pursuit of a gendered strategy of internal demarcation as they attempted to manipulate the gendering process by the gender assignment and differential evaluation of radiography skills to their advantage. They did this through discursive strategies which sought to establish an equivalence between maleness and technical skills, and femaleness and patient-centred skills, whilst simultaneously elevating technical and downgrading caring skills in the radiographer's work. Why did male radiographers resort to such strategies and did they succeed?

A study of the gendering process in radiography cannot ignore the complex inter-occupational relations in which radiographers were embroiled in the medical division of labour around X-ray work. The emergence of radiography as a para-medical occupation occurred at the same time as the emergence of radiology as a specialism within the medical profession. Indeed, inter-occupational relations between radiologists, who were qualified and registered members of the medical profession specialising in medical X-ray diagnosis and treatment, and radiographers, who were X-ray technicians responsible for the production of X-ray images upon which medical diagnosis depended, form more than simply the backdrop to the analysis of the gendering process in radiography. Rather, these inter-occupational relations of medical dominance and para-medical subordination came increasingly to be articulated within patriarchal parameters, as patterns of male authority became embedded in the hierarchical structure of the occupational division of labour around the medical application of X-ray technology. They are therefore essential to an analysis of the

gendering process in radiography. How, then, did the occupational division of labour around the use of X-ray technology in
medical diagnosis and treatment take shape? What is its significance for an understanding of the gendering process in
radiography?

RADIOGRAPHER AND RADIOLOGIST: THE DIVISION OF LABOUR IN X-RAY WORK

Following the discovery of X-rays by Roentegen in 1895, the first
X-ray photograph in Britain appeared in the *British Medical Journal*
in 1896 (Larkin 1983: 61). The medical profession was quick to
recognise the potential medical applications of X-rays and medical
interests were prominent in the various organisations, such as the
Roentegen Society formed in 1897, which sprung up in the early
days following the discovery of X-rays. The Electro-Therapeutic
Society, which formed in 1902, concerned itself solely with clinical
and scientific matters and by 1907 had become a section of the
Royal Society of Medicine (Barclay 1942: 352). In 1917 medical
men formed their own society, the British Association for the
Advancement of Radiology and Physiotherapy (BARP), which
later became the British Institute of Radiology in 1924. The primary aim of BARP was to establish radiology as a medical specialism with consultant status and its own post-graduate diploma. In
1920 the first examination for a Cambridge Diploma in Medical
Radiology and Electrology secured 'a single portal of entry into
radiology as a specialist medical subject' (*British Journal of Radiology*
1932: 17).

But medical men were not the only group interested in X-ray
technology, nor in its medical uses. The first X-ray photograph
which appeared in the *British Medical Journal* in 1896 was taken by
an electrical engineer, Campbell Swinton (Larkin 1983: 61). Early
membership of the Roentegen Society was diverse, encompassing
physicists, industrial manufacturers, photographers and amateurs
as well as medical men (*British Journal of Radiology* 1932: 10).
Nevertheless, a sense of medical proprietorship of X-rays quickly
developed and by 1903 complaints were appearing in the medical
press about lay radiographers (Larkin 1983: 63). But X-ray work
was unregulated in these early years, and was characterised by a
diversity of practices and personnel. In 1900, X-ray equipment was
under the charge of the honorary dentist at Nottingham General

Hospital, and X-ray pictures of fractured limbs were taken by the theatre beadle at St Mary's Hospital in London (Stevens 1966: 33). As hospitals purchased X-ray equipment, nurses, porters, dispensers or even handymen might be called upon to operate it (*British Journal of Radiology* 1937: 127). In addition, X-ray equipment could be purchased and operated privately, often by an electrical engineer or a chemist.

The evolution of the distinct occupational roles and spheres of competence of the 'radiologist', a medically trained specialist, and the 'radiographer', a non-medical technical assistant, has been thoroughly documented by Gerald Larkin (1978, 1983). As Larkin demonstrates, the social organisation of X-ray work hinged upon the dual process of the emergence of the radiologist as a specialist within the medical profession and the emergence of radiographers acting at the behest of radiologists in the capacity of technical aides close to but excluded from important diagnostic processes in modern medicine. This emerging division of labour in turn depended upon the construction and maintenance of a distinction between the *production* of X-ray plates or radiographs, which involved positioning the subject, operating the equipment, and the technical production of the X-ray images, on the one hand, and the *interpretation* of the information conveyed by the X-ray images, on the other. Medical radiologists argued that the interpretation or reporting of the information conveyed by the X-ray image was a diagnostic process which required expert medical and scientific knowledge and which should only be undertaken by specially trained doctors (Barclay 1942: 352). The crux of medical radiologists' demarcationary strategy was their insistence that for the non-medically trained radiographer, the end result was the radiograph, and not the interpretive skills with regard to the information conveyed by the X-ray image nor the clinical skills of medical diagnosis. 'The radiographer must operate the equipment, look after the comfort of the patient while in his charge, and closely and carefully follow the instructions of the radiologist' (*British Journal of Radiology* 1930: 497).

The essence of the radiologists' struggle was to place the exclusive prerogative over the process of interpretation within the sphere of competence and control of the medical profession, whilst simultaneously establishing for radiologists consultant status within the profession, where the doctor would request a report on his patient from a medically qualified radiologist, not a radiographer (*British Journal of Radiology* 1930: 98).

However, as Larkin notes, there was a lack of consensus amongst medical men about whether the medically trained radiologist alone should be responsible for the total process of technical production and clinical interpretation, or whether the technical production could be left to a lay radiographer (Larkin 1983: 64–6). The resolution of this issue became a matter of urgency due to the extensive use of X-ray techniques during the first world war and the prospect of ex-army radiographers and radiologically experienced army doctors flooding the market in the immediate post-war period. Propelled by the prospective chaos of an unregulated post-war labour market for radiographers and radiologists, the British Medical Association considered the need for a post-war policy on radiology and recommended that radiographers be placed under the direct supervision of qualified medical practitioners (Larkin 1983: 68).

In 1918 the initiative to organise radiographers into a society came from the British Association for the Advancement of Radiology and Physiotherapy (BARP), which represented those medical interests concerned to limit and control the work of lay radiographers. As part of this initiative BARP approached the Institution of Electrical Engineers, one of the prominent interest groups in the early days of X-ray technology (Larkin 1983: 69). Under the watchful eye of BARP, the Institution of Electrical Engineers together with a small number of male hospital radiographers from London made the first moves to organise radiographers (*British Journal of Radiology* 1932). The Institution of Electrical Engineers did much of the preliminary work to get the Society of Radiographers legally constituted (*British Journal of Radiology* 1930: 459) and in 1920 the first council of the society was composed of equal numbers of radiographers, radiologists and electrical engineers (Larkin 1983: 69). The original articles of association of the Society of Radiographers had incorporated the General Medical Council's ruling that radiographers should work under the direction of a qualified medical practitioner. However, by 1924 medical radiologists were expressing concern that this rule was not being strictly observed and that radiographers 'were taking upon themselves the functions of qualified medical men, and working without the supervision and direction of qualified medical practitioners' (*British Journal of Radiology* 1927: 37).

In 1924 a special meeting of the society was called and it was proposed to add to the original articles of association a clause prohibiting any member of the Society of Radiographers from making a 'report or diagnosis on any radiograph or screen examination' (Minutes of the Society of Radiographers 1924: 155, *British Journal of Radiology* 1927: 37).

The Institution of Electrical Engineers were prepared to accept a ban on reporting to patients, but were not prepared to accept a ban on reporting their findings to medical practitioners (Larkin 1983: 72). The Institution of Electrical Engineers represented the interests of radiographers in private practice, who purchased, operated and maintained X-ray apparatus themselves and who were therefore keen to retain a degree of autonomy from the medical profession. It was still the case that doctors could and frequently did by-pass radiologists and request radiographic information from radiographers in private practice (Larkin 1983). So, whilst some radiographers were 'content to produce the best possible pictures' (*British Journal of Radiology* 1927: 258) for the medical radiologist to interpret and report on, the Institution of Electrical Engineers was not prepared to accept such a restricted sphere of competence. They were not content simply to produce good pictures. But the Institution of Electrical Engineers were in a minority and lost the day, largely because any opposition to the General Medical Council's demand implied antagonising the radiologists, who threatened to withdraw their patronage of radiographers and bar them from the British Institute of Radiology if laymen continued to report (Larkin 1983: 73). Unable to protect the interests of private radiographers, the Institution of Electrical Engineers withdrew from the society (Minutes of the Society of Radiographers 1925: 176, *British Journal of Radiology* 1927, Larkin 1983: 83).

The advent of the radiologist and the successful incorporation of the skill of interpreting the radiograph within the medical diagnostic process had served to de-skill the radiographer in private practice. During the 1920s the medically trained and qualified radiologist became a more familiar sight in hospitals, and the younger generation of medical practitioners increasingly consulted hospital radiologists rather than use the services of a radiographer in private practice. By 1927, one radiographer in private practice lamented that the radiographer in private practice was regarded by medical practitioners 'as something of a quack'

(*British Journal of Radiology* 1927: 257). Radiographers now had to be 'content to produce the best possible pictures . . . [and] make our work so good that they [radiologists] cannot get on without us' (*British Journal of Radiology* 1927: 257).

The role of medical radiologists as the architects of the medical division of labour around X-ray work, the acquiescence of a group of largely hospital radiographers to their restricted and subordinate role within this division of labour, and the dissension within the ranks of radiographers over the issue of reporting, were key processes in the evolution of the distinct occupational roles of radiographer and radiologist. But how did these events have a bearing on the gender composition of radiography?

Larkin's discussion of sexual divisions within radiography is disappointingly perfunctory. At one point he simply suggests that radiography attracted middle-class daughters in search of a husband, although hastily admits there is no evidence for this! More perceptively, Larkin notes that the manual skills of radiography that had been shed by the medical profession were redefined as 'scientific' yet in some sense 'suitably female'. He also observes that the predominance of women in radiography 'buttresses the authority of the predominantly male medical profession and a much smaller group of male radiographers' (Larkin 1983: 83, 85).

Nonetheless, Larkin fails to unpick the significance of gender relations in his analysis of the emergence of the inter-occupational relations between medical radiologists and X-ray technicians. This is largely because he underemphasises the mediating role of patriarchal relations in processes of occupational demarcation within the medical division of labour.

Inter-occupational relations between radiologists and radiographers were increasingly articulated within partriarchal parameters as the intensification of the radiographer's subordination to the medical radiologist within the emerging medical division of labour around X-ray technology was accompanied by an increasingly gendered discourse of radiographer–radiologist relations. By 1938 the relationship between the radiographer and the radiologist was likened to 'friendship, tinged with deference to the "chief"' whilst the radiographer had come to sound more like the radiologist's secretary or wife than a technician. 'We, as radiographers should aim at the smooth running of the department. Let us cope with the petty grievances and upsets, so that the radiologists are only asked to settle the major difficulties' (*Radiography* 1938: 184). By 1952 the description of radiography work finds an explicit parallel in housework. 'Like the housewife's tasks, a technician's work is never done' (*Radiography* 1952).

The advice meeted out to the 'ideal X-ray technician' to 'keep him in clean white coats, see that his hair, possibly askew by removal of lead apron, head mirror or red goggles is combed before he confronts a patient' reads like the advice to a young radiographer-bride embarking on the hazardous career of pleasing her radiologist-husband who will, we are told, 'pout and fidget at these things and say he is henpecked, but he will like it' (*Radiography* 1952: 137)!

Paradoxically, then, male hospital radiographers' active involvement in the negotiation of their subordination to medical radiologists generated some of the pre-conditions for their own demise, as the intensification of their subordinate role was accompanied by the discursive construction of inter-occupational relations between radiologists and radiographers in terms of gendered positions.

Dissension within the ranks of radiographers over the issue of reporting and the defection of the Institution of Electrical Engineers over this issue also had ramifications for the gender composition of radiography. Larkin (1983) suggests that there is a causal relationship between the defection of the Institution of Electrical Engineers from the Society of Radiographers in 1925 and the shift from a predominantly male to a predominantly female membership of the society in the late 1920s. This is unconvincing, though, because women were qualifying as radiographers in greater numbers than men as early as 1923. Rather, the significance of the defection of the Institution of Electrical Engineers for the gender composition of the society is to be found primarily in the fact that henceforth the Society of Radiographers came to represent the interests of radiographers employed in hospitals, as distinct from self-employed radiographers in private practice, whose interests had been represented by the Institution of Electrical Engineers. Women were to be found largely in hospital radiography departments, engaged in the practice of radiography within an employment relationship rather than as independent practitioners.

GENDER AND OCCUPATIONAL CLOSURE IN RADIOGRAPHY

The Society of Radiographers was formed in 1921 largely in order to regulate the practice of radiography and promptly instituted its own diploma in radiography. As we saw above, the initiative to organise radiographers had come from medical radiologists in BARP, whose concern was largely with restricting and regulating the practice of radiography. Electrical engineers and male hospital radiographers were involved, but not female hospital radiographers although they were employed as hospital radiographers. The society received an application for membership as late as 1935 from a Miss Crump of St George's Hospital in London, although she had been working as a radiographer since 1910 (Minutes of the Society of Radiographers 1935: 77). In 1930 another application for membership came from Miss Vaughan, who stated that when the society had been formed she had been a radiographer at Great Ormond Street Hospital, but had not been given the opportunity to join. She had been trained at Guy's Hospital in 1920 and had been employed as a radiographer in various hospitals since then (Minutes of the Society of Radiographers 1930: 182).

The gender of the main actors involved in organising radiographers is significant. The presence of women in unregulated X-ray work had not gone unnoticed (*Archives of Radiology and Electrotherapy* 1921). Male radiographers hoped that the formalisation of access to X-ray work by means of credentialist tactics would exclude women. This becomes clear from the following retrospective account by one of the self-confessed conspirators:

> An examination for membership was instituted, with the idea of making it difficult for any, other than the most intelligent male citizens, to become qualified radiographers. So far, so good. But to the confusion of the conspirators, Eve marched cooly into the lairs of the examiners, and emerged garbed in the protecting mantle which is embroidered M.S.R.; and lo, all their politics were confounded.
>
> (*British Journal of Radiology* 1932: 572)

In 1920 fifty men and only nine women received the first diploma of the society (*Archives of Radiology and Electrotherapy* 1921) followed by five men and four women the following year. But from 1923 onwards there were at least three times as many women as men training and qualifying as radiographers annually. Credentialist tactics had not excluded women from radiography, and the tide of feminisation was rapidly in train.

By the mid-1930s radiographers were expressing concern about the oversupply of trained radiographers, which was explicitly linked to 'the question of sex' (Report of a Special Meeting of Members of the Society of Radiographers 1935). The seeds for this association between the presence of women in radiography, overcrowding and low salaries had been sown by an article which appeared in the *Daily Telegraph* advocating radiography as an ideal career for women. The relatively brief (i.e. one-year) and inexpensive training in radiography was contrasted to 'the three-figure fees and five-year training of many professions', which many women found prohibitive. Radiography was hailed as a 'quick return career' which made it particularly attractive to women especially as:

So many women nowadays inevitably abandon their careers on marriage that women rather than men are compelled to look for vocations that will yield a quick return for the time and money spent on training. The vocation, too, should be one to which the married woman can return, if need be, and rapidly regain her footing. . . . This profession is one not yet overcrowded, and as it costs only 20 guineas to qualify in radiography, its well-paid appointments represent a good investment of cash and capability.

(*Daily Telegraph* 2 July 1930, *British Journal of Radiology* 1930: 435)

The Society of Radiographers was clearly perturbed by this article and responded promptly in a letter to the editor, pointing out that the article was misleading and also that work with X-rays was inherently dangerous (*Daily Telegraph* 8 July 1930, *British Journal of Radiology* 1930: 435–6). In 1934 the Society received a letter from a male radiographer complaining about the preponderance of female members of the society, but it declined to take action (Minutes of the Society of Radiographers 1934: 119).

By 1935 three-fifths of the society's membership were women (*Radiography* 1935: 155) and in this year a special meeting of the Society of Radiographers was called in response to increasing concern about the precarious professional status of radiographers. At this meeting a causal link between the presence of women in radiography and overcrowding, low salaries and unemployment was explicitly articulated. Interestingly, low salaries were identified as a problem for male radiographers rather than for the female radiographers who actually received them! 'The snag of the profession was the question of sex. . . . The Society had been flooded with cheap labour; it was all very well for a woman who wanted pin-money, she was "O.K."' (Report of a Special Meeting of Members of the Society of Radiographers 1935). There were two responses to this statement. The chairman immediately intervened to forestall any discussion of the principle of equal pay for male and female radiographers, whilst making his own personal view on the matter quite clear. He did not think that women should receive equal pay with men for the same work. But Miss Kitty Clarke, who was to be elected as the first woman president of the society later in that same year, took exception to this view and argued that 'It was not at all to be supposed that because a woman worked in a profession her only object was to earn pin-money. Many of these women had responsibilities equal to those of men'.

The society did not commit itself to the principle of equal pay in the 1930s, despite the fact that an advisory committee on salaries had advised the society to recommend to the British Hospitals Association that 'No difference should be made between men and women'(Minutes of the Society of Radiographers 1933: 71). In addition, the society displayed a reluctance to intervene on behalf of its female members who frequently sought official support for their protests against long hours and low salaries. In 1930 a complaint from the West London X-ray department about the excessive working hours of the female staff was simply referred to the radiologist-in-charge for clarification (Minutes of the Society of Radiographers 1930). This is a clear instance of the society relying on the good will and patronage of medical radiologists to act on their behalf in matters concerning hospital employment. In 1931 a female radiographer asked if the council would support her if she joined other members of staff in rejecting a cut in salary, but the council of the society declared 'that this was a matter entirely out of their jurisdiction' (Minutes of the Society of Radiographers 1931). Again, when the society received a request from a female radiographer for support in her resignation from the Royal Infirmary in Bristol over unsatisfactory hours of duty, it 'could not advise' (Minutes of the Society of Radiographers 1932).

But how was the society to respond to what was perceived by a section of its membership as a crisis of professionalisation that was being exacerbated by the mixed gender composition of the occupation? It decided that the period of training for the society's diploma should be extended from one year to two years, on the grounds that:

> It was realised that such a rule might make it difficult for some to undertake a two years' period of training, but on the other hand, it might have the effect of reducing the number entering the profession, and also of raising the standard of candidates . . . and help to bring the training of radiographers more into line with other professions.
>
> (*Radiography* 1936: 59)

This amounted to an intensification of credentialist tactics attempting to regulate entry into radiography. And yet credentialist tactics had previously failed to exclude women, so it was difficult to see why they should be any more successful now. Indeed, they were not, and women continued to make up the vast majority of newly qualified radiographers (see Table 6.1).

Anxiety about the presence of women in radiography was also being expressed on another level by male radiographers, this time through discursive strategies. In the 1930s male radiographers were using the pages of their journal *Radiography* to engage in what can only be described as retrospective reconstructions of the early days of unregulated X-ray work. They were representing the history of pioneer work with the new X-ray technology as the exclusive work of men, the 'electricians, porters and engineers of the hospitals' (*Radiography* 1937: 127). There was an insistence on the necessity for electrical and engineering skills in the early days of radiography, and an emphasis on ingenuity as well as 'a distinct flair for inventing and adapting'. In the days of the temperamental Coolidge gas tube 'it was necessary for the radiographer to be an expert electrician' (*Radiography* 1937: 110). By 1939 the male radiographer is being singled out for his 'academic outlook' and for being technically minded, in contrast to the 'press-the-button radiographer' whose lack of knowlege about 'what happens when the button is pressed' is a mark of her inferiority, for we can, I think, safely assume that the 'press-the-button' radiographer is female.

By appealing to the engineering pedigree of radiography skills, male radiographers were mobilising a discursive equivalence between 'technical competence' and 'masculinity' in order to stamp radiography skills as inherently masculine. This was accompanied

179

Table 6.1 Examination passes for diploma of MSR (Membership of the Society of Radiographers) 1921–37

	Women	Men
1921	9	50
1922 (Jan)	4	5
(July)	10	5
1923 (Jan)	11	2
(Dec)	10	3
1923 (Dec)	5	3
1925	(no figures available)	
1926		
1927 (June)	11	3
(Dec)	11	2
1928 (June)	23	4
(Dec)	18	10
1929 (June)	30	1
(Dec)	27	13
1930 (June)	39	7
(Dec)	18	12
1931 (June)	16	3
(Dec)	26	10
1932 (June)	35	12
1933	(no figures available)	
1934 (Dec)	57	14
1935 (June)	55	13
(Dec)	55	17
1936 (June)	19	5
1937 (June)	50	10
(Dec)	62	6

Sources: 1921 Archives of Radiology and Electrotherapy, 1922–24 Minutes of the Society of Radiographers; 1927–32 British Journal of Radiology, 1932–37 Radiography

by a parallel move to deny the value and legitimacy of patient-centred skills in radiography, whilst the discursive equivalence between 'nursing' and 'femininity' was mobilised in order to associate these patient-centred skills with the female radiographer.

There were, then, two levels at which gender struggle in radiography was occurring: through closure strategies, as we have seen from the anxiety about overcrowding and how this was linked to the presence of women in radiography; and also through discursive strategies, as male radiographers were intent upon distinguishing between technical and caring skills in radiography, establishing discursive equivalences between technical skills and masculinity, on the one hand, and caring skills and femininity, on the other, whilst simultaneously elevating the value of the technical and denying the legitimacy of the caring skills in radiography. I now want to pose some 'why' questions in relation to the preceding discussion. First, in relation to the failure of credentialism to exclude women from radiography or to halt the tide of feminisation, why were women able to establish a presence in regulated X-ray work in the first place and to continue to represent the majority of radiography trainees and workers? Second, why did male radiographers attempt to discursively reconstruct radiography as an enduringly technical and by association male specialism? In order to answer these questions, it is necessary to look more closely at the history of women's involvement in work with X-ray technology.

THE FEMINISATION OF RADIOGRAPHY

We have seen that credentialist tactics failed to exclude women from radiography in the first place, and that the intensification of credentialism in the 1930s failed to stem the tide of feminisation of radiography. So how were women able to establish a presence in unregulated X-ray work and to maintain their presence in regulated X-ray work, quickly coming to represent the majority of radiography trainees and workers?

Women had been involved in operating X-ray apparatus from the outset. In 1896, only a year after the discovery of X-rays by Roentegen, 'a woman assisted in the taking of radiographs' (*Radiography* 1935: 155). But it was in their capacity as hospital nurses that women initially gained hands-on experience of the new X-ray technology and established their presence in radiography in the days before the regulation of radiography practice and training. Male radiographers' discursive reconstruction of the early days of X-ray work was partial because they ignored the fact that, as one angry correspondent to the journal *Radiography* commented:

When X-ray departments were very young, the work which today has reached a degree of efficiency in the hands of qualified technicians was then carried out for the most part by nurses. These nurses had no theoretical knowledge of the work they were doing. They were taught practically and they got on with the job. Often they became very interested in their work, their departments grew, and they became 'Sisters-in-charge'.

(*Radiography* 1937: 74)

As early as 1915 an article appeared in the *Nursing Times* about X-ray work for nurses, claiming that 'women can in many places take the place of the male assistants now employed as operators'. The article drew attention to the use of X-ray nurses by radiographers in private practice, and to the post of X-ray sister who 'in smaller institutions does the work for which a resident [radiographer] would otherwise be responsible'. The X-ray sister was in charge of X-ray nurses and she was also called upon to 'interpret the radiograms (the ignorance many doctors have of them is surprising) and see that they are properly taken by her staff' (*Nursing Times* 1915: 1599). There was also reference to training in X-ray work in some nurse training schools. By 1921 an American nurse writing in the *British Journal of Nursing* (1921: 59) was describing X-ray work as 'a vast field open to nurses'.

The use of nurses to operate newly installed X-ray apparatus in hospitals is extremely important in explaining both how women initially got their hands on X-ray technology and how they gained access to regulated radiography training and practice. Because women's access to radiography work was predominantly by way of hospital nursing and because the society's diploma was based on hospital training programmes, then they were able to take advantage of radiography training. Women had already established themselves within the institutional context of the hospital and there were less likely to be formal barriers to the entry of women into hospital-based professional training, unlike university-based professional education.

However, once women have gained access to an occupation, patterns of internal gender segregation can be constructed in order to protect men from female competition for certain jobs, and avoid the substitution of cheaper female labour for more expensive male labour. This can be done by distinguishing between and differentially evaluating gender-specific bundles of skills and competencies. Male radiographers were indeed attempting to internally segregate the occupation by gender and especially coveted the senior radiography posts. But surely, then, we would have expected them to associate 'technical skills' with the male radiographer and 'nursing skills' with the female radiographer, and then to declare technical as somehow superior to and more valuable than nursing skills in senior radiography posts? But, paradoxically, instead they appeared to be engaged in an attempt to reassert the sole value of technical skills, whilst completely denying the relevance and legitimacy of nursing skills in radiography work. In retrospect, they would appear to have been, and indeed were, hastening their own demise. So why were they resorting to this tack in the face of the escalating feminisation of radiography?

The 'nurse-radiographer' and 'X-ray sister'

The historical association between nursing and radiography practice for women was significant not simply because this meant that it was in their capacity as nurses that women initially got their hands on X-ray technology. It was also significant because custom and practice in some hospitals meant that nurses were not only called upon to operate newly installed X-ray apparatus, but might also be put in charge of newly established X-ray departments, particularly in smaller hospitals where X-ray duties might be combined with a sister's ward duties elsewhere in the hospital (*British Journal of Radiology* 1928: 439). Indeed, it was even argued that the X-ray sister preceded the radiographer in hospitals, and that the emerging distinction between the two was a dubious one (*Radiography* 1937: 74). Some X-ray sisters took advantage of the training and formal qualifications offered by the Society of Radiographers from 1921 onwards (although one lamented the fact that few trained nurses were availing themselves of the diploma in radiography, recalling only three instances in eight years at her particular nurse training school).

A pamphlet of the Central Employment Bureau of Women included radiography in its list of careers for educated women, noting that 'a Radiographer is not necessarily a trained nurse, but for the practical obtaining of posts, there is no doubt that the woman with three years' hospital experience is preferred' (Central Employment Bureau of Women, undated). Hospitals would sometimes advertise specifically for an X-ray sister in preference to a radiographer and, if they could not appoint a dually qualified woman, would frequently prefer to appoint a state registered nurse with experience in X-ray work rather than a radiographer who was not a trained nurse (*Radiography* 1937: 75). The important point about such practices was that they put some women at a distinct advantage in the market for X-ray workers, particularly for senior posts in charge of X-ray departments, because the demand for nurse-radiographers, X-ray sisters and trained nurses with practical experience in X-ray work was a sex-specific demand for female X-ray workers. The problem for male radiographers was the view held in some quarters that 'of two radiographers of otherwise equal ability, the one trained as a nurse, and the other not, the former would be unquestionably more valuable in every instance' (*Radiography* 1937: 190).

Of course this was a problem for radiographers across the board, whether male or female, because it amounted to a blurring of occupational boundaries between nursing and radiography and was a symptom of the lack of any real controls over who could and could not be appointed to operate X-ray apparatus. Radiographers had not resorted to legalistic tactics of occupational closure, which involved the petitioning of parliament for a statutory register of qualified radiographers (*British Journal of Radiology* 1930: 490). Instead they relied upon the patronage and good will of medical radiologists to ensure that qualified radiographers were appointed to hospital posts and to assist radiologists in private practice. It was not until 1960 that the Professions Supplementary to Medicine Act provided for the registration of radiographers along with six other medical auxiliary occupations (Larkin 1983: 176–9).

But the immediate problem for male radiographers in the 1920s and 1930s was that they not only had to compete for posts with trained women radiographers, but also had to compete for some of these posts at a considerable disadvantage, when custom and practice favoured the employment of trained nurses either with or without formal qualifications in radiography. And so one begins to see why some male radiographers argued that nurse training had no value in radiography and that nursing skills were largely peripheral to the work of the radiographer. It was argued, for example, that:

> the nursing is so elementary that there is no justification for an extensive 4-year training as a nurse if one intends to

specialise in radiography. If one is doing radiography one is not doing nursing and vice versa. . . . All the nursing required can easily by acquired from a course of St John Ambulance work. . . . The SRN has no practical value in radiography.

(*Radiography* 1937: 111–2)

The denigration of nursing qualifications and skills in radiography was accompanied by the elevation of technical skills, as the radiographer's role was defined in relation to the apparatus, not the patient:

The Radiographer is responsible for anything from £1,000–£2,000 worth of apparatus, he is responsible for the maintenance of it and its well-being, he is responsible for the quality of the work produced, and is responsible for the economic running of the department. . . . An experienced radiographer is one who has an intelligent knowledge of the apparatus being used, who can locate a breakdown and, within limits, repair it.

(*Radiography* 1937: 111–2)

The radiographer's role was also defined in relation to the diagnostic process, which was the responsibility of the radiologist who was, in turn, responsible to the patient. This was to produce diagnostically good radiographs (*Radiography* 1939: 217), for which the requisite skills and knowledge were claimed to be technical, not medical. Technical skill was presented as gender-specific, as it was the male radiographer who was reputed to be technically minded.

Thus, the reason why male radiographers' appeal to the engineering origins of radiographic skills was accompanied by an insistence that nursing skills had no value and legitimacy in radiography (cf *Radiography* 1937: 111–2, 189) was that they aimed at removing the competitive advantage for posts (as distinct from any real advantage in the form of salary) enjoyed by female nurse-radiographers, most particularly for those senior hospital posts held by X-ray sisters.

Male radiographers' invectives against nursing qualifications and skills were simultaneously invectives against the gender-specific skills of women in X-ray work. As one woman who herself held a dual qualification in radiography and nursing observed:

I see no reason for the sarcastic comments that O.M. Alexander pours on the heads of M.S.R.s who also have their S.R.N. I shrewdly suspect that in reality it is all female radiographers that he aims at, but desists in all probability either from fear of bringing a hornets' nest about his ears, or, what is more likely, feels that X-ray sisters, being in the minority, offer a better subject for abuse. There is no reason why any S.R. nurse who wishes to do so should not take up radiography, any more than there is for an engineer to take up radiography.

(*Radiography* 1937: 159)

The role of nursing qualifications and skills were defended by women who were qualified as both nurses and radiographers. Nurse training was advocated as essential to duties such as handling fractured limbs in the X-ray department, administering Lipiodol injections and looking after patients under anaesthetic. In other words, it was argued, radiography was not just about apparatus. It was also about the patient. 'Radiography is not only a matter of locating breakdowns, turning knobs, and saving films – an engineer can do the first two, and anybody the third – there is also the patient for whose sake this expensive apparatus is congregated together' (*Radiography* 1937: 160).

A medical radiologist sprung to the defence of the nurse-radiographer, arguing that she was more valuable to the radiologist than the radiographer precisely because the radiographer's role was essentially a medical one, not a purely technical one. Interestingly, medical knowledge was deemed to be essential not only in relation to patient care but also for the purposes of taking diagnostically good radiographs:

It is not merely that a nurse is better able to look after a sick patient, to ease broken limbs, and to face with equanimity the various emergencies of medical life. . . . It is also [that] a knowledge of the working human physiology of the lungs, the liver, the gall-bladder, the kidneys, and the intestines, and of the various changes that can take place in these organs in disease, does often give the nurse the hint as to where and how and when to take that extra film, outside the routine set usually demanded, which may make possible a correct diagnosis in a difficult case.

(*Radiography* 1937: 191)

A further perspective on the legitimacy of nursing skills in radiography occupied what may be termed the 'middle ground'. It was argued that nursing skills were necessary for the job and that more adequate training in medical and nursing care of the patient was desirable for radiographers, although it was by no means necessary to be a fully trained and qualified nurse to practise as a radiographer (*Radiography* 1937: 189, 141–3). This was an argument for incorporating elements of medical and nurse training into the course requirements of the diploma of the Society of Radiography. But patient care was rapidly becoming indelibly stamped as 'women's work' in radiography and the official incorporation of medical and nurse training into the radiography syllabus was likely to be resisted. Men staunchly defended a definition of the radiographer's role as essentially a technical one, resisting any formal identification of patient-centred or nursing skills with radiography. Only one male radiographer entered the annual Reid competition run by the Society of Radiographers for the best essay on 'The care and comfort of patients in radiotherapy and X-ray therapy', a fact that led the then president of the society to point out that 'it was just as important for a man to know how to look after a patient as it was for a woman' (Minutes of the Society of Radiographers 1936).

Gender segregation in radiography

Male radiographers' attempts in the 1930s to denigrate the value of nursing skills in radiography and inflate the value of technical ones may be seen as a last ditch attempt to stem the tide of feminisation in radiography. It is difficult to see what gains there were to be made, except to secure for male radiographers exclusive access to those senior radiography posts which they coveted, but which were still being filled in some hospitals by X-ray sisters. But employer practices were hastening the feminisation of radiography and the demise of the male radiographer, as was the failure of the Society of Radiographers to press for equal pay for male and female radiographers.

Nurse radiographers and X-ray sisters were employed as radiographers at the lower salary of nursing staff. In hospitals where probationer nurses had been employed in junior radiography posts, there was a reluctance to employ junior radiographers of the Society of Radiographers in their place because of the higher salaries demanded by radiographers. The appointment of women to posts as radiographers was accompanied by the payment of a lower salary. This is demonstrated by the following case, where a hospital radiologist requested a female radiographer from the appointments bureau run by the Society of Radiographers. There were no female radiographers on the books, so the names of some male radiographers were suggested. However, it was pointed out that 'the salary was insufficient' and the radiologist did eventually appoint a male radiographer but 'at a suitable salary' (Report of a Special Meeting of Members of the Society of Radiographers 1935). There were, it was said, 'posts that will always be occupied by women, others essentially for men' (*Radiography* 1935: 155). The radiologist in private practice frequently sought a secretary-radiographer and was described as 'very particular as to the type of person he employed', that is, a female radiographer. But industrial employers demanded engineering in addition to radiography, which generated sex-specific demand for male radiographers, who were more likely than women to have engineering qualifications (*Radiography* 1935: 158). By the 1930s, then, patterns of gendered segregation in radiography were very much in evidence, and were being generated by employer practices, which often amounted to a preference for female labour, whether as a secretary-radiographer in private practice, or as a nurse-radiographer or X-ray sister in hospitals.

CONCLUSION

Male hospital radiographers had quickly conceded to the demarcationary strategy of de-skilling pursued by medical radiologists in relation to radiographers. Paradoxically, male hospital radiographers' active involvement in the negotiation of their subordinate role vis-à-vis medical radiologists in the newly emerging medical division of labour around X-ray work generated some of the pre-conditions for their own demise, as the intensification of the radiographers' subordinate role was accompanied by a gendered discourse of inter-occupational relations, which constructed an equivalence between radiologists and radiographers and male–female relations. But, whilst the importance of inter-occupational relations between radiologists and radiographers has been well documented by Larkin (1978, 1983), the relationship between radiography and the nursing profession has been neglected by comparison. This relationship would appear to be crucial in explaining the process of feminisation of radiography, especially given the importance of nurse-radiographers and X-ray sisters.

The debate about the legitimacy of nursing skills in radiography provides considerable insights into points of tension surrounding questions of the skill mix in the evolving occupation of radiography in the 1920s and 1930s, and into the gendering process. We have seen how there was a tension between skills relating to the 'apparatus' and those relating to 'patient care' and that this tension assumed gendered connotations. Indeed, Cockburn's (1985) study of contemporary developments of X-ray technology and the gendering process reveals that this tension between 'technology' and 'caring' skills has reemerged now that male radiographers are once again a growing minority.

Women had originally accessed radiography work through the occupation of nursing, and had established a presence in hospital radiography work prior to the formalisation of routes of access to radiography. The strong presence of women in hospital employment explains why organised male radiographers had hoped in vain that women would be excluded by means of credentialist tactics in the form of a diploma in radiography. In addition, dually qualified women or nurses with experience of radiography were appointed in preference to qualified radiographers in some hospitals, providing a source of cheap labour for hospitals with new radiography departments. Employer practices were putting women at a distinct advantage in the labour market for radiographers. This trend was not abated by the Society of Radiographers because it did not adopt the principle of equal pay, so radiologists could and did prefer to appoint female radiographers at a lower salary than male radiographers. However, male radiographers did attempt to stem the tide of feminisation by deploying discursive strategies around issues of the appropriate skill mix in radiography. They did this largely in order to remove the competitive advantage for senior posts enjoyed by women who could combine nursing and radiography skills and experience. There was, then, a conflict between men and employers over the use of female labour in radiography. The material basis for internal demarcation between male and female radiographers emerged as a result of employer practices, whilst male radiographers engaged

189

in a rearguard discursive strategy which sought to de-legitimise the material grounds for employer preferences for female labour in senior posts and replace these with a rejuvenated emphasis upon technical skills in radiography as enduringly masculine skills.

Inter-occupational relations between nursing and radiography were also important in another sense. The debate about the roles of the nurse-radiographer and X-ray sister in radiography departments also revealed a more general anxiety about the professional status of radiographers in the medical division of labour. It was feared that nurses would 'flood' radiography and that radiography would become simply 'an insignificant branch of the nursing service' (*Radiography* 1935: 103). In particular, it was the involvement of matrons in decisions regarding the appointment and conditions of service of hospital radiographers which was resented, and it was argued that it was the radiologist 'who should know what particular type of radiographer is required in his department' (*Radiography* 1935: 168). The authority of the matron in relation to radiographers would have been further strengthened by the practice of appointing X-ray sisters, a practice which was itself attributed to the influence of matrons, who might prefer to have trained nurses in charge of hospital departments. The authority of the matron also presented an alternative set of authority relations to that between the radiographer and the medical radiologist. Radiographers' strategy of dual closure was very much dependent upon the patronage of medical radiologists, to whom they looked to ensure that only qualified radiographers were appointed as hospital radiographers. In short, the professional subordination of radiography to the medical profession was preferred to the subsumption of radiography within the nursing profession. It was argued that radiographers should not come under the jurisdiction of the matron (*Radiography* 1935: 118), who was blamed for the long hours and low salaries endured by many radiographers, and that the radiographer's proper authority was the medical radiologist, particularly as there were so many male radiographers (*Radiography* 1937: 141).

The subordination of male radiographers within a female chain of command headed by the matron involved the dislocation of the patriarchal ordering of occupational roles and authority relations that characterised the medical division of labour within the hospital. As it was, the male radiographer already occupied a somewhat ambiguous position within the medical division of labour for 'if the radiographer is a man he is always thought to be a doctor by the patient' (*Radiography* 1937: 140). And yet, by attaching themselves to the coat-tails of radiology in a subordinate and supervised role, male radiographers hastened their own demise because they had acceded to medical radiologists' demarcationary strategy of de-skilling in the early days of organised radiography. It was not so much what the radiographers did, but the inter-occupational relations within which they did it which had precipitated the feminisation of the occupation.

7

CONCLUSION

In this book I have been mainly concerned with developing some conceptual tools that might be useful for an analysis of the relation between gender and the occupational politics of closure, particularly in relation to professional projects. Because I have insisted on the historical specificity of professional projects, and investigated those of four occupational groups in a related division of labour, further questions about the applicability of this model to current developments in professionalisation and in other occupations remain open questions which need further investigation. In addition, the relation between gender and professionalisation has been the main focus, and class factors a secondary one, which some readers may, with a measure of justification, feel has been understated. However, in this chapter I do wish to pick up some implications of my analysis of the relation between gender and professionalisation for an understanding of the historical formation of the service class. First, though, the overall argument and substantive evidence will be pulled together, and some of the links between these different professional projects will be pulled out.

GENDER, CLOSURE AND PROFESSIONAL PROJECTS

The gender of actors involved in professional projects has been identified as a necessary factor in analysing the form and outcome of professional projects, mainly because men and women had unequal access to the various resources which were necessary to stake a successful claim to 'professional status' in the nineteenth and early twentieth centuries. I have defined professional projects as projects of occupational closure, and proposed a model of four different strategies of occupational closure. This model elaborated

192

a four-fold distinction between exclusionary, inclusionary, demarcationary and dual closure strategies. In particular, it was geared towards excavating the specifically gendered dimensions of closure strategies.

Exclusion and inclusion: the case of the medical profession

Following Parkin (1979) exclusionary strategies were defined as involving the downwards exercise of power in a process of subordination as an occupational group seeks to secure, maintain or enhance privileged access to rewards and opportunities in the occupational labour market. In addition, exclusionary strategies are concerned with mechanisms of intra-occupational control, attempting to regulate access to and the internal affairs of a particular occupational group. In line with other commentators (Parry and Parry 1976, Waddington 1984, Larkin 1983) I identified the case of medical professionalisation in the nineteenth century as a paradigmatic case of exclusionary closure. But, unlike other commentators, I concentrated on the relation between the professionalisation and masculinisation of medical practice in the nineteenth century. It seems to me that the exclusion of women from the practice of medicine was an important plank of professional closure in modern medicine, and one that is understated in mainstream analyses of medical professionalisation. This is surprising given how the historical conjuncture of masculinisation and professionalisation in medical practice has been extensively documented in feminist analyses (Ehrenreich and English 1973a, 1973b, 1979, Oakley 1976, 1984, Verluysen 1980). Nonetheless, it appears that some feminist analyses overstate the continuity in forms of male control over women's engagement in various healing practices, and fail to fully appreciate both the gender-specific forms which women's activities took prior to the nineteenth century, as well as the significance of broader structural changes for women's participation, particularly the escalating importance of market provision as distinct from domestic and community provision in a rapidly expanding market for medical services in the eighteenth and early nineteenth centuries. Women's involvement in healing practices would appear to have been predominantly within domestic and community arenas, whilst their professional practice was largely circumvented by marriage and family relations. Consequently, it was both the relocation of medical services

193

from a predominantly domestic and community arena to a predominantly market arena, together with the ability of men to collectively organise and construct organisational forms in the new sphere of civil society, that signalled the demise of the female practitioner in those areas of regulated medical practice which unified in 1858 under the Medical (Registration) Act.

The male professional project in medicine used gendered collectivist criteria of exclusion against women and these were embedded in the institutions of civil society, in the universities and medical corporations which made up the nineteen state-legitimated portals of entry onto the medical register. In other words, it was the credentialist tactics of professionalisation which provided the most effective means of excluding women from the medical profession, whilst legalistic tactics, which are also central to professional projects, but represent heteronomous means of professionalisation, only indirectly secured women's exclusion from medicine. I emphasised how legal rules of gendered exclusion were not codified into the 1858 Medical (Registration) Act and how the General Medical Council, when forced to consider the whole issue of the admission of women, baulked at the prospect of being seen to call for the elaboration of legal rules of exclusion. This is important, because it suggests that gendered strategies of exclusion were only indirectly secured within the institutional arena of the state.

Indeed, it became clearer that the state was the weak link in the chain of patriarchal closure in the nineteenth-century medical profession when I turned my attention to the ways in which women who wished to practice medicine challenged the exclusive male prerogative to do so. Here, the concept of an inclusionary strategy proved useful in unpicking the campaign by women in the 1860s and 1870s to gain entry to the medical profession. Aspiring medical women's inclusionary strategy was essentially a usurpationary struggle, a countervailing response on the part of an excluded group and in tension with an exclusionary strategy. Thus, the exclusive male prerogative over legitimate medical practice was immediately challenged by aspiring medical women, who engaged in a protracted usurpationary struggle. It began with the isolated attempt by Elizabeth Garrett in the 1860s, and continued at Edinburgh University where, between 1869 and 1873, a group of women attempted to receive medical lectures and present themselves for medical degrees. It culminated in attempts between 1874 and 1876 to secure women's access to medical education, examination and registration by means of act of parliament. By distinguishing between credentialist and legalistic tactics of occupational politics, and between equal rights and separatist tactics of gender politics, different facets of women's campaign to enter the medical profession were identified.

The well-documented episode at Edinburgh revealed the use of countervailing credentialist tactics and amounted to a typical equal rights struggle, as women sought entry to existing, male-dominated institutions of medical education and examination on equal terms with men. In other words, they sought to replace gendered collectivist criteria of exclusion with non-gendered individualist criteria of inclusion. It is important not to assume that exclusion on the grounds of gender and race is an 'informal' element of credentialing (as Freidson 1986 does). Rather, as Crompton (1986) argues, and this case study demonstrates, gendered exclusionary mechanisms were embedded in the formal credentialing process. This is why, as Crompton and Sanderson (1989) show in their analysis of pharmacy and accountancy, the 'qualifications lever' is a vital element of women gaining access to an occupation. When this credentialist, equal rights tactic failed, women turned to separatism, and set up their own London School of Medicine for Women. It is interesting to note the wide-spread adoption of separatist methods by middle-class women as they forged spaces within which they could participate in the public sphere, and Vicinus (1985) also emphasises this as a distinctive feature of middle-class (and particularly single) women's movements into other areas, such as philanthropy.

Aside from establishing the robustness of the twin concepts of exclusionary closure and inclusionary usurpation along their gendered dimensions, the case study of the mid-nineteenth century medical profession also underscored a number of points that I made in connection with the necessity of moving the sociology of the professions onto a less androcentric terrain. Here, I stressed the importance of gendering the agents of professional projects, distinguishing between 'male' and 'female' professional projects, and of structurally grounding these within the parameters of patriarchal capitalism. In the case of gendered exclusion embedded in the male professional project in medicine, it was the sphere of civil society within which male power was most effectively institutionalised and organised and where it was most resilient to the usurpationary claims of women. This may be deduced from the evident failure of women's usurpationary struggle when it focused its efforts on countervailing credentialist, equal rights tactics. The modern universities and professional corporations proved remarkably resilient to these. So Larson's (1979) distinction between autonomous and heteronomous means of professionalisation is important in tracing the relation between gender and professional projects, as the universities and medical organisations were key institutions within which autonomous means were mobilised.

Nonetheless, whilst the resources of male power were most effectively institutionalised within the modern university and medical corporations, it was the nineteenth-century patriarchal capitalist state which proved the weaker link in the chain of patriarchal closure. Again, Larson's analysis suggests that state-sponsorship of the professional project represents a heteronomous means of professionalisation, as members of an occupation rely on the support of members of the dominant élite. But this support is terribly fragile, as both Johnson (1982) and Larson (1977) suggest was historically the case, and Crompton (1990) demonstrates is currently the case – witness the concerted attacks on the occupational or market monopolies of opticians, solicitors and doctors. When aspiring medical women eventually concentrated upon legalistic tactics, they were successful. In 1876 an enabling bill was passed and this established that universities and medical corporations could not use their existing powers to exclude women – but neither could they be forced to include them! But the crucial point to be made here is that this was something of a Pyrric victory because these institutions admitted and were governed exclusively by men, who were able to continue to use their powers to exclude women from access to the systematic training and testing necessary to engage in medical practice, if they so wished.

The twin concepts of exclusion and inclusion thus provided useful analytical tools for unravelling the ways and means of gender struggles around access to modern medical practice. It was as women challenged their exclusion from medicine that the precise ways and means of male power became clearer. But these two concepts only capture some of the complex and varied processes of occupational closure in the emerging medical division of labour. This led me to propose another set of closure strategies, which I term demarcationary and dual closure strategies.

Professional dominance and occupational demarcation: medical men, midwives and nurses

Demarcation, like exclusion, was identified as a closure strategy engaged in by dominant occupational or social groups. But whereas exclusion referred to processes of intra-occupational control, demarcation described processes of inter-occupational control in the form of attempts to control and regulate the labour of other, related occupations in a division of labour. Gendered strategies of demarcation were defined as those concerned with the creation and control of boundaries between gendered occupations in a division of labour. They entail the encirclement of women within a related but distinct sphere of competence within a division of labour and, invariably, precisely because these occupations are gendered, involve their subordination to a male occupation.

The paradigmatic case of gendered strategies of demarcationary closure within the emerging medical division of labour was the troubled inter-occupational relations between medical men and midwives in the latter half of the nineteenth century. My analysis of the protracted debate about the issue of midwives' registration revealed the need for a concept of demarcationary as distinct from exclusionary closure. But it also revealed how, although gender homology facilitates alliances (as indeed Kanter (1976) establishes in discussing the gender ordering of managerial hierarchies), male solidarity is not pre-ordained but has to be constructed and may be tenuous. There is, as Hartmann (1979) says, a hierarchy among men. Gender politics were pressed into the service of medical politics and the intra-professional rivalries of medical men.

Medical men did not speak with one voice over the issue of midwives' registration. There were two demarcationary strategies, each pursued by different groups of medical men. One was a demarcationary strategy of de-skilling, which sought to preserve the independent occupation of midwifery, although in a clearly de-skilled and subordinate position in the medical division of labour. The other was a demarcationary strategy of incorporation, which sought to 'end' not 'mend' the midwives' role, and replace the midwife by the obstetric nurse, who could not be called out to a client in the first instance, but could only attend the woman under the instruction of a doctor. This latter solution, as we saw,

197

sought to abolish the independent midwifery practitioner and establish an exclusive medical prerogative over the provision of all midwifery services. But the independent midwife was not destroyed, because the demarcationary strategy of de-skilling eventually won through. Why should this have been the case? I suggested that one of the reasons was that doctors simply could not have met the total demand for midwifery services, and sought to segment the market according to the social class of the client and the gender of the practitioners. Female midwives would meet the demand for routine midwifery services from the poor, whilst medical men would supply midwifery services to the richer segments of society and deal with all cases of abnormal labour.

At the same time as championing the cause of the independent midwife, medical advocates of the de-skilling option were acutely aware that the boundaries between midwifery and medical practice would have to be monitored and controlled. As we saw, by the mid-nineteenth century the occupational boundaries between midwifery and medical practice had been constructed around a division between assistance in the process of 'normal' labour (the midwife's permitted sphere of action) and intervention in the process of 'abnormal labour' (the medical man's exclusive prerogative). The term 'discursively constructed' is highly appropriate here, because these very conditions, one normal and one abnormal, were being socially constructed. The major problem for medical men advocating the preservation of the independent midwife was how to ensure that the independent midwife who would be called out in the first instance would know when it was appropriate to call for the doctor and do so. It was therefore imperative that medical men monitored and controlled, and indeed determined, the knowledge base of midwifery and the practice of trained midwives. I suggested how this was ensured through pre-emptive credentialism, as medical men of the Obstetrical Society initiated a programme of midwifery training and examination, and through pre-emptive legalism, as this same group of medical men championed the state-sponsored registration of midwives whilst simultaneously ensuring that the medical profession effectively controlled the occupational infrastructure of midwifery by ensuring majority representation on any statutory midwives' board.

The highly complex intersections between gender and medical politics are worth noting here. First, there are interesting links between obstetricians' stances on midwives and women doctors.

Obstetricians were, of course, amongst the most vocal opponents of aspiring women doctors whilst simultaneously providing the necessary male sponsorship for midwives' own quest for a system of state registration. Obstetricians specialised in midwifery, obstetric surgery and the treatment of diseases of women and children. Yet, women's strongest moral claim to the right to practice as fully qualified medical practitioners was the right of women patients to consult medical practitioners of the same sex. This right was articulated in the context of Victorian moral propriety, but also on the grounds that women doctors were more fitted than male doctors to diagnose diseases of women (Blackwell and Blackwell 1860). Indeed, Vicinus's (1985) emphasis on separatism as a means of middle-class women entering public spheres emerges as important once more, because aspiring women doctors also articulated their anticipated role as medical practitioners in terms of their special, gender-specific interest in the treatment of the diseases of women and children. And of course, for Elizabeth Blackwell and others, medical women's role was to extend beyond treatment in the curative or palliative senses and into 'prevention' in the form of educating working-class wives and mothers in the habits of health and hygiene (Blackwell 1902). But the main point here is women's claim to special competence in the treatment of women, because this was precisely the obstetricians' own jealously guarded sphere, a sphere which was not wholly accepted even by fellow members of the medical profession, many of whom had little time for the modern day successors of 'men-midwives' (cf Donnison 1977). Many women preferred to consult a doctor of their own sex, particularly for gynaecological conditions, whilst their reluctance to consult male doctors endangered their health (Blackwell 1902, Jex-Blake 1886, Manton 1965). An important thread linking the exclusionary and demarcationary strategies of those medical men specialising in obstetrics must surely have been that midwives with a partial medical training and in a clearly demarcated and subordinated position vis-à-vis medicine were a lesser threat than female doctors with a full medical education and in direct competition.

There is a further way in which the case studies in gender politics are interrelated and, in turn, are linked to intra-professional rivalries between medical men. Whilst a group of medical obstetricians provided crucial support for a system of midwives' registration, another group of medical men, this time general practitioners, simultaneously opposed midwives' registration but supported the campaign for nurse registration. I have suggested that this group of medical men felt excluded from the profitable monopolies over medical practice enjoyed by the élite of surgeons and physicians, and were most exposed to the vagaries of the open market. One of the reasons why they so vehemently opposed midwives' registration was because they feared the competitive threat posed by a new class of independent midwifery practitioners in the medical division of labour. And yet it was this same section of the medical profession which provided loyal support for the nurses' campaign for nurse registration. I suggested that the key to this support was to be found in the politics of 'occupational populism', or the championing of the rights of the ordinary ranks of medical practitioners to control the affairs of the medical profession, rather than the élite sections of physicians and surgeons, who defended what was keenly felt to be an inequitable, multi-portal system of medical credentialism. Why should this section of the medical profession have adopted such contrary positions, supporting one group of female practitioners whilst opposing another? Donnison (1976) has also noted this link, but explains this by suggesting that general practitoners' advocacy of the cause of nurse registration was simply insincere. I don't think it was, as their support for the system of nurse registration envisaged by Mrs Bedford-Fenwick was clearly something from which they would benefit, both in terms of gaining some representation on nurses' statutory central board and of curbing the power of élite bodies of the medical profession by ensuring that these latter gained no representation. Further, their strategy of incorporation, which aimed to abolish midwives as independent practitioners with their own clients, involved the redefinition of midwives as 'obstetric nurses' so, from the 1880s onwards, the British Medical Association proposed bills for the registration of general, surgical *and* obstetric nurses.

Female professional projects

One of the points I have been particularly concerned to establish has been that women have engaged in professional projects. I introduced the term 'dual closure' to describe these. The concept of dual closure proved a useful one with which to unpick the sociological dimensions of the struggles of nurses and midwives to consolidate their own positions in the emerging medical division of labour. A dual closure strategy contains both usurpationary and exclusionary dimensions, as actors resist subordination from above and simultaneously seek to close off an occupation and restrict entry to its ranks. At the same time, female professional projects assumed various and empirically complex forms, and it proved possible to distinguish between two different forms in the case of midwives' attempts to secure a place for themselves in the emerging medical division of labour in the nineteenth century.

The earlier, more radical, dual closure project pursued by midwives in the 1860s sought to 're-skill' the midwife and ensure her status as an independent practitioner with her own clients, as well as to ensure that she was able to intervene in as well as attend to women in labour. This female professional project was described as a revolutionary dual closure project, and one which concentrated on credentialist rather than legalistic tactics. The later, less radical, campaign for a system of state-sponsored registration of midwives was a more accommodative dual closure project, which broadly accepted the de-skilled and restricted sphere of competence of the midwife favoured by pro-registration medical men, but which nonetheless ensured that midwives continued to exist, were educated and registered, and retained the status of independent practitioners with their own clients, to which they could be called out in the first instance. My analysis of the form assumed by this more accommodative professional project of midwives pointed to the close co-operation between midwives and medical men involved in the campaign for midwives registration. Medical men, for their part, stood to gain because the market for midwifery services could be segmented, with midwives for the poor and medical men for the richer segments of society. Midwives also stood to gain because they could utilise the programme of midwifery education and examination introduced by medical men of the Obstetrical Society, so securing a form of credentialism for midwives, and, as they concentrated on legalistic tactics, they could rely on medical men advocating midwife registration to represent their interests at the level of the state. In discussing female professional projects in the nineteenth century, I emphasised the necessity of women to mobilise proxy male power in this way in order to mobilise the heteronomous means of occupational closure and secure state-sponsorship for their professional projects.

In the case of nurses, the concept of dual closure was used to scrutinise the campaign for nurse registration spearheaded by Mrs Bedford-Fenwick, a figure who has been neglected in the history of nursing. I have shown how Mrs Bedford-Fenwick's campaign for nurse registration was a female professional project, and contained strongly usurpationary and strongly exclusionary dimensions. Her vision of 'nurses' self-government' was a bid to centralise control over nurse training, examination and practise in a state-sponsored body on which nurses were to form a clear majority. But her vision posed a strong challenge to existing sets of power relations in the emerging hospital system of health care, and drew forth strong opposition from voluntary hospitals as well as from hospital nurses and matrons, who sought to defend the gains of the Nightingale reform, particularly the enhanced occupational role of the matron within the voluntary hospital. Mrs Bedford-Fenwick's vision of a supra-institutional, centralised body to control the affairs of nurses challenged the newly found autonomy of the nursing staff within the voluntary hospitals and they threatened to undermine the symbiotic relation which had come to exist between the new, reformed system of nursing and the management needs of the voluntary hospital. I have also argued that the eventual passage of the Nurse Registration Act in 1919 was, however, not a victory for pro-registrationist nurses but a significant defeat. The nurses' professional project was never realised and, indeed, has resurfaced in the 1980s in the form in initiatives around nurse education and training in the form of 'Project 2000'. The severing of nurse education from the staffing needs of hospitals is one of the aims of Project 2000, which was very much a part of Mrs Bedford-Fenwick's vision one hundred years ago.

The major aim of subjecting the campaigns of both midwives and nurses to sociological scrutiny using some of the tools of closure theory was to make the point that professional projects as collective projects of occupational closure which have historically employed credentialist and legalistic tactics, most notably by securing state-sponsorship, have been engaged in by women as well as men. The relative success or failure of such projects has been, as many writers have argued, historically contingent. What I have attempted to establish is that the gender of the actors engaged in professional projects was also an important factor, and that female professional projects assumed a distinctive form best described as dual closure strategies. In other words, the gender of collective actors is not fortuitous or contingent, but a necessary factor in explaining the form and the outcome of such projects.

Internal demarcation and discursive strategies

The case study of gender and radiography introduced a further concept, that of internal demarcation. This described a sub-type of exclusion because it was geared towards intra-occupational control, but described the attempts by male radiographers to internally demarcate between male and female spheres of competence within an occupation. Although the main focus of this book has been on the gendered dimensions of closure strategies, the concept of a discursive strategy (cf Pringle 1989, Chua and Clegg 1990) proved a particularly useful one in the analysis of gender struggle in radiography during the 1920s and 1930s.

There is no immediately obvious explanation for the rapid feminisation of the occupation of radiography, particularly because the radiographer's skills were 'scientific' and 'technical' ones, not usually amenable to feminine gender-typing. And yet, as Larkin (1983) observes, they were. I suggested a number of reasons for this. First, male radiographers had formalised the route of access to radiography in 1921 through the setting up of a diploma, and yet women quickly made up the majority of qualifying radiographers. So why had credentialism failed to exclude women? I argued that women had already gained access to radiography skills and hands-on experience of X-ray technology in the early days of the introduction of X-ray equipment into hospitals, and that they had done so largely in their capacity as nurses. Second, because radiography training was hospital-based, women were able to take advantage of this formal training because they had already established a presence in hospitals and their training schools. Third, because the inter-occupational relations within which radiographers were embroiled in the medical division of labour increasingly came to be articulated within the parameters of patriarchal male–female authority relations. I also suggested that female nurse-radiographers or X-ray sisters enjoyed a distinct gender-specific competitive advantage for posts as radiographers, and this was largely the result of employer strategies, particularly in small hospitals where employers sometimes preferred to appoint nurse-radiographers or X-ray sisters at the lower salary of nursing.

Male radiographers in the 1930s were acutely aware of the seemingly inexorable process of feminisation, and engaged in internal demarcationary strategies, but largely at the discursive level. They attempted to discursively reconstruct the early pioneer days of X-ray work as days when male radiographers ruled the roost, to establish discursive equivalence between 'technical' skills and maleness, and between 'caring, patient-centred' skills and femaleness, whilst simultaneously denying the value of the latter in radiography. But the combined effects of the fact that X-ray technology was all the time becoming more predictable and routinised, together with the increasing articulation of the radiographer–radiologist relation within patriarchal authority relations (even to the extent of explicitly using discursive parallels between radiographers and 'housewives'), sealed the fate of male radiographers as a dwindling minority of X-ray technicians.

GENDER, CLOSURE, CLASS FORMATION AND THE STATE

Let me now turn to a consideration of the implications of my analysis of the relationship between gender and professional projects for an understanding of broader processes of service class formation. After all, professional closure is regarded by many writers as an integral feature of the formation of the middle classes in modern societies (Parkin 1976, Parry and Parry 1979, Abercrombie and Urry 1983), whilst Goldthorpe (1982) emphasises the role of exclusionary strategies (particularly through the use of formal qualifications to control entry to more desirable locations in a division of labour) as a significant feature of service class formation. I want to suggest here how my analysis of gender and professional projects suggests that there were important ways in which the historic formation of service class places was simultaneously a gendered process.

The concept of a 'service class' has become an increasingly popular one in analyses of the contemporary configuration of class places (cf Goldthorpe 1982, 1987, Abercrombie and Urry 1983, Lash and Urry 1987, Savage et al. 1991), although it was first used in 1924 by Karl Renner to describe the rise of the professional manager and the decline of the owner-manager, and popularised by Dahrendorf, who used the term to refer to 'salaried employees who occupy positions that are part of a bureaucratic hierarchy' (Dahrendorf 1959: 55). As common sociological currency, it refers

broadly to higher-level white-collar occupational groups in advant-
aged positions in modern societies: namely professional, administrative and managerial employees (cf Goldthorpe 1982). But most
service class theorists have to deal with the problem of 'boundary
definition' in relation to determining where the boundary falls
between the higher-level white collar occupations which constitute
the service class and those lower-level ones which do not. Signi-
ficantly, this is a gendered boundary, and, indeed, gendered
criteria do slip into various attempts to draw this boundary –
although unobtrusively. So, for example, Abercrombie and Urry
(1983) simultaneously establish both the proletarian *and* feminine
character of routine white-collar work which they subsequently
exclude from their category of the service class. But what they do
not probe is the corollary of this, which is the masculine character
of those managerial, administrative and managerial positions
which form part of their designated service class. Indeed, it may be
argued that existing attempts to specify the basis of the service class
have failed precisely because they have not theorised the gendered
basis of the service class.

Another key distinguishing characteristic that marks lower-level
white-collar occupations off from the higher-level occupations of
the service class are the different market and work situations of
these two groups (Goldthorpe 1982, Abercrombie and Urry 1983),
the former relating to the level of rewards and opportunities, the
latter to the degree of autonomy and discretion enjoyed. But, by
looking at processes at the core of the historical development of
the service class, such as professional projects, then it is possible to
see the very constitution of this white-collar hierarchy as having
been intimately related to *gendered* processes of occupational formation. In other words, gendered processes have played a role in
shaping the hierarchical arrangement of work and market situations which go to make up the occupational structure. It is already
firmly established that vertical segregation by gender is a key factor
in facilitating the movement by male clerical workers up through
and out of clerical work and into more managerial roles (cf
Crompton and Jones 1984). But this is to track the movement of
gendered persons through existing jobs slots or places, when I
think a stronger argument can be sustained, which traces how
gendered patterns of closure in the labour market have provided
key resources in the very social construction of those occupational
places that go to make up the service class. This may be argued

more generally with reference to the formation of professional, managerial and administrative hierarchies in nineteenth-century Britain, showing how they depended upon the maintenance of gendered exclusion and the manipulation of occupational boundaries by means of gendered demarcation in the labour market. Here, I simply want to highlight some particular issues that arise out of my discussion of gender and professional projects.

First, the focus on gender and collective projects of occupational closure highlights one of the ways in which the structure of occupational positions is not 'always already there' or simply functionally determined, but that the structuring of occupational positions, i.e. of their specific functions, their relative work and market situations, their symbolic standing in society, is the outcome of collective processes involving groups such as trade unions and professional associations engaged in distributive struggle (cf Crompton 1989), and that one force for cohesion or basis for collective action has been gendered solidarity.

Second, the professional project of medicine was facilitated by the ability of medical men to incorporate gendered criteria of exclusion vis-à-vis women into their professionalisation strategy, and so helped in the process of securing privileged access to rewards and opportunities – that is a relatively privileged *market* position. Third, the patriarchal structuring of the institutions of civil society and the state facilitated the institutionalisation of male privilege within the emerging medical division of labour between medicine and related occupations. In other words, it facilitated the hierarchical structuring of the relative *work* positions of medicine and paramedical occupations. So, the gender of the practitioners played some considerable part in the evolution of the distinctive and unequal market and work situations of these various occupations.

Fourth, as regards the formation and consolidation of medical professional service class positions during the latter half of the nineteenth century, Waddington (1984) makes the important point that the 1858 Medical Act secured institutional closure, but not social closure, which was a more gradual and fraught process. However, the ensuing struggle to secure relatively privileged material and symbolic rewards was considerably aided by the fact that the medical profession had secured a *gendered* form of social closure as part and parcel of institutional closure. It facilitated, for example, the forging of a discursive equivalence between 'gentlemanly status' and the occupation of medicine, particularly for the lower ranks of general practitioner (Parry and Parry 1976). But most critically, at this particular historical juncture, the formation of male occupational monopoly was facilitated by the patriarchal structuring of the institutions of the state and civil society, the latter the sphere where free occupational association was forged (Durkheim 1984). The institutionalisation of male power in both these spheres facilitated the monopolistic claims of men in professional service class positions. When we survey the disparate work and market situations of health care professionals today, it must be recognised that these are the product of past struggles by occupational groups, whose access to the resources of occupational professionalisation were facilitated or constrained by gender.

This argument, in turn, suggests that radical attempts to distinguish between 'people' and 'places' are flawed. Places are not formed through purely economic processes, as Hartmann (1979) suggests, arguing that capitalism provides the places whilst sexism and racism determine who fills them. It also suggests that gendered processes are significant not simply in the selection and allocation of personnel to fill places, as a number of class theorists now recognise, but also in the very constitution of these places. This point has recently been acknowledged by Marshall et al. who recognise that 'the manner in which the class structure is (at least in part) constituted through relations between the sexes is also, in our view, intrinsic to class analysis' (1988: 84). Crompton (1989) has also suggested that 'within the occupational structure, the impact of class factors cannot be isolated from gender, which is a central element in the structuring of occupations'. My analysis of gender and professionalisation in the medical division of labour provides one instance of how the historic construction of service class positions was related to gendered strategies of closure within the labour market.

Gender and the state

Another recent body of literature directs attention to the relation between gender and the state (Watson 1990, Franzway et al. 1989, Eisenstein 1981, 1984, Mackinnon 1982, Harrison and Mort 1980, Holter 1984, Showstack Sassoon 1987) and a 'feminist theory of the state' is emerging. Some writers have addressed the relation between the state and women's oppression but argued that the state is a fundamentally capitalist state and does not function as a directly repressive mechanism of women's subordination (McIntosh 1978, Barrett 1980, Harrison and Mort 1980). Other writers have argued that the state is a patriarchal state and therefore directly implicated in women's subordination (Hanmer 1978, Barker 1978, Hartmann 1979, Walby 1986, 1990a, Eisenstein 1981, 1984, Mackinnon 1982). Mackinnon argues that the state *is* (essentially) male, whilst Eisenstein operates with a more materialist, 'relative autonomy' framework to argue that the state is a capitalist patriarchal institution, but that it is more 'relative' than 'autonomous' along its patriarchal dimensions. There is a strong sense in which Eisenstein is suggesting the 'patriarchal interests' are more securely represented through the state because they are, literally, 'embodied' in male state managers in a more indissoluble way than 'capitalist interests', which are (as Miliband demonstrated in his classic thesis) forged through social networks.

However, the current trend in theorising about the state is towards a general drift away from these overly functionalist renderings of the state–society relation, and this drift is occurring in both mainstream sociology (cf Urry 1980, Jessop 1982, McLennan 1984) and in feminist studies (cf Franzway et al. 1989, Watson 1990, Showstack Sassoon 1987). In relation to this drift towards what I think we may call an 'institutional' theory of the state as less a monolith and more a constellation of competing interests, my analysis of gender struggles and professionalisation suggests that these were importantly displaced onto the state. This is what Offe (1984) argues in relation to social conflict in welfare capitalism generally although it would be incautious to draw direct parallels here, primarily because of the different historical period I have examined. Nonetheless, female professional projects, albeit mediated by proxy male power, did have considerable effectiveness at the level of the state. Indeed, we have seen how women were more successful in the pursuit of legalistic tactics seeking state sponsorship, than they were in credentialist ones. And specifically in the case of the medical profession it would appear that male dominance was only weakly institutionalised in the sphere of the state, but proved most resilient in the sphere of civil society. This would seem to suggest, contra Eisenstein, that the state is more autonomous than relative along its patriarchal dimensions. But it also underscores the need to move well beyond a 'relative autonomy' framework and to draw on post-marxist (Urry 1980, Jessop

1982) or pluralist marxist (McLennan 1984) theories of the state which acknowledge the plurality of social contradictions and political struggles, as well as their complex interrelations at the level of the state.

The state can only 'embody' male interests if these are institutionalised within the state apparatus. This approach appears to me as the way forward, and indeed it should be clear by now that I discuss 'patriarchal structures' generally in terms of the institutionalisation of male privilege in sites of social relations.

This line of sociological reasoning in relation to gender relations generally and gender and the state in particular is characteristic of the work of Connell (1987) and Franzway et al. (1989). Of course, Giddens (1984) defines institutions as enduring practices and the process of institutionalisation as the creation of conditions that make cyclical practice possible. Connell develops Giddens' notion of the cyclical durability of practices that make up 'institutions', although I would diverge from Connell on the grounds that he associates patriarchy with 'categoricalism', and so underemploys the concept, and prioritises the sphere of reproduction in his theorisation of gender relations. Nonetheless, he does usefully emphasise how gender is institutionalized through a network of links formed by cyclical practices, and how it is stabilised 'to the extent that the groups constituted in the network have interests in the conditions for cyclical rather than divergent practice' (Connell 1987: 181).

Insofar as we may speak of 'patriarchal structures' then these do not need to be conceptualised as 'deep structures', as Walby (1990a) maintains, but refer to the institutionalisation of gendered social practices, which are 'patriarchal' in the sense of systematically maintaining male power and privilege. In relation to discussions of the 'patriarchal state' then we are speaking here of the institutionalisation of male power. But, as Franzway et al. (1989) perceptively argue, this is both historically and nationally variable, and women have used the state to advance their own interests contra men. But, crucially, my analysis of how gender struggles in the sphere of occupational politics become displaced onto the state provides some grist to the mill for their argument that 'the state participates in constituting antagonistic interests in sexual politics and can become a vehicle for advancing those interests' (Franzway et al. 1989: 41). It was the organisations of civil society which provided the 'outer ditches' of the institutionalisation of male power in professional projects and which assumed central importance in facilitating and sustaining the institutionalisation of male privilege within professional hierarchy. The state proved the weaker link in the institutional chain of male privilege which sustained patriarchal closure in the context of professionalisation.

BIBLIOGRAPHY

Abel-Smith, B. (1960) *A History of the Nursing Profession*, London: Heinemann.
—— (1964) *The Hospitals 1800–1948*, London: Heinemann.
Abercrombie, N. and Urry, J. (1983) *Capital, Labour and the New Middle Classes*, London: Allen & Unwin.
Abrams, P. (1982) *Historical Sociology*, London: Open Books.
Acker, J. (1973) 'Women and Social Stratification', *American Journal of Sociology*, 78: 936–45.
—— (1989) 'The problem with patriarchy', *Sociology*, 23 (2): 235–40.
Alexander, S. and Taylor, B. (1981) 'In Defence of Patriarchy' in R. Samuel (ed.) *People's History and Socialist Theory*, London: Routledge & Kegan Paul.
Allen, S. (1982) 'Gender Inequality and Class Formation' in A. Giddens and G. Mackenzie (eds) *Social Class and the Division of Labour: Essays in Honour of Ilya Neustadt*, Cambridge: Cambridge University Press.
Amsden, A.H. (ed.) (1980) *The Economics of Women and Work*, Harmondsworth: Penguin.
Anderson, G. (1988) 'The white-blouse revolution' in G. Anderson (ed.) *The White-Blouse Revolution*, Manchester: Manchester University Press.
Aveling, J. (1872) *English Midwives: Their History and Prospects*, London: J. & J. Churchill.
Baly, M.E. (1980) *Nursing and Social Change*, London: Heinemann Medical Books (Second Edition).
—— (1987) 'The Nightingale Nurses: the Myth and the Reality' in C. Maggs (ed.) *Nursing History: The State of the Art*, London: Croom Helm.
Banks, O. (1981) *Faces of Feminism*, Oxford: Martin Robertson.
Barclay, A.E. (1942) 'The Passing of the Cambridge Diploma', *British Journal of Radiology*, Vol. 15: 351–4.
Barker, D. Leonard (1978) 'The Regulation of Marriage: Repressive Benevolence' in G. Littlejohn, B. Smart, J. Wakeford and N. Yuval-Davis (eds) *Power and the State*, London: Croom Helm.
Barrett, M. (1980) *Women's Oppression Today*, London: Verso (Second Edition 1987).

211

Barrett, M. and McIntosh, M. (1980) 'The "Family Wage": Some Problems for Socialists and Feminists', *Capital and Class*, 11, Summer: 51–72.
Barron, R.D. and Norris, G.M. (1976) 'Sexual Divisions and the Dual Labour Market' in D. Leonard Barker and S. Allen (eds) *Dependence and Exploitation in Work and Marriage*, London: Longman.
Beechey, V. (1977) 'Some Notes on Female Wage Labour in Capitalist Production', *Capital and Class*, 3, Autumn: 45–66.
—— (1978) 'Women and Production: a critical analysis of some sociological theories of women's work' in A. Kuhn and A. Wolpe *Feminism and Materialism: Women and Modes of Production*, London: Routledge & Kegan Paul.
—— (1979) 'On Patriarchy', *Feminist Review*, 3: 66–82.
—— (1982) 'The Sexual Division of Labour and the Labour Process: a critical assessment of Braverman' in S. Wood (ed.) *The Degradation of Work?*, London: Hutchinson.
—— (1986) 'Recent Approaches to Women's Employment in Great Britain' in *Unequal Work*, London: Virago.
Beechey, V. and Perkins, T. (1986) *A Matter of Hours*, Cambridge: Polity Press.
Bell, E. Moberly (1953) *Storming the Citadel: The Rise of the Woman Doctor*, London: Constable.
Bellaby, P. and Oribabor, P. (1980) '"History of the Present" – Contradiction and Struggle in Nursing' in C. Davies (ed.) *Rewriting Nursing History*, London: Croom Helm.
Berlant, J.L. (1975) *Profession and Monopoly*, Berkeley: University of California Press.
Blackwell, E. (1902) *Essays in Medical Sociology*, London: Ernest Bell (reprinted 1972, New York: Arno Press and The New York Times).
—— (1914) *Pioneer Work for Women*, London: J.M. Dent & Sons.
Blackwell, E. and Blackwell, R. (1860) 'Medicine as a Profession for Women', *English Woman's Journal*, Vol. 5, 27, May: 145–56.
Blau, F.D. and Jusenius, C.L. (1976) 'Economists' Approaches to Sex Segregation in the Labour Market' in M. Blaxall and B. Reagan (eds) *Women and the Workplace: The Implications of Occupational Segregation*, Chicago: University of Chicago Press.
Borchorst, A. and Siim, A. (1987) 'Women and the Advanced Welfare State – a new kind of patriarchal power?' in A. Showstack Sassoon (ed.) *Women and the State*, London: Hutchinson.
Bosanquet, N. and Doeringer, P.B. (1973) 'Is There a Dual Labour Market in Great Britain?', *The Economic Journal*, June: 421–35.
Bradley, H. (1976) 'Technological Change, Management Strategies and the Development of Gender-based Job Segregation in the Labour Process', in D. Knights and H. Willmott (eds) *Gender and the Labour Process*, Aldershot: Gower.
—— (1989) *Men's Work, Women's Work*, Cambridge: Polity Press.
Branca, P. (1976) 'Image and Reality: the myth of the idle Victorian woman' in M. Hartmann and L. Banner (eds) *Clio's Consciousness Raised*, New York: Octagon Books.

Braverman, H. (1974) *Labour and Monopoly Capital*, New York: Monthly Review Press.

Braybon, G. (1981) *Women Workers in the First World War: The British Experience*, London: Croom Helm.

Breay, M. (1897) 'Nursing in the Victorian Era', *The Nursing Record and Hospital World*, Vol. 19, June: 493–502.

Brenner, J. and Ramas, M. (1984) 'Rethinking Women's Oppression', *New Left Review*, March–April: 33–71.

Bruegel, I. (1979) 'Women as a Reserve Army of Labour: a note on recent British experience', *Feminist Review*, 3: 12–23.

Cain, G.C. (1976) 'The Challenge of Segmented Labour Market Theories to Orthodox Theory: a survey', *Journal of Economic Literature*, Vol. 14, 4, December.

Cameron, H.C. (1954) *Mr Guy's Hospital 1726–1948*, London: Longmans Green.

Carchedi, G. (1977) *On the Economic Identification of Social Classes*, London: Routledge & Kegan Paul.

Carpenter, M. (1977) 'The New Managerialism and Professionalism in Nursing' in J. Woodward and D. Richards (eds) *Health Care and Popular Medicine in Nineteenth Century England*, London: Croom Helm.

Carr-Saunders, A.M. and Wilson, P.A. (1933) *The Professions*, London: Oxford University Press.

Chamberlain, M. (1981) *Old Wives' Tales: Their History, Remedies and Spells*, London: Virago.

Chodorow, N. (1978a) 'Mothering, Male Dominance and Capitalism' in Z.R. Eisenstein (ed.) *Capitalist Patriarchy and the Case for Socialist Feminism*, New York: Monthly Review Press.

—— (1978b) *Mothering: Psychoanalysis and the Social Organization of Gender*, Berkeley: University of California Press.

Chua, T. and Clegg, S. (1990) 'Professional Closure: the case of British nursing', *Theory and Society*, Vol. 19, No. 2: 135–72.

Clark, A. (1919) *Working Life of Women in the Seventeenth Century*, London: George Routledge (Reprinted 1981, London: Virago).

Clark, G. (1964) *A History of the Royal College of Physicians of London*, Vol. 1, Oxford: Clarendon Press.

—— (1966) *A History of the Royal College of Physicians of London*, Vol. 2, Oxford: Clarendon Press.

Cockburn, C. (1983) *Brothers: Male Dominance and Technological Change*, London: Pluto Press.

—— (1985) *Machinery of Male Dominance: Men, Women and Technological Change*, London: Pluto Press.

—— (1986a) 'The Material of Male Power' in *Feminist Review* (ed.) *Waged Work: A Reader*, London: Virago.

—— (1986b) 'The Relations of Technology: what implications for theories of sex and class?' in R. Crompton and M. Mann (eds) *Gender and Stratification*, Cambridge: Polity Press.

—— (1988) 'The Gendering of Jobs: workplace relations and the reproduction of sex segregation' in S. Walby (ed.) *Gender Segregation at Work*, Milton Keynes: Open University Press.

Collins, R. (1975) *Conflict Sociology: Toward an Explanatory Science*, New York: Academic Press.
—— (1979) *The Credential Society: an Historical Sociology of Education and Stratification*, New York: Academic Press.
Connell, R.W. (1987) *Gender and Power*, Cambridge: Polity Press.
Connelly, P. (1978) *Last Hired, First Fired: Women and the Canadian Workforce*, Toronto: The Women's Press.
Cook, E.T. (1914) *The Life of Florence Nightingale*, Vol. 2 (1862–1910), London: Macmillan.
Cooke, A.M. (1972) *A History of the Royal College of Physicians of London*, Vol. 3, Oxford: Clarendon Press.
Cope, Z. (1959) *The Royal College of Surgeons in England: a History*, London: Anthony Blond.
Corr, H. (1990) 'Politics of the Sexes in English and Scottish Teachers' Unions 1870–1914' in H. Corr and L. Jamieson (eds) *The Politics of Everyday Life*, London: Macmillan.
Cowell, B. and Wainwright, D. (1981) *Behind the Blue Door: The History of the Royal College of Midwives 1881–1981*, London: George Routledge.
Crompton, R. (1986) 'Women and the Service Class' in R. Crompton and M. Mann (eds) *Gender and Stratification*, Cambridge: Polity Press.
—— (1987) 'Gender, Status and Professionalism', *Sociology*, 21: 413–28.
—— (1989) 'Class Theory and Gender', *British Journal of Sociology*, 40(4).
—— (1990) 'Professions in the Current Context', *Work, Employment and Society*.
Crompton, R. and Gubbay, J. (1977) *Economy and Class Structure*, London: Macmillan.
Crompton, R. and Jones, G. (1984) *White Collar Proletariat? De-skilling and Gender in Clerical Work*, London: Macmillan.
Crompton, R. and Sanderson, K. (1989) *Gendered Jobs and Social Change*, London: Unwin Hyman.
Crow, G. (1989) 'The Use of the Concept of 'Strategy' in Recent Sociological Literature', *Sociology*, 23: 1–24.
Cullingworth, C.J. (1878) 'The Registration of Midwives', *Contemporary Review*, March.
Dahrendorf, R. (1959) *Class and Class Conflict in an Industrial Society*, London: Routledge & Kegan Paul.
Daly, M. (1978) *Gyn/Ecology: The Metaethics of Radical Feminism*, Boston: Beacon Press.
Davidoff, L. and Hall, C. (1987) *Family Fortunes: Men and Women of the English Middle Class*, London: Hutchinson.
Davies, C. (ed.) (1980a) *Rewriting Nursing History*, London: Croom Helm.
—— (1980b) 'A Constant Casualty: nurse education in Britain and the USA to 1939' in C. Davies (ed.) *Rewriting Nursing History*, London: Croom Helm, 102–22.
—— (1982) 'The Regulation of Nursing Work: an historical comparison of Britain and the USA', *Research in the Sociology of Health Care*, Vol. 2: 121–60.
Davies, M. (1979) 'Woman's Place is at the Typewriter: the feminization

of the clerical labour force' in Z.R. Eisenstein (ed.) *Capitalist Patriarchy and the Case for Socialist Feminism*, New York: Monthly Review Press.

Delphy, C. (1984) 'The Main Enemy' in *Close to Home*, London: Hutchinson.

Dex, S. (1985) *The Sexual Division of Work*, Brighton: Wheatsheaf.

Dingwall, R. and McIntosh, J. (1978) *Readings in the Sociology of Nursing*, London: Churchill Livingstone.

Dingwall, R., Rafferty, A.M. and Webster, C. (1988) *An Introduction to the Social History of Nursing*, London: Routledge.

Doeringer, P. and Piore, M. (1971) *Internal Labour Markets and Manpower Analysis*, Massachusetts: D.C. Heath.

Donegan, J.B. (1978) *Women and Men Midwives: Medicine, Morality and Misogyny in Early America*, Connecticut and London: Greenwood Press.

Donnison, J. (1976) 'Medical Women and Lady Midwives: a case study in medical and feminist politics', *Women's Studies*, Vol. 3: 229–350.

—— (1977) *Midwives and Medical Men*, London: Heinemann.

Doyal, L. (1986) 'Women, Health and Medicine' in V. Beechey and E. Whitelegg (eds) *Women in Britain Today*, Milton Keynes: Open University Press.

Doyal, L., Rowbotham, S. and Scott, A. (1973) 'Introduction' in B. Ehrenreich and D. English, *Witches and Midwives and Nurses: A History of Women Healers*, London: Writers and Readers Publishing Co-operative.

Drake, B. (1920) *Women in Trade Unions*, London: Labour Research Department (Virago 1984 offset edition).

Durkheim, E. (1984) *The Division of Labour in Society*, London: Macmillan.

Dworkin, A. (1981) *Pornography: Men Possessing Women*, London: The Women's Press.

Dyhouse, C. (1981) *Girls Growing Up in Late Victorian and Edwardian England*, London: Routledge & Kegan Paul.

Edholm, F., Harris, O. and Young, K. (1977) 'Conceptualising Women', *Critique of Anthropology*, Vol. 3.

Edmunds, J. (1864) *Inaugural Address to the Female Medical Society*, London (pamphlet).

Edwards, R. (1979) *Contested Terrain: The Transformation of the Workplace in the Twentieth Century*, New York: Basic Books.

Ehrenreich, B. and Ehrenreich, J. (1977) 'The Professional Managerial Class', *Radical America* 11(2): 12–17.

Ehrenreich, B and English, D. (1973a) *Complaints and Disorders: The Sexual Politics of Sickness*, New York: Feminist Press.

—— (1973b) *Witches, Midwives and Nurses: A History of Women Healers*, London: Writers and Readers Publishing Co-operative.

—— (1979) *For Her Own Good: 150 Year of the Expert's Advice to Women*, London: Pluto Press.

Eisenstein, Z.R. (1979) 'Developing a Theory of Capitalist Patriarchy and Socialist Feminism' in Z.R. Eisenstein (ed.) *Capitalist Patriarchy and the Case for Socialist Feminism*, New York: Monthly Review Press.

—— (1981) *The Radical Future of Liberal Feminism*, New York: Longman.
—— (1984) *Feminism and Sexual Equality*, New York: Monthly Review Press.
Elliott, P. (1972) *The Sociology of the Professions*, London: Macmillan.
Etzioni, A. (1969) *The Semi-Professions and their Organization*, New York: Free Press.
Feldberg, R.L. and Glenn, E.N. (1979) 'Male and Female: Job versus Gender Models in the Sociology of Work', *Social Problems*, Vol. 26, 5: 524–38.
Firestone, S. (1974) *The Dialectic of Sex: The Case for Feminist Revolution*, New York: Morrow.
Fogarty, M.P., Allen, I. and Walters, P. (1981) *Women in Top Jobs*, London: Heinemann Education Books.
Forbes, T.R. (1964) 'The Regulation of English Midwives in the Sixteenth and Seventeenth Centuries', *Medical History*, Vol. 8: 235–44.
Franklin, R.E. (1950) 'Medical Education and the Rise of the General Practitioner', PhD Thesis, University of Birmingham.
Franzway, S., Court, D., and Connell, R.W. (1989) *Staking a Claim: Feminism, Bureaucracy and the State*, Cambridge: Polity Press.
Fraser, N. and Nicholson, L. (1988) 'Social Criticism Without Philosophy: an encounter between feminism and post-modernism' in A. Ross (ed.) *Universal Abandon? The Politics of Post-Modernism*, Edinburgh: Edinburgh University Press.
Freidson, E. (1970a) *Professional Dominance: The Social Structure of Medical Care*, New York: Atherton Press.
—— (1970b) *Profession of Medicine: A Study of the Sociology of Applied Knowledge*, New York: Harper & Row.
—— (1977) 'The Future of Professionalism' in M. Stacey and M. Reid (eds) *Health and the Division of Labour*, London: Croom Helm.
—— (1983) 'The Theory of Professions: State of the Art, in R. Dingwall and P. Lewis (eds) *The Sociology of the Professions*, London: Macmillan.
—— (1986) *Professional Powers: A Study of the Institutionalisation of Formal Knowledge*, Chicago and London: University of Chicago Press.
Gamarnikow, E. (1978) 'Sexual Division of Labour: the case of nursing' in A. Kuhn and A. Wolpe (eds) *Feminism and Materialism*, London: Routledge & Kegan Paul.
Garnsey, E. (1978) 'Women's Work and Theories of Class Stratification', *Sociology*, Vol. 17: 223–43.
Giddens, A. (1980) *The Class Structure of the Advanced Societies*, London: Hutchinson.
—— (1982) 'Labour and Interaction' in J.B. Thomson and D. Held (eds) *Habermas: Critical Debates*, London: Macmillan.
—— (1984) *The Constitution of Society*, Cambridge: Polity Press.
Glazer, P.M and Slater, M. (1987) *Unequal Colleagues: The Entrance of Women into the Professions, 1890–1940*, New Brunswick and London: Rutgers University Press.
Glucksman, M. (1985) 'In a Class of Their Own? Women Workers in the New Industries', *Feminist Review*, 24.
—— (1990) *Women Assemble*, London: Routledge.

Goldthorpe, J. (1982) 'The Service Class: its formation and future' in A. Giddens and G. MacKenzie (eds) *Social Class and the Division of Labour*, Cambridge: Cambridge University Press.

—— (1983) 'Women and Class Analysis: a defence of the conventional view', *Sociology*, Vol. 17: 465–88.

—— (1987) *Social Mobility and Class Structure in Modern Britain*, Oxford: Clarendon Press (Second Edition).

Gordon, D.M., Edwards, R. and Reich, M. (1982) *Segmented Work, Divided Workers*, Cambridge: Cambridge University Press.

Gramsci, A. (1971) *Selections from Prison Notebooks*, (ed.) Q. Hoare and P. Nowell Smith, London: Lawrence & Wishart.

Grandjean, B.D. and Bernal, H.H. (1979) 'Sex and Centralisation in a Semi-Profession', *Sociology of Work and Literature*, Vol. 6.

Greenwood, E. (1957) 'The Attributes of a Profession', *Social Work* 2: 44–55.

Hakim, C. (1979) *Occupational Segregation: A Comparative Study of the Degree and Pattern of the Differentiation between Men's and Women's Work in Britain, the United States and Other Countries*, Department of Employment Research Paper, Department of Employment, London.

—— (1987) 'Homeworking in Britain: key findings from the national survey of home-based workers', *Employment Gazette*, February: 92–104.

Hanmer, J. (1978) 'Violence and the Social Control of Women' in G. Littlejohn, B. Smart, J. Wakeford and N. Yuval-Davis (eds) *Power and the State*, London: Croom Helm.

Harre, R. (1981) 'Philosophical aspects of the micro-macro problem' in K. Knorr-Cetina and A.V. Cicourel (eds) *Advances in Social Theory and Methodology: Towards an Integration of Micro- and Macro-Sociologies*, Boston: Routledge.

Harrison, R. and Mort, F. (1980) 'Patriarchal Aspects of Nineteenth Century State Formation; Property Relations, Marriage and Divorce, and Sexuality' in P. Corrigan (ed.) *Capitalism, State Formation and Marxist Theory*, London: Quartet Books.

Hartmann, H. (1979) 'Capitalism, Patriarchy and Job Segregation by Sex' in Z.R Eisenstein (ed.) *Capitalist Patriarchy and the Case for Socialist Feminism*, New York: Monthly Review Press.

—— (1981) 'The Unhappy Marriage of Marxism and Feminism: towards a more progressive union' in L. Sargent (ed.) *Women and Revolution*, New York: Monthly Review Press.

Hearn, J. (1982) 'Notes on Patriarchy, Professionalization and the Semi-Professions', *Sociology*, Vol. 16.

—— (1987) *The Gender of Oppression*, Brighton: Wheatsheaf.

Hector, W. (1973) *The Work of Mrs Bedford-Fenwick and The Rise of Professional Nursing*, London: Royal College of Nursing.

Hernes, H.M. (1987) 'Women and the Welfare State: the transition from private to public dependence' in A. Showstack Sassoon (ed.) *Women and the State*, London: Hutchinson.

HMSO (1892) *Report from the Select Committee on the Registration of Midwives, House of Commons*, London: HMSO.

217

—— (1904) *Report from the Select Committee on Registration of Nurses, House of Commons*, London: HMSO.

—— (1905) *Report from the Select Committee on Registration of Nurses, House of Commons*, London: HMSO.

Holcombe, L. (1973) *Victorian Ladies at Work: Middle-Class Working Women in England and Wales, 1850–1914*, Newton Abbot: David & Charles.

Holter, H. (ed.) (1984) *Patriarchy in a Welfare Society*, Oslo: Universitetsforlaget.

Hughes, M. (1943) *Women Healers in Medieval Life and Literature*, New York: King's Crown Press.

Humphries, J. (1977) 'Class Struggle and the Persistence of the Working Class Family', *Cambridge Journal of Economics*, 1 (September) 241–58.

—— (1981) 'Protective Legislation, the Capitalist State and Working-class Men: the case of the 1842 Mines Regulation Act', *Feminist Review*, 7: 106–9.

—— (1983) 'The Emancipation of Women in the 1970s and 1980s; from latent to the floating', *Capital and Class*, 20, Summer: 6–28.

Hunt, F. (1985) 'Opportunities Lost and Gained: Mechanization and Women's Work in the London Bookbinding and Printing Trades' in A.V. John (ed.) *Unequal Opportunities; Women's Employment in England 1800–1918*, Oxford: Blackwell.

Hurd-Mead, K. Campbell (1937) *A History of Women in Medicine*, London: Longwood Press.

Hutchins, B. and Harrison, A. (1911) *A History of Factory Legislation*, London: Bell & Son.

Jamous, H. and Peloille, B. (1970) 'Changes in the French University Hospital System' in J.A. Jackson (ed.) *Professions and Professionalisation*, Cambridge: Cambridge University Press.

Jessop, B. (1982) *The Capitalist State*, Oxford: Martin Robertson.

Jex-Blake, S. (1886) *Medical Women: A Thesis and a History*, Edinburgh: Oliphant, Andersen & Ferrier.

John, A. (1980) *By the Sweat of their Brow: Women Workers in Victorian Coal Mines*, London: Croom Helm.

—— (1981) 'Letter in Response to Jane Humphries', *Feminist Review* 8: 106–9.

—— (ed.) (1986) *Unequal Opportunities: Women's Employment in England 1800–1918*, Oxford: Blackwell.

Johnson, T. (1972) *Professions and Power*, London: Macmillan.

—— (1977) 'Professions in the Class Structure' in R. Scase (ed.) *Industrial Society; Class, Cleavage and Control*, London: Allen & Unwin.

—— (1982) 'The State and the Professions; peculiarities of the British' in A. Giddens and G. Mackenzie (eds) *Social Class and the Division of Labour: Essays in Honour of Ilya Neustadt*, Cambridge: Cambridge University Press.

Kanter, R.M. (1975) 'Women in the Structure of Organizations' in M. Millman and R. Kanter (eds) *Another Voice*, New York: Anchor Books.

—— (1976) *Men and Women of the Corporation*, New York: Basic Books.

Kobrin, F.E. (1966) 'The American Midwife Controversy: a crisis of professionalisation', *Bulletin of the History of Medicine*, Vol. 40: 350–63.

218

Kreckel, R. (1980) 'Unequal Opportunities Structure and Labour Market Segmentation', *Sociology*, Vol. 4: 525–50.

Lander, K. (1922) 'The study of anatomy by women before the nineteenth century, *Proceedings of the 3rd International Congress of the History of Medicine*, London, pp. 125–134.

Larkin, G. (1978) 'Medical Dominance and Control: Radiographers in the Division of Labour', *Sociological Review*, Vol. 26: 843–58.

—— (1983) *Occupational Monopoly and Modern Medicine*, London: Tavistock.

Larson, M. (1977) *The Rise of Professionalism*, California: University of California Press.

—— (1979) 'Professionalism: Rise and Fall', *International Journal of Health Services*, Vol. 9.

Lash, S. and Urry, J. (1987) *The End of Organized Capitalism*, Cambridge: Polity Press.

Leggatt, T. (1970) 'Teaching as a Profession' in J.A. Jackson (ed.) *Professions and Professionalization*, Cambridge: Cambridge University Press.

Lewis, J. (1984) *Women in England 1870–1950: Sexual Divisions and Social Change*, Brighton: Wheatsheaf.

Liff, S. (1986) 'Technical Change and Occupational Sex-typing' in D. Knights and H. Willmott (eds) *Gender and the Labour Process*, Aldershot: Gower.

Lowe, G. (1987) *Women in the Administrative Revolution*, Cambridge: Polity Press.

Lown, J. (1983) 'Not so Much a Factory, More a Form of Patriarchy: gender and class during industrialisation' in E. Gamarnikow et al. *Gender, Class and Work*, London: Heinemann.

—— (1990) *Women and Industrialization*, Cambridge: Polity Press.

Lutzker, E. (1974) 'The London School of Medicine for Women: origin and important contributions to medicine by a few graduates', *Proceedings of the XXIII Congress of the History of Medicine*, Vol. 1: 357–66.

MacDonald, K.M. (1985) 'Social closure and occupational registration', *Sociology*, 19: 541–56.

McIntosh, M. (1978) 'The state and the oppression of women' in A. Kuhn and A. Wolpe (eds) *Feminism and Materialism*, London: Routledge & Kegan Paul.

Mackinnon, C.A. (1982) 'Feminism, Marxism, Method and the State: an agenda for theory' in N.O. Keohane, M.Z. Rosaldo and B.C. Gelpi (eds) *Feminist Theory: A Critique of Ideology*, Brighton: Harvester Press.

McLennan, G. (1984) 'Capitalist State or Democratic Polity? Recent Developments in Marxist and Pluralist Theory' in G. McLennan, D. Held and S. Hall (eds) *The Idea of the Modern State*, Milton Keynes: Open University Press.

McNally, F. (1979) *Women for Hire: A Study of the Female Office Worker*, London: Macmillan.

Maggs, C.J. (1983) *The Origins of General Nursing*, London: Croom Helm.

—— (ed.) (1987) *Nursing History: The State of the Art*, London: Croom Helm.

Manton, J. (1965) *Elizabeth Garrett Anderson*, London: Methuen.

Mark-Lawson, J., Savage, M. and Warde, A. (1985) 'Gender and Local Politics: struggles over welfare policies 1918–1939' in L. Murgatroyd, D. Shapiro, J. Urry, S. Walby, A. Warde with J. Mark-Lawson (eds) *Localities, Class and Gender*, London: Pion.

Mark-Lawson, J. and Witz, A. (1988) 'From "Family Labour" to "Family Wage"?: the case of women's labour in nineteenth-century coal-mining', *Social History*, Vol. 13 (2): 151–74.

—— (1990) 'Familial Control or Patriarchal Domination?: the family system of labour in nineteenth-century coalmining in Britain' in H. Corr and L. Jamieson (eds) *The Politics of Everyday Life*, London: Macmillan.

Marrett, C.B. (1972) 'Centralization in Female Organizations: reassessing the evidence', *Social Problems*, Vol. 19, Winter: 348–57.

Marshall, G., Rose, D., Newby, H. and Vogler, C. (1988) *Social Class in Modern Britain*, London: Unwin Hyman.

Martindale, H. (1938) *Women Servants of the State 1870–1938: A History of Women in the Civil Service*, London: Allen & Unwin.

Medick, H. (1976) 'The Proto-Industrial Family Economy: the structural function of household and family industry during the transition from peasant society to industrial capitalism', *Social History*, 1(3).

Mercato, A.P. del (1981) 'Social Reproduction and the Basic Structure of the Labour Market' in F. Wilkinson (ed.) *The Dynamics of Labour Market Segmentation*, New York: Academic Press.

Milkman, R. (1976) 'Women's Work and Economic Crisis: some lessons from the Great Depression', *Review of Radical Political Economy*, Vol. 8, 1, Spring: 73–87.

—— (1983) 'Female Factory Labour and Industrial Structure: control and conflict over "woman's place" in auto and electrical manufacture', *Politics and Society*, Vol. 12, 2: 159–203.

—— (1984) *Gender at Work: The Dynamics of Job Segregation by Sex during World War II*, Urbana and Chicago: University of Illinois Press.

Millerson, G. (1964) *The Qualifying Associations: A Study in Pro-fessionalisation*, London.

Millet, K. (1972) *Sexual Politics*, London: Paladin.

Mincer, J. (1980) 'Labor Force Participation of Married Women: A Study of Labor Supply' in A.H. Amsden (ed.) *The Economics of Women and Work*, Harmondsworth: Penguin.

Mincer, J. and Polachek, S. (1974) 'Family Investments in Human Capi-tal', *Journal of Political Economy*, Vol. 82, 2, March–April: 76–108.

Mitchell, J. (1975) *Psychoanalysis and Feminism*, Harmondsworth: Penguin.

Morgan, G. and Hopper, D. (1982) 'Labour in the Woollen and Worsted Industry: a critical analysis of dual labour market theory' in G. Day et al. (eds) *Diversity and Decomposition in the Labour Market*, Aldershot: Gower.

Morley, E.J. (1914) *Women Workers in Seven Professions*, London: George Routledge.

Morrell, C. (1981) *'Black Friday' and Violence Against Women in the Suffragette Movement*, London: Women's Research and Resources Centre.

Murgatroyd, L. (1985) 'Gender and Occupational Segregation' in L. Murgatroyd, D. Shapiro, J. Urry, S. Walby, A. Warde with J. Mark-Lawson (eds) *Localities, Class and Gender*, London: Pion.

Murphy, R. (1983) 'The Struggle for Scholarly Recognition: The Development of the Closure Problematic in Sociology', *Theory and Society*, Vol. 12: 631–58.

—— (1984) 'The Structures of Closure: a critique and development of the theories of Weber, Collins and Parkin', *British Journal of Sociology*, Vol. 35: 547–67.

—— (1985) 'Exploitation or Exclusion?', *Sociology*, Vol. 19: 225–43.

—— (1986) 'Weberian Closure Theory: a contribution to the ongoing assessment', *British Journal of Sociology*, Vol. 37: 21–41.

—— (1988) *Social Closure: The Theory of Monopolization and Exclusion*, Oxford: Clarendon Press.

Myrdal, A. and Klein, V. (1956) *Women's Two Roles*, London: Routledge & Kegan Paul.

Navarro, V. (1978) *Class, Struggle, the State and Medicine*, London: Martin Robertson.

Neff, W. (1929) *Victorian Working Women: An Historical and Literary Study of Women in British Industries and Professions*, London: Frank Cass (1966 Reprint of First Edition).

Newman, C. (1957) *The Evolution of Medical Education in the Nineteenth Century*, London: Oxford University Press.

Nicholson, L.J. (1986) *Gender and History*, New York: Columbia University Press.

Nutting, M.A. and Dock, L.L. (1907) *A History of Nursing*, New York: G.P. Putman.

Oakley, A. (1976) 'Wisewomen and Medicine Men: changes in the management of childbirth' in J. Mitchell and A. Oakley (eds) *The Rights and Wrongs of Women*, Harmondsworth: Penguin.

—— (1984) *The Captured Womb*, Oxford: Blackwell.

Offe, C. (1984) *Contradictions of the Welfare State*, London: Hutchinson.

Oppenheimer, V.K. (1969) *The Female Labour Force in the United States: Demographic and Economic Factors Governing its Growth and Changing Composition*, Population Monograph Series No. 5, California: University of California Press.

Parkin, F. (1971) *Class Inequality and Political Order*, St Albans: Paladin.

—— (1974) 'Strategies of Social Closure in Class Formation' in F. Parkin (ed.) *The Social Analysis of Class Structure*, London: Tavistock.

—— (1979) *Marxism and Class Theory: A Bourgeois Critique*, London: Tavistock.

Parry, N. and Parry, J. (1976) *The Rise of the Medical Profession*, London: Croom Helm.

Parsons, T. (1954) 'The Professions and Social Structure' in *Essays in Sociological Theory*, New York: Free Press.

Pelling, M. and Webster, C. (1979) 'Medical Practitioners' in C. Webster (ed.) *Health, Medicine and Morality in the Sixteenth Century*, Cambridge: Cambridge University Press.

Phillips, A. (1987) *Divided Loyalties: Dilemmas of Sex and Class*, London: Virago.

Phillips, A. and Taylor, B. (1984) 'Sex and Skill' in *Feminist Review* (ed.) *Wages Work: A Reader*, London: Virago.

Pinchbeck, I. (1930) *Women Workers and the Industrial Revolution* (Reprinted 1981 London: Virago).

Piore, M. (1975) 'Notes for a Theory of Labor Market Stratification' in R.C. Edwards, M. Reich and D. Gordon (eds) *Labor Market Segmentation*, Massachusetts: D.C. Heath.

Power, E. (1921) 'Women Practitioners of Medicine in the Middle Ages', *Proceedings of the Royal Society of Medicine*, 15 (Section on History of Medicine).

Pratt, E.A. (1897) *Pioneer Women in Victoria's Reign*, London: George Newnes.

Pringle, R. (1989) *Secretaries Talk: Sexuality, Power and Work*, London: Verso.

Pybus, F.C. (1928–9) 'The Company of Barber-Surgeons and Tallow Chandlers of Newcastle-on-Tyne', *Proceedings of the Royal Society of Medicine*, 22 (Section on History of Medicine): 7–16.

Reader, W.J. (1966) *Professional Men: The Rise of the Professional Classes in Nineteenth-Century England*, London: Weidenfeld & Nicholson.

Reich, M., Gordon, D.M. and Edwards, R.C. (1980) 'A Theory of Labor Market Segmentation' in A.H. Amsden (ed.) *The Economics of Women and Work*, Harmondsworth: Penguin.

Reynolds, M. (1920) *The Learned Lady in England 1650–1760*, Cambridge: The Riverside Press.

Rich, A. (1976) *Of Woman Born: Motherhood as Experience and Institution*, London: Virago.

—— (1980) 'Compulsory Heterosexuality and Lesbian Existence', *Signs*, Vol. 5, 3, Spring: 389–417.

Richards, E. (1974) 'Women in the British Economy since about 1700: an interpretation', *History*, Vol. 59, 197: 337–57.

Rowbotham, S. (1981) 'The Trouble with Patriarchy' in R. Samuel (ed.) *People's History and Socialist Theory*, London: Routledge & Kegan Paul.

Rubery, J. (1978) 'Structured Labour Markets, Worker Organisation and Low Pay', *Cambridge Journal of Economics*, Vol. 2, 1, March: 17–36.

Rubery, J. and Tarling, F. (1982) 'Women in the Recession', *Socialist Economic Review*, London: Merlin.

Rubin, G. (1975) 'The Traffic in Women' in R. Reiter (ed.) *Toward an Anthropology of Women*, New York: Monthly Review Press.

Rueschemeyer, D. (1983) 'Professional Autonomy and the Social Control of Expertise' in R. Dingwall and P. Lewis (eds) *The Sociology of the Profession: Lawyers, Doctors and Others*, London: Macmillan.

—— (1986) *Power and the Division of Labour*, Cambridge: Polity Press.

Sachs, A. and Wilson, J.H. (1978) *Sexism and the Law: A Study of Male Beliefs and Legal Bias in Britain and the United States*, Oxford: Martin Robertson.

Sanderson, K. (1990) 'Meanings of Class and Social Mobility: the public and private lives of women civil servants' in H. Corr and L. Jamieson (eds) *The Politics of Everyday Life*, London: Macmillan.

Sarah, E. (1983) 'Christabel Pankhurst: reclaiming her power (1880–1958)' in D. Spender (ed.) *Feminist Theorists: Three Centuries of Women's Intellectual Traditions*, London: The Women's Press.

Savage, M. (1985) 'Capitalist and patriarchal relations at work; Preston cotton weaving 1890–1940' in L. Murgatroyd, D. Shapiro, J. Urry, S. Walby, A. Warde with J. Mark-Lawson (eds) *Localities, Class and Gender*, London: Pion.

—— (1987) *The Dynamics of Working Class Politics*, Cambridge: Cambridge University Press.

—— (1988a) 'Women and Work in the Lancashire Cotton Industry, 1890–1939' in J.A. Jowitt and A.J. McIvor (eds) *Employers and Labour in the English Textile Industries, 1850–1939*, London: Routledge.

—— (1988b) 'Trade unionism, sex segregation and the state; women's employment in 'new industries' in inter-war Britain', *Social History*, 13(2), 209–29.

Savage, M., Barlow, J., Dickson, P. and Fielding, P. (1991) *Property, Bureaucracy and Culture: Middle Class Formation in Contemporary Britain*, London: Routledge.

Sayer, D. (1984) *Method in Social Science*, London: Hutchinson.

Scharlieb, M. (1924) *Reminiscences*, London: Williams & Norgate.

Seccombe, W. (1974) 'The Housewife and her Labour under Capitalism', *New Left Review*, 83: 3–24.

—— (1975) 'Domestic Labour – Reply to Critics', *New Left Review*, 94: 85–96.

—— (1986) 'Patriarchy Stabilized: the construction of the male breadwinner norm in nineteenth century Britain', *Social History*, Vol. 11, 1, January: 53–76.

Sen, G. (1980) 'The Sexual Division of Labor and the Working-Class Family: towards a conceptual synthesis of class relations and the subordination of women', *The Review of Radical Political Economics*, Vol. 12, 2, Summer: 76–86.

Simpson, R.L. and Simpson, I.H. (1969) 'Women and Bureaucracy in the Semi-Professions' in A. Etzioni (ed.) *The Semi-Professions and their Organization*, New York: Free Press.

Showstack Sassoon, A. (1987) (ed.) *Women and the State*, London: Hutchinson.

Smith, F.B. (1982) *Florence Nightingale: Reputation and Power*, London: Croom Helm.

Spender, D. (1982) *Women of Ideas – and what men have done to them*, London: Routledge & Kegan Paul.

Stacey, M. (1981) 'The Division of Labour Revisited or Overcoming the Two Adams' in P. Abrams, R. Deem, J. Finch and P. Rock (eds) *Practice and Progress: British Sociology 1950–1980*, London: Allen & Unwin.

Stansfeld, J. (1877) 'Medical Women', *Nineteenth Century*, Vol. 1, 5: 889–901.

Stevens, R. (1966) *Medical Practice in Modern England*, New Haven and London: Yale University Press.

Strachey, R. (1935) *The Cause*, London: Virago.
Summerfield, P. (1984) *Women Workers in the Second World War*, London: Croom Helm.
Thompson, P. (1983) *The Nature of Work: An Introduction to Debates on the Labour Process*, London: Macmillan.
Thorne, I. (1915) *Sketch of the Foundation and Development of the London School of Medicine for Women*, London: Women's Printing Society.
Turner, B.S. (1985) 'Knowledge, Skill and Occupational Strategy: the professionalisation of paramedical groups', *Community Health Studies*, Vol. 9: 38–48.
—— (1987) *Medical Power and Social Knowledge*, London: Sage.
Urry, J. (1980) *The Anatomy of Capitalist Societies*, London: Macmillan.
Vaughan, P. (1959) *Doctors' Commons: A Short History of the British Medical Association*, London: Heinemann.
Verluysen, M. (1980) 'Old Wives' Tales? Women Healers in English History' in C. Davies (ed.) *Rewriting Nursing History*, London: Croom Helm.
Vicinus, M. (1985) *Independent Women: Work and Community for Single Women 1850–1920*, London: Virago.
Vogel, L. (1983) *Marxism and the Oppression of Women: Towards a Unitary Theory*, London: Pluto Press.
Vollmer, H.M. and Mills, D.L. (1966) *Professionalisation*, New Jersey: Englewood Cliffs.
Waddington, I. (1977) 'General Practitioners and Consultants in Early Nineteenth Century England: the sociology of an intra-professional conflict' in J. Woodward and D. Richards (eds) *Health Care and Popular Medicine in Nineteenth Century England*, London: Croom Helm.
—— (1984) *The Medical Profession in the Industrial Revolution*, Ireland: Gill & MacMillan.
Walby, S. (1983) 'Patriarchal Structures: the case of unemployment' in E. Gamarnikow, D. Morgan, J. Purvis, D. Taylorson (eds) *Gender, Class and Work*, London: Heinemann.
—— (1985a) 'Segregation in Employment in Social and Economic Theory', Paper Presented to *Segregation in Employment, ESRC Social Stratification Seminar Symposium*, University of Lancaster, 10–12 July.
—— (1985b) 'Spatial and Historical Variations in Women's Employment' in L. Murgatroyd, D. Shapiro, J. Urry, S. Walby, A. Warde with J. Mark-Lawson (eds) *Localities, Class and Gender*, London: Pion.
—— (1986) *Patriarchy at Work*, Cambridge: Polity Press.
—— (1988a) 'Flexibility and the Changing Sexual Division of Labour' in S. Wood (ed.) *The Degradation of Work?* London: Hutchinson (Second Edition).
—— (1988b) 'Introduction' in *Gender Segregation at Work*, Milton Keynes: Open University Press.
—— (1989) 'Theorising patriarchy', *Sociology*, Vol. 23, 2: 213–34.
—— (1990a) *Theorizing Patriarchy*, Oxford: Basil Blackwell.
—— (1990b) 'Women's Employment and the Historical Periodisation of Patriarchy' in H. Corr and L. Jamieson (eds) *The Politics of Everyday Life*, London: Macmillan.

Wall, C., Cameron, H. and Underwood, E.A. (1963) *A History of the Worshipful Society of Apothecaries of London*, Oxford: Oxford University Press.

Watson, S. (1990) *Playing the State*, London: Verso.

Weber, M. (1968) *Economy and Society*, G. Roth and C. Wittich (eds), New York: Bedminster Press.

West, J. (1978) 'Women, Sex and Class' in A. Kuhn and A. Wolpe (eds) *Feminism and Materialism*, London: Routledge & Kegan Paul.

Westwood, S. (1984) *All Day, Every Day: Factory and Family in the Making of Women's Lives*, London: Pluto Press.

White, R. (1976) 'Some Political Influences surrounding the Nurses Registration Act 1919 in the United Kingdom', *Journal of Advanced Nursing Studies*, Vol. 1.

—— (1978) *Social Change and the Development of the Nursing Profession*, London: Henry Kimpton.

Widdowson, F. (1983) *Going up into the Next Class*, London: Hutchinson.

Wilensky, H. (1964) 'The Professionalisation of Everyone', *American Journal of Sociology* 70: 137–48.

Williams, G. (1976) 'Trends in Occupational Differentiation by Sex', *Sociology of Work and Occupations*, Vol. 3, 1, February: 38–62.

Williams, K. (1980) 'From Sarah Gamp to Florence Nightingale: a critical study of hospital nursing systems from 1840 to 1897' in C. Davies (ed.) *Rewriting Nursing History*, London: Croom Helm.

Wilson, E. (1980) *Only Halfway to Paradise. Women in Postwar Britain: 1945–1968*, London: Tavistock.

Wood, S. (1982) *The Degradation of Work?*, London: Hutchinson.

Woodward, J. and Richards, D. (1977) *Health Care and Popular Medicine in Nineteenth Century England: Essays in the Social History of Medicine*, London: Croom Helm.

Wyman, A.L. (1984) 'The Surgeoness: The Female Practitioner of Surgery 1400–1800', *Medical History*, Vol. 28: 22–41.

Zimmeck, M. (1986) 'Jobs for the girls: the expansion of clerical work for women' in A. John (ed.) *Unequal Opportunities: Women's Employment in England 1800–1918*, Oxford: Blackwell.

—— (1988) 'The New Women and the Machinery of Government: a spanner in the works' in R. McLeod (ed.) *Government and Expertise: Specialists, Administrators and Professionals 1860–1919*, Cambridge: Cambridge University Press.

Zweig, F. (1952) *Women's Life and Labour*, London: Victor Gollancz.

NAME INDEX

Abel-Smith, B. 50, 128, 130,
133–7, 139–41, 159–62
Abercrombie, N. 4, 52, 54–5,
204–5
Acker, J. 3, 42
Alexander, S. 13
Allen, S. 2
Anderson, G. 31, 32
Aveling, Dr J. 106–7, 113–14, 118

Baly, M.E. 50, 129, 131, 155
Barclay, A.E. 170–1
Barker, D. Leonard 208
Barlow, J. 204
Barrett, M. 3, 4, 11–12, 16, 208
Barron, R.D. 4
Bedford-Fenwick, Dr 130, 135
Bedford-Fenwick, Mrs 124–5,
144–55, 157, 161, 163, 166,
167, 200, 202
Beechey, V. 2, 4, 12
Bell, E. Moberly 90, 98
Bellaby, P. 48, 129, 139, 163
Berlant, J.L. 42–3, 75
Blackwell, E. 84–7, 93, 119, 199
Blackwell, R. 199
Bonham-Carter, Henry 134, 136
Borchorst, A. 3
Bradley, H. 3–4, 22–4, 26–7, 30–1
Branca, P. 31
Braverman, H. 4
Braybon, G. 13, 25
Breay, M. 138
Brenner, J. 27

British Journal of Nursing 129,
132–6, 145–54, 158, 161–2, 182
British Journal of Radiology 170–4,
176–7, 180, 183–4
British Medical Journal 77, 96,
110–13, 115, 127, 155, 158–9
Burdett, Henry 132, 134
Burstyn 35

Cameron, H.C. 80–1, 139–40
Campbell 75
Carchedi, G. 54
Carpenter, M. 139, 163
Carr-Saunders, A.M. 1
Chamberlain, M. 75, 77
Chodorow, N. 13
Chua, T. 7, 142, 203
Clark, A. 75, 77–8, 81, 106
Clark, G. 106
Clegg, S. 7, 142, 203
Cockburn, C. 4, 11–14, 18–21, 26,
29, 36, 63, 169, 189
Collins, R. 65
Connell, R.W. 209
Cook, E.T. 141
Cooke, A.M. 86, 100–1
Cope, Z. 80, 86, 100
Corr, H. 31
Court, D. 205–7
Cowper-Temple, William 73, 83,
93–5
Crompton, R. 2–4, 31, 40, 43–4,
52, 54, 65, 195–6, 205–7
Crow, G. 51

SUBJECT INDEX

British Association for the
Advancement of Radiology and
Physiotherapy 170, 172, 176
British Institute of Radiology 170,
173
British Medical Association 99;
and midwife registration 109,
111; and nurse registration
135, 136, 151, 155–9, 161–2,
200; and radiology 172
British National Council of
Women 154–5
British Nurses Association *see*
Royal British Nurses Association

capitalist-patriarchy 11, 13–14
Central Committee for the State
Registration of Nurses 135–6,
152, 161; draft registration bill
of 158–9
Central Employment Bureau of
Women 183
civil society 29, 37, 54, 65–8, 73–4,
82–3, 88, 91, 97, 99, 102–3,
194–6, 207, 208–9
closure 5, 39, 43–4, 48–50, 102–3,
192; autonomous means of
58–9, 65–6, 68, 74, 102, 118,
125, 196; and class formation 5;
and gender 5–7, 43–50, 61;
heteronomous means of 58–9,
65–6, 68, 71, 89, 102–3, 144,
146, 194, 196; neo-Weberian

theory of 36, 43–4, 46, 48–9,
50–1, 59, 65; patriarchal 66, 68,
74, 87–8, 93, 97, 102–3; and
professionalisation 5, 39, 42–4,
102–4
College of Nursing 160–2, 163;
and Mrs Bedford-Fenwick 161;
and Sir Arthur Stanley 151–62
credentialism 43, 195, 64–5, 67
credentialist tactics 64–5, 67, 194;
countervailing 88–92, 101–2,
195–6; of midwives 117–20,
125; of nurses 144–7, 165, 167;
of radiographers 168, 176–9,
189, 203

demarcation 30, 36–7; strategy of
6, 44–8, 68–9, 75, 104–5, 108,
117, 156, 168, 170–5, 191, 193,
196–206; and deskilling 69,
104, 105–7, 109–110, 112–17,
122, 125, 127, 188, 191, 197–8;
and incorporation 104, 105,
109–12, 116, 122, 126, 197–8;
internal 6, 169, 188–91, 203–4
discursive strategy 6–7, 206; and
midwives 126–7, 198; and
nurses 141–3; and
radiographers 169, 174,
179–81, 188–9, 203–4
dual closure, strategy of 6, 48–50,
69, 104–6, 108, 117, 128, 144,
147–55, 156, 165–7, 193, 201,

230